REFLECTIONS
on

New Farm

REFLECTIONS

on

New Farm

COMPILED BY

Gerard Benjamin & Gloria Grant

NEW FARM & DISTRICTS HISTORICAL SOCIETY INC.

Compiled and designed by Gerard Benjamin and Gloria Grant
on behalf of the New Farm & Districts Historical Society Inc.

Typeset in 11.5/14 Arno Pro Regular, by Gerard Benjamin, Newstead
Printed by: Ligare Pty Ltd, Riverwood NSW 2210

First published in Australia in 2008 by:
New Farm & Districts Historical Society Inc.
PO Box 1141, New Farm Qld 4005
The NFDHS office is located at the front of the Ron Muir Meeting Room,
adjacent to the New Farm Library, 135 Sydney Street, New Farm Qld 4005
Office opening hours: Every Thursday 2-4 pm
Email: newfarmhistory@yahoo.com

Enquiries should be addressed to the publisher.

ISBN 978-0-9805868-0-0

This project has been kindly funded by
the Gambling Community Benefit Fund.

Funded by

Gambling
**Community
Benefit Fund**
Queensland Government

Additional copies of this book may be ordered from the New Farm & Districts Historical Society Inc. by e-mailing: newfarmhistory@yahoo.com

Front Cover: *CSR Refinery by Shirley Miller, ca. 1980s.* — Not only is the CSR tower the second most recognisable piece of New Farm skyline after the Holy Spirit Church's steeple, but the refinery was the first substantial industry in New Farm. It lasted over 100 years, provided much employment and helped make New Farm a working suburb.

Title Page: *Doctor's House, corner of Moreton Street and Bowen Terrace, watercolour by Gladys Blundell 1997.* This large residence once stood on the site of the present-day Palm Lodge Nursing Home.

Contents

Threads Well Woven...

From the President

A S A MEMBER of a family that has dwelled in New Farm since 1888 and having lived here all of my life (more than 60 years), I commend this book to you for your enjoyment. I trust that it will help you to understand a little of the history of this old suburb which has had such varied social structures since the early days of Brisbane.

How fortunate we are that there are people living today who are able to share their own memories and record their family's story in relation to New Farm, so as to help us to understand our past and build on it into the future.

Gloria and Gerard have skilfully woven the threads of the stories into an enjoyable and informative read. The loose ends that exist from that weaving will undoubtedly be taken up in the future, to weave another portion of the unfinished 'tapestry' we know as New Farm.

We are very grateful to have received a grant from the Gambling Community Benefit Fund. The Grant has enabled us to embark upon preserving the history of New Farm using oral histories recorded over the past 30 years.

Enjoy!

Ross Garnett
President, New Farm & Districts Historical Society.
November 2008

The office of the New Farm and Districts Historical Society is at the front of the Ron Muir Meeting Room, next to the New Farm Library in Sydney Street.

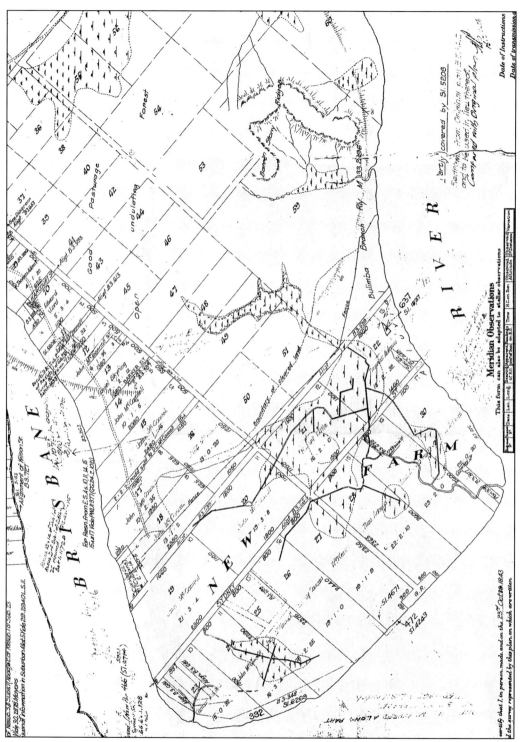

A portion of Wade's survey of eastern suburban allotments (New Farm) 1843. The thoroughfares later to become Brunswick Street, Merthyr Road and Sydney Streets are clearly marked. The various swampy areas and watercourses are prominent. — *B1234.2 courtesy of Department of Natural Resources.*

New Farm Panorama

Foreword by Councillor David Hinchliffe

As a child newly arrived from provincial Toowoomba in the 60s, I considered New Farm to be very "grown up" (I didn't know the meaning of the word "cosmopolitan" back then). We lived in three-storey brick flats at 113 Merthyr Road, built and owned by recently arrived Italian families. Their units were always filled with the scent of pasta and Bolognese sauce and the sound of happy families eating and conversing animatedly. Our next door neighbours on one side spoke Yugoslav and on the other side Greek. One of my best friends had a full set of dentures at the age of 12, knocked out by a combination of a tough schoolyard and an even tougher home. We travelled by tram. New Farm was about as different from Toowoomba as you could imagine. It was exciting, colourful, loud and exuberant — but definitely not for the faint-hearted.

The fact is that New Farm back in the 60s was going through one of its many "stages". For the last 150 years, since it was identified as the 'new farm' for the fledgling penal colony, New Farm has been evolving. It evolved first from the hunting and fishing ground swamp which the local Turrbal people inhabited prior to white settlement. They would trek down by the side of the cliff from their camp in the Spring Hill area, following a route which later became known as Bowen Terrace, to make their way to the fertile swamplands now known as New Farm Park.

New Farm has passed through stages — as an indispensable food source for the convict station, as a prized settlement in its own right for new free settlers, as the residential suburb of some of our finest citizens — even one of the architects of Australia's constitution and federation — as well as being a suburb for countless working families.

It fulfilled a role as the dormitory suburb of the city between wars, with a number of substantial brick art deco flats providing accommodation for workers and visitors from the country.

During World War II, General Douglas MacArthur regularly visited the New Farm area to oversee the local submarine base. New Farm back then became the very epicentre of the 'Brisbane Line' defence strategy for Australia in the face of possible Japanese invasion. Our suburb's footpaths were alive with regular "GI Joes", helping to win the war.

Post-war, we opened our arms to the peoples of Europe who fled the destruction and detritus of Europe, racked as it was then with upheaval, guilt and uncertainty. These immigrants were determined to build a new life in a new world and for many — particularly the Italian community — New Farm became their 'New Home'. The crowded schoolyards at New Farm State and Holy Spirit Schools performed the rites of passage for thousands of sons and daughters of immigrants, making their way into the mainstream of Australian society. The new migrants left their mark. Not only did they bring the sweet aromas of the cuisine of their native land as well as their sense of *joi de vivre* but they set to work literally re-building parts of New Farm.

Council planning policies of the 60s allowed high rise construction in significant parts of New Farm and the first of our 'skyscraper' residential apartments was built on the corner of Sydney Street and Oxlade Drive on the site of the former Merthyr Bowls Club. As a 12 year old, I delivered the afternoon *Telegraph* to residents in this 13-storey behemoth, little realising 40 years later I would be among its 100 residents.

The population declined in the 70s and 80s, as the sons and daughters of post-war immigrants forged a life for themselves in the emerging suburbs. Old New Farm had become *passe*. Grand old homes declined, some were tragically bulldozed to make way for the new era of high-rise, and others were converted to boarding houses for people who were down on their luck. Many of the houses that once teemed with the sounds of children became sad, declining homes for their sole remaining and ageing residents. The 1974 Australia Day flood had wreaked havoc in low-lying New Farm and that event — as much as any other — seemed to mark the turning of the tide in the suburb's popularity.

Just as quickly, the pendulum swung in the opposite direction, and suburbanisation gave way to a sense of new urbanism. It was the advent of Council's Urban Renewal program in the 90s that saw New Farm become 'new' again for a new generation. While the height of major buildings was actually reduced, the scale of development increased as old industrial land, the nearby woolstores, the Coca Cola and Fosters factories, the CSR Refinery and gypsum store were recycled for residents who were flocking back, eager to live, cuddled once again in the bend of the river and next to the city.

This, of course, brought new challenges and opportunities. Some old New Farmers weren't sure that they liked the new look. Traffic increased. New styles emerged — but with that came the growth of our schools, which had plummeted from 1,000 children at New Farm in the 60s to just over 100 in the 80s. The Powerhouse had been left dormant for 30 years after it ceased its role of generating electricity to power Brisbane's trams. With Urban Renewal, it was recycled and reinvigorated to

generate something quite different — a sense of the vibrant culture and lifestyle excitement which now had the new New Farm as its focus. Restaurants and delis opened. New Farm was alive again, embracing its new era.

So — has New Farm stopped changing? Of course not! This is a suburb that is constantly re-inventing itself. It has become the most sought-after suburb in Brisbane, appealing to 'empty-nesters' from the suburbs and provincial Queensland, as well as to young professionals wanting to live close to work. It also has a strong heart and recognises that a truly cosmopolitan and 'rich' community welcomes people from all walks of life and backgrounds.

Prospective buyers of home units at *Glenfalloch* in 1962 were assured that they could "live elegantly and easily" at "a prestige address."— *Courtesy D. Hinchliffe.*

As long as we have organisations such as the local New Farm Neighbourhood Centre providing a caretaker role for the 'soul' of our suburb, and the New Farm & Districts Historical Society recording the area's history, New Farm's future will be as interesting, exciting and as caring as its past!

A panorama of New Farm, as seen by long-time resident, community representative and artist, David Hinchliffe. —*'View From My Window 2,' oil on canvas, 2008.*

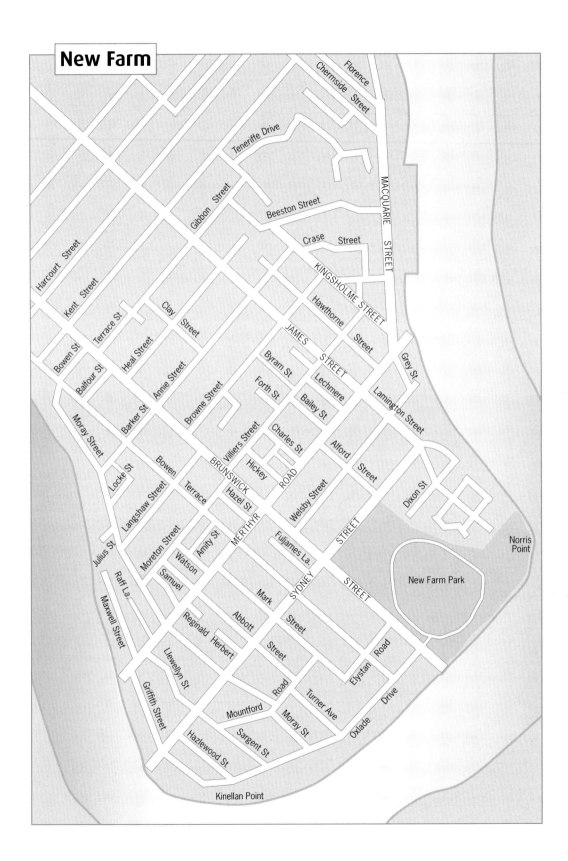

Breathing Life into the Past

Introduction

SYDNEY · STREET · MOUNTFORD · SARGENT

Judging by this portion of the pictorial panorama ca. 1901 that hangs in the NFDHS office, New Farm looked very different 107 years ago. There was clearly an air of rusticity about Sargent Street and Mountford Road. — *Presented in 1981 by the Hon. Don Lane, Minister for Transport and Member for Merthyr.*

T HE HISTORY OF New Farm is a wide canvas indeed, so wide that it cannot be covered in one volume. Our modest objective has been to sketch out certain parts only. To these, we have added detail and highlight, knowing full well that other books will follow in order to keep bringing new life to New Farm's past.

A key reference has been the New Farm & Districts Historical Society's oral history file which contains numerous transcripts, the earliest of which was recorded 34 years ago in 1974. From these invaluable recollections of New Farm residents, extracts have been chosen so as to illustrate a variety of topics. Further factual data has been added to provide an historical context for the stories that have come to light. The historical narrative has been interspersed with italic quotations from more than 30 contributors.

* * *

FOR A COMPARATIVELY small suburb on the fringe of Brisbane's CBD, it is remarkable how wide New Farm's 'brand recognition' is and just how many people are likely to have had, or know someone who has had, a New Farm connection. Mention a local street and before long someone will say, "I once lived just around the corner from there. The house is gone of course. There's a block of flats there now. It was such an interesting place…" or "Our old house in New Farm just sold for over a million dollars. Can you believe that?"

* * *

ONE OF THE benefits of the two photos shown in this Introduction is to enable readers to look afresh at places and events and see them in a different perspective. Knowing how and why things happened in the past gives a new understanding about why things are the way they are today, good, bad or indifferent.

Perhaps what you read in this book will also add to your pleasure as you walk the streets of New Farm, looking past the contemporary home-styles in order to glimpse earlier episodes in the life of the same streets today.

If this exercise sparks an urge to reconnect with the hidden seams of the locality's past, then you are warmly invited to contact the New Farm & Districts Historical Society where you will have access to archives of local relevance, plus the joy of meeting kindred spirits.

This book, which addresses the historic substratum of modern-day New Farm, has been a long time in coming. It draws on the work of many dedicated individuals who have contributed their efforts towards preserving the stories about New Farm's past, and that's why there is such a long list of acknowledgements at the end of this book.

Needless to say, there are many more stories and photos that you could have added to this volume. Let's just say that if this book impels you to record your family's story about life in New Farm, then this first compilation is sure to spark sequels.

Gerard Benjamin & Gloria Grant

Another view from Sargent Street looking towards the single house on this section of Moray Street. Behind it among the trees of Turner Avenue is the sizeable residence, *Kinellan*. Who could have imagined then how New Farm would develop! — *Presented in 1981 by the Hon. Don Lane, Minister for Transport and Member for Merthyr.*

1   **Whitefellows come to Binkin-ba**

The strangers make themselves at home...

MANY CURIOUS EYES must have watched intently — both from the high places of *Binkin-ba*, the 'place of the land tortoise', and its lower-lying areas — as strange white people began to appear more frequently, coming by river around the peninsula later known as New Farm.

When John Oxley surveyed the Brisbane River in October 1823, he was guided by John Finnegan who, along with fellow ex-convicts Pamphlet and Parsons, had been marooned on Moreton Island after a shipwreck and had survived with the help of local Aborigines.

Oxley returned the next year with botanist Allan Cunningham. Near Breakfast Creek, an Aborigine took Oxley's hat, possibly impelled by the same motive as the schoolboys from Bowen Terrace who, during World War II, souvenired the cap of a US serviceman while he slept in New Farm Park. Unfortunately for the Aborigine, he was shot several days later by Lieutenant Butler at Toowong.

After another year (around May 1825), many more whites arrived and began to set up a permanent camp which was to become the Moreton Bay penal station on the Brisbane River adjacent to William Street. The Turrbal people appear not to have been overly concerned since "the banks of the river were being used as a natural 'highway' by all adjacent Aboriginal groups, with the Turrbal long accustomed to playing the role of tolerant hosts." [1]

Besides, the Aboriginal people felt themselves to be superior in strength and numbers. Cunningham observed that 'the ordinary stature of the Aborigines at Moreton Bay' was 'about six feet' (1.8m), while the average height of the white male incomers was about 5 feet 4 inches (1.6m). [2] Regarding numbers, the conventional assessment was that there were almost 5,000 Aborigines nearby in the mid-1840s, even after de-population by smallpox. This meant that pre-contact numbers may have been *double* this figure. [3]

It is little wonder that the convict station, which was intended to be a "particularly brutal secondary detention centre," [4] but having an initial population below 200, was commenced with "some trepidation and a distinct presentiment of siege." [5]

In the light of this, by 1827-28 when the convict population may have increased to around 700 (with 100 military personnel), [6] the need to help sustain the settlement with its own food supply was a pressing matter. A 'new farm' was needed to supplement the existing agriculture on the south side of the river.

* * *

HAVING LIVED AMONG local Aborigines and been well treated, the rescued Finnegan had tried to impress upon officials in Sydney in the mid-1820s that "at Moreton Bay, the blacks were in thousands ... and were far more advanced in civilised life than the Aborigines about Sydney."[7]

Matthew Flinders and later observers offered supporting evidence of the Aborigines' structured social pattern, thereby countering the assumption that they simply 'ranged over' the land, and thus did not 'possess' or 'reside within' designated areas. Holding to these assumptions made it easy to rationalise the "territorial usurpation" that followed, reinforced by the perception that, "compared with the Englishman's rationality and emotional command, the Aborigine's impulsiveness was viewed as a measure of his volatility and unpredictability."[8]

As to the apparent Aboriginal tolerance and at times even friendliness towards the "usurpers", one explanation is that the whitefellows were seen as *reincarnations* of the Aborigines' departed ancestors. To the living, the ways of the "white spirits" might seem unconventional and strange but this was accommodated, much as one might show understanding and hospitality to a long-staying, unruly house-guest. Even if the host's patience and resources were sorely tried, one would never expect the guest to try to eject the host and take over his domain, especially if it was a "veritable Garden of Eden."

Sometime between 1827 and 1828, the penal settlement's Commandant, Captain Patrick Logan, established a 'new farm', clearing around 240 acres (97 hectares) at the lower end of the New Farm peninsula to supply corn and a variety of fruit and

This is possibly the first photo of the New Farm area, taken from the windmill on Wickham Terrace, ca. 1861. On the left is All Saints' Anglican Church, Wickham Terrace. Looking beyond Kangaroo Point, New Farm appears lightly forested. Markings on the picture point out *Ravenswood*, the home of solicitor Daniel Foley Roberts, which stood on Bowen Terrace overlooking what later became Moray Street — *John Oxley Library 110130*

vegetables. The convict gangs were marched from their prison barracks near Queen Street, via a track roughly following the later Bowen Terrace. Even if escapees managed to cross the river, they would still have to deal with local Turrbal groups who were rewarded with blankets and axes by authorities for returning 'bushrangers.'[9]

It is estimated that two kilometres of post and rail fencing were erected by convict work gangs to protect the crops from larger animals and trespassers. The convict gangs also accomplished another major task which was to improve conditions at New Farm by draining the swamps, most likely by a system of simple channels.

> SURVEYOR HENRY WADE wrote to the Colonial Secretary in 1843 describing the construction of drains built by convict labour to expel excess water from the many swamps of the paperbark forests utilised for planting crops. The surveyor mapped the extensive three-kilometre network of drains at the new farm that linked the respective watercourses at the southern and eastern points.[10]

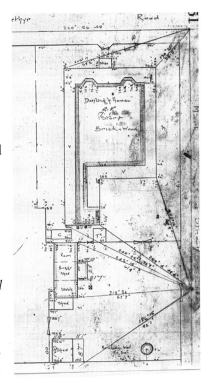

The 'brick-edge well', regarded by the Gilmours as a 'convict well' is marked on the bottom of this 1913 Sewerage Plan for *Denbigh House* on the corner of Merthyr Road and Mark Street. Between it and the house are a stable and buggy shed. — *Plan courtesy of Paul Lewis.*

While the settlement's maize-growing efforts in 1832 allowed for a surplus to be sent to Sydney, succeeding years weren't as successful. By 1836, Commandant Fyans complained that the crop at New Farm would be lost because there were not enough convicts to keep the weeds down.[11] It seems that the only building erected at New Farm during the convict era was a tool shed, somewhere on the south-east portion of the farm,[12] although a number of 'crow-minder' huts were also built. Tom Petrie's *Reminiscences of Early Queensland* (which first appeared in 1902) give some insight into the convict arrangements:

> FATHER HAS OFTEN seen the convicts cultivating the ground about Brisbane, and it was all done by hoe — not plough. "I have seen," he says, "the poor fellows march with chains on their legs to their work at New Farm and back again." On each cultivated part when the corn was in cob, a prisoner was put on guard to keep away the crows and cockatoos. He was dubbed the "crow-minder," and he had what was called a clapper to make a noise to frighten these birds.
> These "crow-minders" were prisoners under short sentence, and they were not chained like the others. The man who watched the land running along the river … had a hut built up in the fork of a gum tree on the bank of the river. This gum tree had steps made of pieces of iron… and it was called "the crow-minder's tree." …

(He) used to climb up to his hut and watch that the blacks did not swim across from Kangaroo Point, or come in a canoe to steal the corn or sweet potatoes. The "crow-minder" at New Farm had a similar tree and hut; it stood on the riverbank near where the residence of Sir Samuel Griffith now stands.[13]

While there is no remaining tangible evidence of New Farm's convict past, Father John Rosenskjar (b. 1917) who grew up at 902 Brunswick Street (now Merthyr Village Shopping Centre) recalls:

WE WERE ONLY a couple of doors from the corner of Welsby Street. In our day, there were no houses on the block from Welsby Street to Sydney Street. When they were building the houses, I heard that they were finding leg-irons and hand-cuffs. I don't think that they found them in abundance, but some were found.[14]

Margaret Gilmour, from her childhood at 3 Mark Street near the corner with Merthyr Road, has a more remarkable recollection:

THERE WAS A paddock next door belonging to the house on the corner. People named Hassall owned it. It was a big house, and he must have been a business man. Mr. Hassall built a house next door for his daughter when she got married. In part of his backyard, which was rather overgrown, was actually a convict well, a covered-over convict well. My father told me they used to find leg irons and things. This house would have been built in the late 1880s.[15]

In notes accompanying her diagram, Margaret explained that the well was covered with a cement or brick dome-like structure big enough for her and her sister Florence (later Lady Joh Bjelke-Petersen) to jump on as children. She did not know if there was water in it and it was filled in when a house was built on the land around 1939. Her house has been in the family since her Gilmour grandparents bought it in 1891-92, from where they witnessed the 1893 flood, so the 'convict-well' had long been part of family lore.

Notes

1.   Raymond Evans, "On the Utmost Verge: Race and Ethnic Relations at Moreton Bay, 1799-1842", in *Queensland Review*, Vol. 15, No. 1, 2008, p.12.
2.   *ibid.*, p. 8.
3.   *ibid.*, p. 7.
4.   *ibid.*, p. 2.
5.   *ibid.*, p. 12.
6.   J. G. Steele, *Brisbane Town In Convict Days 1824-1842*, Uni. of Qld Press, St Lucia, 1975, p. 4.
7.   Evans, *op. cit.*, p. 5.
8.   *ibid.*, p. 8.
9.   John Schiavo, "New Farm: A Study of Land Use and Settlement To 1999," Brisbane City Council — Local Community History Grants Program, p. 11.
10.   *ibid.*, p. 11.
11.   W. Ross Johnston, *Brisbane: The First Thirty Years*, Boolarong, Bowen Hills, 1988, p. 45.
12.   *Brisbane Courier*, 12 May 1906, p. 12.
13.   Petrie, Constance Campbell, *Tom Petrie's Reminiscences of Early Queensland*, University of Queensland Press, St Lucia, 1992, pp. 223-224.
14.   Oral History: John Rosenskjar, 2008.
15.   Oral History: Margaret Gilmour, 2007.

2 Prime Spot from the Start

...Fletcher, Jones, Griffith...

During his 1851 visit to Brisbane, Conrad Martens sketched the Jones'"New Farm" residence and was keenly observed in this activity by nine year old Frances Sophia Jones, who kept this signed pencil sketch for many years. — *Courtesy: The Colonial Diaries.*

AMONG THE MANY famous figures who have chosen to make New Farm their home, perhaps the most pre-eminent was Sir Samuel Walker Griffith (1845-1920), first Chief Justice of the High Court and twice Premier of Queensland. In 1879-1880, he built *Merthyr,* a grand house on a location now occupied by the *Amity* nursing home at 193 Moray Street. It is possible that the spot he chose was the site of the first household in New Farm.

When Brisbane town closed as a penal station in 1840 and was opened to free settlement in 1842, John McConnell quickly acquired most of the Eastern Suburban Allotments between Brunswick Street and the river, including the area occupied by the 'new farm' worked by convicts years earlier. On these allotments, John and his brother David established several farms sized around 22-34 acres (9-13.7 ha) and these were leased to tenant farmers along with their 'cottages, gardens, outbuildings and reservoirs.'

Among the influx of newcomers in 1844 was Richard Jones and family including their youngest daughter, two year old Frances. The ill-fated explorer Ludwig Leichhardt happened to be on the same ship from Sydney. In March 1847, Mr Jones, a merchant and the first Brisbane member in the NSW Parliament, purchased 93 acres (37.6 ha) between Brunswick Street and the river, part of it having been the 'new farm'. The family took up residence in a cottage previously occupied by a retired army lieutenant named George Fletcher who had operated a dairy. In 1846 Fletcher was described as the person who "occupied the only household at New Farm." [1]

Perhaps the cottage was added to or rebuilt, but as the Jones' residence, it was named *New Farm*, and the long, low, wooden dwelling was depicted by the artist Conrad Martens when he visited Brisbane in 1851.

In 1930, 88 year old Frances Sophia Jones was interviewed by Florence Lord about her early memories of that abode, and recalls that she stood behind the artist when he did the drawing. Stating that Mrs Jones' memory was wonderful and that she could recount old events and dates as if they belonged to the present, the interviewer's record was illuminating:

TRACES OF THE convict farm were still evident when the Jones family went to live there, and an old dead tree, in which the overseer of the convicts used to sit and watch them at work, still stood on the farmland. In this tree had been fastened or cut out of the wood a sort of seat for the overseer's use, and a ladder led up to it from below. Mrs Jones also tells me that in the centre of what was then, or a few years later, used as the racecourse, now the New Farm Park, there stood a large tree stump, round which was the mark of a chain. To this, the poor unfortunate convicts were chained and then flogged. On their land at 'New Farm', Mrs Jones says they made a splendid fruit and vegetable garden and there was also a plot of sugar cane. Of the shade trees planted, there are two great bunya pines still standing in the Merthyr grounds. Beautiful water was obtained from a well sunk in the ground.

(Present day) Sydney Street formed a boundary and "on that side was a waterhole on which wild fowl of many kinds congregated, and which my father protected from the guns of sportsmen." 'New Farm' had its own landing on the river. There were only two other houses in the vicinity, the cottage of Mr George Raff, 'Moraybank', and that of a Mr Wise, situated near the water's edge at what is now the end of Brunswick Street and the New Farm ferry. Here he grew beautiful strawberries. Mr Raff added a bit here and a bit there to his cottage, until the old rambling home that it became was destroyed by fire in later years.

If it seemed as if the Jones family had few neighbours then this was possibly correct. Of Brisbane's 1851 population of 2543, only a comparative handful lived in New Farm. By one measure, only seven houses were constructed in the suburb when the white population was less than 60.[2] On the other hand, the *Moreton Bay Courier* (1 June 1850, p. 2) had a prophetic word to say about the locality: "Nearer to Brisbane, on the suburban allotments recently sold in the direction of New Farm, a flourishing village is springing up, and is plainly destined at no distant day to become part and parcel of the town."

If homes were few then so were roads. Likely to have been little more than tracks, the two main paths would have been the 'road to New Farm' (Brunswick Street) and the east-west path (Merthyr Road) offering access to the racecourse. When Richard Jones died in 1852, it was easier to remove his body by boat:

IN THOSE PRIMITIVE days, there were no hearses. The body was brought in a rowing boat from New Farm to the South Brisbane Ferry, where the Victoria Bridge now stands. From there it was carried in relays of men to the Cemetery, afterwards known as Milton Cemetery. I well recollect that on visiting the grave with my mother or sister, we were always accompanied by men servants on account of the blacks who at this time were very treacherous.[3]

Frances Sophia Jones assiduously recorded episodes from her family's history. Here she related details of her father's death in 1852, when the family lived at 'New Farm', an estate between Brunswick Street and the river.
— *Courtesy of the Bancroft family collection.*

In 1857 Mrs Richard Jones relinquished *New Farm* and returned to England. Twenty-one acres of the estate were sold to R.R. Mackenzie who, in 1854, had married Louisa, another daughter of Mr and Mrs Jones. The Mackenzies (he was later a Premier of Queensland) built the single storey *Kinellan* (on present-day Turner Avenue) and it was their home until 1870.

Florence Lord reports that not long afterwards, part of the original block owned by Mr Jones came to the attention of an interested party:

> *WHEN VISITING MR and the first Mrs George Raff at their home 'Moraybank' one day while they were still living on Wickham Terrace, Sir Samuel and Lady Griffith mentioned the fact of their wishing to purchase a home, so Mr Raff took them along a bush track and showed them a pretty creeper-covered wooden dwelling, which, I understand, he owned, and in which at the time there lived four bachelors, one of them being Mr Donkin, who afterwards married one of the Misses Raff. As the home took the fancy of Sir Samuel & Lady Griffith, he purchased it.*[4]

It appears that the Griffith family lived in the original *New Farm* dwelling, and some of their children were born there before *Merthyr*, named after Samuel Griffith's birthplace Merthyr Tydfil in Wales, was completed in 1880. The old wooden house was then attached to the verandah of a side wing of the new home. Frances Jones' interviewer concluded, "This old house has stood for 83 years, and holds associations of the greatest interest to us who have a regard

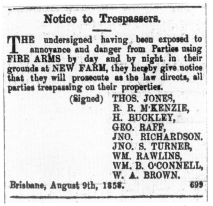

This "Notice to Trespassers" lists some of New Farm's early landholders. — *Moreton Bay Courier, 11 August 1858, p. 3.*

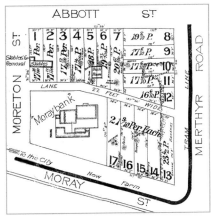

An extract from the 1908 Plan advertising *Moraybank Estate*, showing George Raff's home *Moraybank*. A Scot from Morayshire, Raff was a merchant, sugar grower and politican. — *Estate Plan: State Library of Qld.*

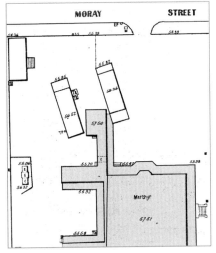

Right: A portion of the 1925 Sewerage Plan for *Merthyr* off Moray Street. It is uncertain which of the three main structures close to the main house may have been the original *New Farm* dwelling associated with the Jones' era. — *Water & Sewerage Board, City of Bris., Plan 167. 1925*

Left: Sir Samuel Griffith aged about 42 in 1887. *Above: Merthyr,* completed in 1880, was admired for its beautiful grounds, flowering shrubbery, blooms, palms and groups of bamboo. — *Image from the collection of the Royal Historical Society of Queensland.*

for the early history of our city." [5] Living close to *Merthyr* was a sought-after Brisbane address and many politicians and key government figures resided nearby, including the Hon. Theodore Unmack whose residence *Moana*, completed around 1886, still stands at 88 Moray Street. [6] *Merthyr* also played its community role:

> ALL THE SUNDAY School teachers and children would assemble at St Michael's and march down to the river flat of Merthyr for the carnival. The Griffith family would stand out in front of their house to greet the parade and welcome the children to their property. Races would be held, followed by a bunfight dinner. [7]

When a committee looking for a permanent home for the new Church of England Grammar School approached Sir Samuel in 1916, he said that he would accept £15,000 for 12 acres of the *Merthyr* property without the house, but Norman Park was chosen instead. [8]

> WHEN SIR SAMUEL Griffith died in 1920, his body was taken from Merthyr in a large black glass-encased hearse drawn by eight black horses resplendent in full regalia, even to the plumage on their heads. [9]

The original *Merthyr* property was gradually subdivided, yielding streets named Griffith and Llewellyn (after the Griffiths' son who died in 1901). The grand house languished, became a boarding house and was demolished in 1963. In the foyer of the *Amity* nursing home are two striking photographs of *Merthyr* along with an account of the house and its famous owner.

Notes

1. John Schiavo, *op. cit.,* p. 16. The early surveyor John Sweatman met Mr Fletcher. See: Jim Allen & Peter Corris (editors) *Journal of John Sweatman,* Uni. of Qld Press, St Lucia, 1977, pp 74-75.
2. *ibid*, p. 17
3. Diary, Bancroft Family collection.
4. Florence E. Lord, *The Queenslander,* 17 April 1930, page 50.
5. Florence E. Lord, *The Queenslander,* 8 May 1930, p. 30. Interview with Mrs Jones.
6. The Hon. T. Unmack was in the Griffith ministry in the 1890s. *Moana,* named after a Hawaiian hotel, was described in 2008 as "the most substantial home in New Farm," when on the market for $8M.
7. Contributed by George Yardley of Lime Street, in 'Old Farm', *New Farm News,* ca 1990s.
8. John R Cole, *op. cit.,* p. 55.
9. Oral History: Russell Stevens, 1992-94.

3

Julius Street

Early industry raises fire risk...

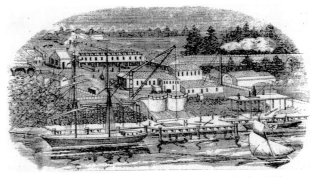

An etching from the 1890s shows the Langshaw Planing Mills at Moray Street, operated by James Campbell & Sons. The pair of lime kilns are just behind the wharf. — *Image: JOL 16627*

I N A 1909 publication to celebrate Queensland's 50th year, 78 year old Thomas Roper of Eagle Junction was listed among the living pioneer colonists, having arrived on the *Fortitude* in 1849. Sometime after 1896, he penned his reminiscences of Brisbane, writing as "The Old Colonialist." References to New Farm are brief, but contain useful hints about residents and geography:

> THE OLD RACECOURSE at New Farm was a place of note in the early days. Here resided Richard Jones Esq.'s property. North-east of this stood a cottage, the residence of A. S. Lyon the original proprietor of the Moreton Bay Courier, and Mr Adams, a solicitor.[1] On the bank of the river near the late Mr Drury's residence was a little cottage, the home of Mr Doig, one of the clerical staff and contemporary with Mr Wilkes of the local paper. I well remember the Duke of York. He was evidently a Chief whose smile was more courted than his frown.

New Farm was clearly favoured by newspaper editors including Arthur Sydney Lyon,[2] founding editor of the *Moreton Bay Courier*, and Sylvester Doig, an editor of the *Moreton Bay Free Press* about whom it was written in 1892, "What is now called Bowen Terrace then had only one house on it inhabited by Mr Sylvester Doig."

Before at least 1895, Moray Street went no further north than Barker Street and substantial properties extended from the river to Bowen Terrace, including the two-acre *Hawstead* (adjacent to Balfour Street) owned by Edward Robert Drury (1832-1896), general manager of the Queensland National Bank. Completed in 1876, *Hawstead* no doubt sought to reflect its Suffolk namesake, the Drurys' ancestral home. Nearby was *Ravenswood*, home of the prominent citizen, Daniel Foley Roberts.

When it came to ancestral territory, the 'Duke of York's clan' was the name given to the Aborigines occupying Brisbane's inner-city area during the convict period. Its leader evidently cut a memorable figure with Mr Roper. The old colonialist had even more to say about one of New Farm's early industries:

> WHERE THE MUNICIPAL Wharves are erected was then an undulating hollow. There was no retaining wall but a gentle grassy slope from the present road to the river. Here the little ketch Nelson discharged her cargoes of oysters for the purpose

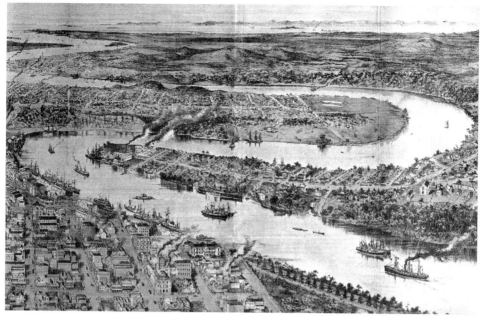

W.A. Clarson's 1888 view of Brisbane shows the New Farm peninsula, including it seems, the sawmill near Julius street (smoke coming from chimney) and a ship docked at a wharf.

of burning for lime. They were burned on kilns built with logs about five feet high. Several tons would be consumed in one burning. These oyster cargoes would be a great attraction to both blacks and juvenile whites. Here they would fraternise and feast on the delicious bivalve. The owners gave free permission providing the shells were left behind. To continue this wholesale destruction would soon have annihilated the oyster from our shores. There were no leased oyster beds or fishing regulations in existence.

'Municipal wharves' may refer to the landing at Merthyr Road, since there are unconfirmed sources that an unofficial ferry operated (during the 1860s and certainly by 1874) between Kangaroo Point and what became Merthyr Road. The activity was clearly an early description of Campbell's lime kiln.

James Campbell arrived from Scotland in 1853 and acquired land on Moray Street by the river adjacent to Langshaw Street during 1876-78, as part of his business to supply building materials including lime, cement, plaster and timber. At the same time, in 1876 *Langshaw Estate* (bounded by Brunswick, Barker and Langshaw Streets, and the river) was advertised,[3] offering large allotments aimed to lure upper-middle class residents.

Campbell sought the permission of the Brisbane Municipal Council (of which he had been an alderman) to establish a lime kiln in 1877. A small wharf was built for schooners to deliver the limestone for burning. In 1882, Campbell opened the Langshaw Planing Mills and Joinery Works on the property and later a second lime kiln was installed.

Built into the side of the river embankment, the pair of kilns received limestone and fuel which were layered from above. The burning at 1000 degrees Celsius lasted three days followed by a cooling period after which the lime could be collected. Alternating the process between the two kilns ensured a steady supply. Remains of a pair of kilns are still visible behind 12 Julius Street, and can be glimpsed from the floating walkway or even the CityCat.[4]

> THE KILN CONSISTED of two vertical brick cylinders, about 40 feet high and 25 feet in diameter. They were no longer in use when we visited them in 1914, when we went fishing in the Brisbane River.[5]

Overlooking the river on a spot close to present-day Julius Street, James Campbell built *Rockybank* for his son, John Dunmore Campbell, who lived there with his young family from at least 1883. Houses were being built along Langshaw Street and were occupied by Campbell's employees. It is worth noting that one of the firm's employees during 1871-1880 was the young James Clark, later to become the 'Pearl King' of Elystan Road.

This early industrial activity, along with the growing number of houses, is likely to have influenced the placement of New Farm's first fire station on the corner of Moray and Langshaw Streets.

The remains of James Campbell's lime kiln on the riverbank below 12 Julius Street. Limestone and fuel were layered from the top of the kiln, and after burning at a high temperature for 3 days, followed by a cooling period, the lime (to be used for mortar in brickwork) could be drawn from the mouth. — *Image supplied courtesy of the Environmental Protection Agency, Queensland.*

> THE FIRST MEETING of the New Farm Volunteer Fire Brigade was held on 11 September 1889, at James Campbell and Sons' sawmill. Campbell offered land for a fire station and by early December that year constructed a fire station for £50 in Moray Street.[6]

Sometime after 1903, the station was removed and rebuilt at 23-27 Heal Street, the property of cordial manufacturer and vice-president of the Volunteer Brigade, William Sargeant.[7] A tall lookout tower was equipped with a large fire bell. In the event of a fire, this was rung with great gusto which not only advised the volunteer firemen but roused the whole neighbourhood. According to Fred Matthews, everyone understood what the rings meant:

> FOLLOWING THE CONTINUOUS ringing, there was a pause, then a code of rings sounded — two for the Valley, three for Spring Hill and four for the City.

Everyone knew this code, and counted the number of rings, then raced outside to see the reflection and judge the size of the fire. If it was a big one, and in a handy location, say in the Valley, everyone would hurry to the scene and watch the firemen in action.[8]

The aftermath of the disastrous fire at the Rosenfeld & Co. timber yard in Moray Street on 18 February 1931. The damage was estimated at £25,000. Ironically, the fire led to the building of the Julius Street flats, a remarkable group of housing apartments.
— *Photo: The Queenslander, 26 February 1931, page 24.*

The 1893 flood probably inundated the lime kilns and Campbells relinquished the property soon afterwards. The site appears to have remained unoccupied for about 20 years. By 1921, timber merchants Rosenfeld & Co. (Qld.) were operating a sawmill from this site and by 1924 the title had passed to Julius Rosenfeld who had timber interests at Ravenshoe in North Queensland from at least 1910.

Oregon

Rosenfeld's Oregon Pine will last for a century. It stands up to the hardest service. Oregon is durable, strong, and does not warp. It is ideal for all building purposes.

We can supply Oregon in any sections, in any sizes, and in any lengths up to 60 feet. Our efficient organisation means to you a delivery service that is perfection in itself. Ask us more about Oregon. 'Phone 5991.

Rosenfeld & Co. (Q.) Limited
Timber Merchants and Importers
MORAY STREET, NEW FARM, BRISBANE

An advertisement for Rosenfeld & Co. (Qld) Limited in a souvenir publication celebrating Brisbane's Centenary (1823-1923).

* * *

WITNESSING A FIRE in the neighbourhood makes an indelible mark on a child's memory, so it is no surprise that many older New Farm residents vividly remembered the day in February 1931 when Rosenfeld's Mill in Moray Street went up in flames. The mill's wharf was a common haunt for children playing and looking for firewood. One of Beattie Dawson's early memories is filling her cart with timber offcuts for her grandmother's copper boiler in the 1920s.

> *I WAS UNDERNEATH the wharf when it happened. We were paddling. We had to go and get wood for my grandmother after school. Quite a few children went to get wood. The parents and grandparents knew that we would play in the water there under the wharves.*

Among the others who remembered this event, Arch Trail could see the smoke from Newstead, Ron Grant remarked that all of New Farm came out to watch, while Bryan Oxlade said, "I remember coming home from school one day about 3pm and it was really alight."

Russell Stevens also remembered the fire:

> ONE LINE OF *freighters used to offload in New Farm. They carried Oregon pine from Canada in large flitches that were re-sawn for construction at a sawmill in Moray Street. The Oregon Pine Mill, as it was known, was completely gutted by fire from Moray Street to the wharf on the river.* [9]

Rather than try to rebuild the mill after the fire on 18 February 1931, a subdivision took place and the result was the Julius Street flats. Constructed between 1934 and 1938, the seven blocks: *Ardrossan, Green Gables, 5 Julius Street, Syncarpia, Ainslie, Pine Lodge* and *Evelyn Court*, epitomised the new era of residential development that was emerging in Brisbane, particularly in New Farm.

New Farm Volunteer Fire Brigade (NFVFB) Lookout c. 1903 on the corner of Moray and Langshaw Streets. The NFVFB shed appears partly-dismantled, so the move to Heal Street may have been imminent. A 1925 plan shows a series of seven houses in Langshaw Street almost identical in design with those at Nos. 75 and 77. — *Image: JOL 141596*

NFVFB at the same spot as above, with Theodore Unmack's residence *Moana* in the background. — *Image: JOL 97498*

Notes

1. Possibly Thomas Adams who commenced as a solicitor in 1843 and was an early landholder of what was to become New Farm Park and the CSR site.
2. Arthur Sydney Lyon, journalist and gentleman who began the *Moreton Bay Courier* on Saturday 20 June 1846, before resigning in December 1847. He died in 1861.
3. *Brisbane Courier*, 4 January 1876, p. 4/1.
4. "Remains of the Langshaw Marble Lime Works" at <www.epa.qld.gov.au/chims/basicSearch.html>.
5. Oral History: Fred Matthews, 1974.
6. K. D. Calthorpe and K. Capell, *Brisbane On Fire: A History of Firefighting 1860-1925*, 1997.
7. The forebears of Don Sargeant (Burwood, Victoria) settled in New Farm in the 1860s. The brigade was disbanded in 1924 when the personnel totalled 25. The fire bell was donated to St Michael & All Angels' Anglican Church, and several pieces of their firefighting equipment are at the Queensland Museum.
8. Fred Matthews, *op. cit.*
9. Oral History: Russell Stevens,1992-94.

4

CSR Refinery

Industry and jobs for more than a century...

The residential precinct of *Cutters' Landing* incorporates several structures of the CSR Refinery which was opened in 1893. — *Photo: Judy Bell.*

Cutters' Landing in Lamington Street marks the spot where mountains of raw sugar, produced from the prodigious labour of countless cane-cutters, went through a refining process so as to be ready for food and drink manufacturing industries, as well as the dinner tables of Queenslanders.

Though delayed by the major floods of February 1893, the Colonial Sugar Refining Company's plant opened on 12 August. Two months later, the steamer *Otter* brought 53 politicians including Premier Thomas McIlwraith to inspect what was to be the first substantial industry in New Farm, one which was to last for over 100 years, provide much employment and help to make New Farm a working suburb.

The decision to expend £4,300 on the purchase of two and a half acres (1 ha) was possibly much discussed on the other side of the New Farm peninsula by Sir Samuel Griffith at his home *Merthyr*. The refinery site had once been part of the 1846 racecourse, was used as a dairy,[1] and was later unsuccessfully advertised as a housing estate. Access to the river would enable ships to deliver raw sugar from North Queensland as well as unload coal for the plant's boilers.

The refinery was designed by James Muir, CSR's chief engineer and the manager of the Pyrmont refinery in Sydney. It comprised of substantial stores to hold both the raw and refined sugar, as well as structures to house the four major steps in the refining process.

Three refinery buildings have survived, including the landmark main processing building with its distinctive tower and a smaller two-storey brick building on its southern side which once served as the refinery's office, both of which have been converted into residential apartments. Dating from 1901, the wooden 'Brown Room' with a verandah on three sides was originally a residence and was later used as a watchman's office, library and staffroom. It continues its life as a gymnasium for the *Cutters' Landing* residential precinct.

Before the refinery's arrival, New Farm was mainly residential. Many employees were drawn from the local area including managers who were sometimes housed on-site.[2] Up to 250 men might be employed. The refinery's arrival was the makings of a

The refinery around 1902. It was a major employer in New Farm for over 100 years. — *Image: JOL 142850*

carrier named George William Cowin who arrived from the Isle of Man in 1881 at the age of 17. In 1890 he married Eliza White, an Irish maid employed by the wealthy produce merchant J. Jackson. Her wise frugality enabled her to buy her own house at 109 Browne Street:

> *In 1892, THE Colonial Sugar Refinery Co. Ltd. called for tenders on two contracts. The first was for the cartage of raw sugar from the Fortitude Valley railhead to the Refinery, while the second was for the cartage of refined sugar from the Refinery to customers. Because the plant was such a major construction, George Cowin reasoned that the government would one day run a rail line to the Refinery, so he only tendered on the second contract — which he won.[3]*

George Cowin was correct in his surmise about a railway. The Queensland Government agreed to construct the Bulimba line (as it was known) which branched from the main line near Bowen Hills, thence to Newstead before following the river to the Refinery, so as to facilitate the delivery of raw sugar. The line's opening in 1897 led to the growth of associated industries such as wool handling and shipping.

* * *

BY 1910 THE Refinery's production had tripled, necessitating its expansion to cover nine acres (3.6 ha). During World War II production almost doubled with the upgrading of equipment. In the years that followed there was modest expansion while innovations produced more efficiencies. A storage area for gypsum was later added adjacent to Dixon Street.[4] The Refinery provided solid, long-term employment for many local workers. It was not unusual to have been employed at the plant for many decades. Interviewed in 1992, Norm Wye and John Cuk had both worked there for 36 years, while Alan Johnson explained, "I started in 1954 at the age of 15, and I've been working at CSR ever since." He began at the bottom of the ladder and after 38 years was Chief Commercial Manager of the Division:

> *THERE WERE NO women working on site. In those days I was the switch-girl and the typist. I did all the typing as well as the telephone work. Finally, three years ago, we had some girls working on site here.[5]*

Before the advent of pallets the work was slow, dangerous and labour-intensive. It was only in the mid-1950s that a Safety Officer was appointed, indicative of a new

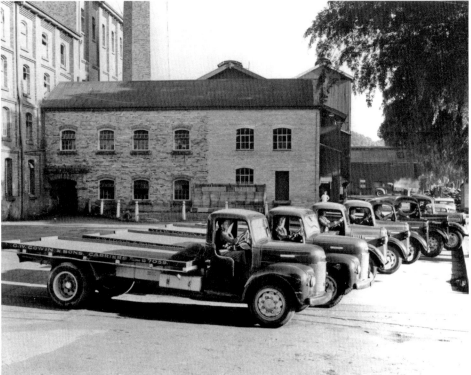

Top: The Refinery's loading area with pre-motor and motor transport belonging to G.W. Cowin & Sons. *Left:* Several decades later at the same spot. The seven trucks parked on the concrete apron beside the river carry signage that reads: 'G.W. Cowin & Sons, Phone B 7059.' — *Photos: George Cowin IV*

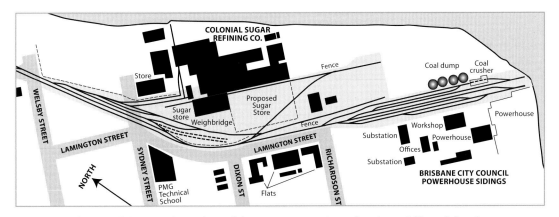

The Refinery and the Powerhouse formed the New Farm terminus of a substantial branch line that followed the river to Newstead before crossing Breakfast Creek Road and joining the main line near Bowen Hills station. — *Graphic: G. Benjamin (from Qld Railways diagrams of 1960 and ARHS 2005).*

approach to work practices at the plant. In earlier times the Refinery was closely identified with the local community:

> THE ATMOSPHERE WAS so different. People lived and worked in those early days around New Farm or the Valley, or over the river. Those types of blokes were real mates. Now people drive long distances (to work at the Refinery each day).[6]

Cowin's Transport continued its arrangement with CSR, and the founder's son George II and grandson George III also worked in the business. By 1960 their trucks made the first bulk delivery of raw sugar. At the same time, when Refinery events were put on for the workers and their families, Cowin's trucks provided the horsepower:

> THE CSR CHRISTMAS Tree was a monster affair. The warehouses now located on the Lamington Street frontage were not there then. It was a lovely grassed area with a few trees around the perimeter. Merry-go-rounds and slippery-slides came in and stalls for knock-ums and hoop-la were erected. Father Christmas arrived on his chariot, a horse drawn dray in the earlier days and a Cowin's truck in later years. Every child received a good quality present, and enjoyed a drink and ice cream during the afternoon. Later the grassed area was lost to the coal heaps, and after that came the warehouses. The canteen and concrete area on the riverside were then used for the event, but it was not the same…

According to Beattie Dawson, local residents could set their clock by the plant: "You always went by the Refinery. The whistle blew at eight o'clock and then at five o'clock. It was a really good time-keeper."[7] Despite the disadvantages of living so close to these industrial operations, including the smoke and the grit, the by-products proved advantageous:

> THERE USED TO be swamp land from near the CSR Refinery through New Farm Park and up to the intersection of Brunswick Street and Merthyr Road. Many areas have been reclaimed over the years with ash and lime from the Refinery,

and later on with ash from the Powerhouse. Some areas of fill may surprise residents, as the levels look very natural now.[8]

In 1952, *Amity*, the home of the prominent politician and businessman Thomas Welsby, was purchased by CSR for the manager's house. Built in 1892 *Amity* adjoins *Cutters' Landing* and still stands.

Despite celebrating its centenary in 1993, the Refinery's long history at New Farm came to a close in March 1998. The Refinery site was bought by the Mirvac Group in 2000 to be converted into a $200 million residential complex with a mix of 329 units and homes. *Cutters' Landing* was completed in 2004.

Above: G.W. Cowin & Sons enjoyed a long term arrangement delivering sugar for the Refinery. In 1936, their fleet of solid tyre motor vehicles was pictured in Villiers Street, in front of what is now the Holy Spirit Primary School. George Cowin III is on the pony. Most drivers were New Farm residents and included: Frank Johnston, Fred Houghton, Vince Belse, Ernie Peterson, Les Brown, Paddy Hackett, Frank Simpson, Percy Peterson with Andy Ferguson standing in front. *Above right:* View of the Refinery ca. 1995 from the corner of Sydney & Lamington Streets. — *Photos: George Cowin IV & Betty Smith.*

Notes

1. "Where the CSR now is, a man named Hastri had a dairy." Unidentified newspaper cutting in *S.W. Jack's Cutting Book No. 2*, pp 28-29.
2. In 1895-96, the *Post Office Directory* showed that "Geo. E. Holyrode, mgr, CSR Co. Ltd" lived at *The Anchorage*, corner of Mark Street and Merthyr Road (on the side closest to *Merthyr*). Later this house was owned by J.S. Hassall who named it *Denbigh*. The house had been built ca. 1889.
3. George Cowin, Talk, 1998.
4. CSR was the first company in Australia to manufacture and market plasterboard. The company entered the gypsum products industry in 1942 with the construction of a plaster mill in Sydney. The company's first plasterboard factory opened there in 1947, followed by a plant in Brisbane.
5. Oral History: Alan Johnson, 2002.
6. *ibid.*
7. Oral History: Beattie Dawson, 2007.
8. Cowin, *op. cit.*

5 Almost a Century of Service

An old-fashioned grocer on James Street...

WITH ADVERTISEMENTS PROCLAIMING Peter's Ice-cream, Horitz Fruit Drinks, King Tea or Persil Soap, and possibly a small billboard promoting the current film at the Rivoli Theatre, New Farm's abundant supply of little corner shops and local stores was a familiar feature of the area when cars were scarce.

The growth of such shops providing day-to-day necessities went hand in hand with the sale of housing sites to accommodate New Farm's increasing population. The 1880s for instance, proved to be a major growth period for the locality. The flood of immigrants meant that more land was needed for housing. Sale posters from this period show that yet more of the larger estates were being subdivided, including *Bowen Terrace Estate* which offered 130 blocks in August 1884. Around 230 lots on *Kingsholme Estate* were advertised for auction in October 1885.

While New Farm has managed to preserve many of its original corner shops in one form or other, one local store continues to occupy a prominent spot in the memory of older residents, even though every trace of the building at 152 James Street was recently removed and the lot levelled ready for a new chapter in its life.

Bert and May, and other members of the large Garnett family, ran a store there, providing everything from household groceries to fruit, vegetables, chook food, chaff for horses, olive oil when the Italians came in the 1950s — and even live birds — for customers all over New Farm. The prices didn't change much and the store offered personalised service, home delivery (usually by bicycle) and compassionate credit when needed. The establishment lasted for around 80 years until just after Coles started in Merthyr Road in the early 1970s.

*   *   *

WHEN YORKSHIREMAN DANIEL Garnett, his wife Mary and six children, arrived in Queensland in 1884, he had a background in stone masonry but the advantages of keeping a shop in the midst of a growing suburb clearly outweighed all else. The Post

In 1926, the Garnett store on James Street was advertising its unique "Kingsholme Blend Tea." On the corner of James and Annie Streets, preparations were underway to build Kingsholme Methodist Church. The corner block is thought to have been sold to the church by Mrs Garnett. — *Photo: Merthyr Road Uniting Church.*

View from the corner of James and Annie Streets during the 1893 flood, with water lapping at the step of the Garnett's Kingsholme Cash Store (No. 152 James Street). Work on the CSR site was under way. To its left is Tom Welsby's riverside house *Amity* with the two chimneys. To the right of the photo are homes on the high side of Lechmere Street including one built by Andrea Stombuco. — *Image: John Oxley Library, API-080-0001-0010*

Office Directory soon listed him in James Street as a grocer and fruiterer between Annie and Browne Streets.

Perhaps the aptitude of their son Ernest for the trade made it easy for Mr Garnett to turn his attention to divine matters because between 1887 and 1915, he served at numerous locations from Redland Bay to Cairns, as a minister of the Primitive Methodists, the keynote of this church being the unadorned essentials of the faith. The twin themes of shopkeeping and churchgoing came to epitomise the growing Garnett family, as if the Methodist Church offered succour on the Sabbath, while Garnett's Store provided the necessities for the locals on every other day of the week and sometimes on Sundays too.

From 1891 onwards, official records show Daniel's son Ernest variously as grocer, fruiterer and 'storekeeper of James Street, Kingsholme'. Following Ernest's marriage to Emma (Moore) in 1890, the educational needs of their children inspired Ernest to serve on the building committee of the proposed New Farm State School which opened in 1901.

Into the new century, while the Garnetts consolidated themselves to the extent that James Street between Annie and Browne Streets was known as *Garnett's Hill*, they also suffered setbacks. Several of Ernest and Emma's young children died and Ernest's father Daniel passed away in 1915, followed by the sudden death of Ernest himself in 1919. Perhaps all of this impelled Ernest's widow Emma to make the property at the corner of James and Annie Streets, "available to the Methodist church for a favourable purchase."

Bert's wife May records a critical period in the family history:

*Bert's father Ernest owned
and ran the shop. During WWI,
he maintained a big shed at the
back which was stacked with kero,
rice, flour, etc. — however, sadly,
he died suddenly and the family
did not know how he worked the
shop so the business gradually ran
down. They owned the land from
the church to the corner of Browne
Street but because they couldn't pay
the rates, they lost a lot of it. Bert
worked for the family for years in
the shop…* [1]

The Garnett residence at 160 James Street,
standing on a block advertised in the sale of the old
Kingsholme Estate in the 1880s. The young man in
the grocer's garb of a long white apron may have
been Ernest Garnett. The house dates from 1887 and
was remodelled in 1971. — *Photo: Garnett family.*

The 1936 Electoral Roll showed
that of Ernest's sons, 'grocer' described
Arthur (of 146 James Street), Victor
and Frank (of Browne Street), while
Herbert of 150 James Street was a
'shop assistant', and their sister Ruby
(Kingsholme Store) was performing
home duties.

Little did Bert know it but when a
young woman named May West came
in 1934 to help in the shop — and live
with Emma, Frank, Bert and Ruby
Garnett at 160 James Street — by the
end of 1939 she and Bert would be
married. The couple began the long
task of building up the business so as
to repay the £300 loan they had taken
out.

"Garnett's store was the centre of
the district" [2] was a sentiment likely
to have been shared by many locals
of that era. The main shop was lined

When Bert Garnett (centre) married May West (right)
in 1939, their reception was at the Canberra Hotel.
They enjoyed a one day honeymoon before starting
work again on Monday morning. Later, May's sister
Audrie (left) helped in the shop. Also pictured is the
all-important delivery bicycle upon which the ladies
are sitting. — *Photo: Garnett family.*

with shelves on three sides and the thick marble counter was where Bert, May, Arthur
and Victor conducted business with the customers. Off to the right was a fruit shop
managed by Frank, and behind this was a hardware and produce section. A six-horse
delivery dray could be backed up the path beside the shop to where there was a
storage shed at the rear to receive deliveries, with groceries to one side and produce to
the other. Also out the back were Frank's aviaries and a two-horse stable.

Sporting badges that say "75yrs", May, Bert and their son Ross stand in front of Garnett's Store which was regarded as 'one of the famous grocers in New Farm.' Bert's grandfather Daniel began shop-keeping in the 1880s, and the family enterprise was sold just months after Bert's death in 1972. — *Photo: Garnett family.*

MAY DID ALL the keeping of the books and writing of cheques and bills. The phone was on from the very beginning and the number was LW 1333. Bert would go to the homes and take a notebook for the orders. Those who had the phone on would ring their order through. When Bert and May had made up all the orders in boxes, Bert would deliver them in the Chevvy.[3]

The shop hours were from 8am to 5pm Monday to Friday, and 8am to noon on Saturday. Emma always closed the shop on Sundays. Sometimes she would serve people who came around but she would not take any money. It had to go on the bill because it was against her Christian beliefs to sell on the Sabbath.

Bert and May's sons Ross and Jeffrie were trained in the family business from a young age. Ross started work in the shop when he was 15 and although Jeffrie worked in the Public Curator's office, there were still chores to be done in the shop before and after work.

Being a veritable pillar of the community, Garnett's store was called upon to take phone messages for people in the neighbourhood and to carry a lot of credit. Bert and Ross even went across the road to lay out the body of Nana Long when she died. Special orders were often made up for big customers such as CSR, or for wool brokers Winchcombe Carson and AML&F (Australian Mercantile Land and Finance Company Limited) when overseas buyers were inspecting the wool.

ALF BARNES WAS taken out of school at the age of twelve and a half to work as a milkman at Mrs Margaret Loughery's dairy in the hollow between Kingsholme and Beeston Streets for 10 shillings a week. He would milk the cows at 3am, clean the dairy, take the cows to a paddock near CSR to graze, then deliver the milk on foot carrying the large cans to all the customers. He carried half-pint and one pint dippers, and filled up the customer's jugs. If they weren't home, he would go into the house, fill the jug and put it into the ice-box. In the afternoon, he would take the cows back to the dairy (often trams and cars had to stop for them to cross the road), milk again at 5 pm, clean up and be home about 7 pm.

One day when he delivered milk to Emma Garnett, she asked, "Do you want to be a milkman all your life?"

"I don't know, M'am."

"What would you like to be?"

"I don't know, M'am."

At dinner that night he told his mother about the conversation. She visited Emma Garnett next morning and asked why she was asking Alf those questions. Emma said that her son Bert needed a strong young man to help in the shop, so Mrs Barnes saw Bert and arranged for Alf to start work. Alf was very happy since the shop work was much easier than in the dairy.[4]

Alf Barnes' charming anecdote perfectly typifies New Farm's steady path from rusticity to suburbia. Alf started in Garnett's Store in 1940 and worked there for 13 years. He could tell innumerable stories about the personalised service that was the keynote of business in those days — such as the lady who ordered a live turkey for Christmas and asked that two be brought to her house so that she could feel which one was the plumper — or the lady in Turner Avenue who habitually phoned at five minutes to 11 and said, "I am entertaining and need Nescafe by 11am," an order that was invariably filled on time.

Bert and Alf's adventure of having to reverse the half-ton utility up the James Street hill as far as the state school — overladen with a ton of supplies from the Roma Street Markets because its first gear could not manage the incline — was another of those stories that became part of Garnett legend.

The store proved to be fascinating for children. James Harrison who attended New Farm State School in the early 30s recalls:

MR GARNETT WAS the old fashioned grocer with a white apron from neck to ankle. He cut his great cheeses with a wire and broomstick handle. The butter came in 56lb butter boxes made of timber, then a grid was passed through the butter cutting it into one or half-pound sections. The whole place smelt of newly-cut ham, cocoa, coffee and tea, and the floor was covered with sawdust (so was the butchers), a regulation at the time.[5]

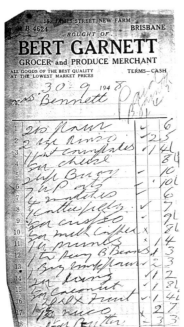

This 1948 account for Mrs Bennett lists flour, Rinso, Cornflakes, Life Buoy soap, matches and baked beans, etc.

George Cowin, whose family had been in business locally even before the Garnetts, reflected on their contribution:

THE GARNETTS WERE famous as grocers of New Farm and played an important role in the suburb's development. Ernest was on the committee to raise funds for the New Farm State School. He was also a leader of the Kingsholme Methodist Church when the church was established.

On the other hand, Frank was a bit of a larrikin. He had a large aviary of Australian birds, some in the protected category. He did a bit of illegal trading in protected birds and animals, and *many other commodities at times. He was also noted for selling the Story Bridge a number of times to American sailors. There were some irate people looking for Frank who was hard to find on occasions. In fact, if you wanted to buy anything during the war, Frank was your man.*[6]

* * *

ROSS GARNETT, who spent the earliest part of his life in the family store, is in the unique position of knowing New Farm and its residents as few others would:

GROWING UP IN a shop was not an easy life for a family. It was unusual in those days for both parents to work and my mother had to be super-organised. From a young age, my brother and I discovered the value of hard work and of "doing our bit" for the family. The shop was also the place where we learned "people skills". Our local customers came from all walks of life and a range of nationalities. I well remember the day when a customer asking for credit was Mr Charles Hope, of Charles Hope Refrigerators' fame.[7] *He had left his wallet at home and assured me that he would come back to pay. My parents gave credit to many folk who couldn't always pay because they were aware of the family's need. Customer service was an essential part of my education from a young age. I value the skills I learnt growing up in a grocer's shop in a suburb as diverse as New Farm was then. There was a great sense of trust in the community, and I certainly became very familiar with my suburb and its people, so much so that I have lived in New Farm all of my life…*

"We were all disappointed when the Garnett name was taken away from that shop because it was such a wonderful place," said Beattie Dawson,[8] while according to Fred Matthews, "It was more than a store. It was an institution and synonymous with New Farm."[9]

Notes

1. May Garnett, in *A History of The Garnett Family Grocery Store 1887-1972,* August 1999.
2. Oral History: Brian Bishop, 2007.
3. May Garnett, *op. cit.*
4. Mrs Margaret Loughery's (originally from Northern Ireland) dependence on employees in her dairy was understandable. Three years after her son in the AIF was killed in Belgium in 1916, she lost her husband. "One of my earliest memories of New Farm was watching Mrs Loughery bring her two cows down Kingsholme Street for their afternoon walk. She always wore a long black dress with a white cap and apron. Sometimes Mum would send us up the hill with a billycan to get some fresh milk, and we would watch fascinated while Mrs Loughery milked the cow. 'Beautiful,' my mother would say when we brought the billy back." (Elaine Boyd, "What New Farm Means to Me", March 1992.) Beattie Dawson recalls another dairy near the State School, that of Mrs McGregor's in Annie Street next to the Methodist Church hall. "Mrs McGregor had Freddie Blanch to look after the cows and next door was the paddock where the church was. There was a little lane down which he'd take the cows to the park every morning… That is why so many mushrooms grew there." (Beattie Dawson, 2007).
5. James Harrison, in *Memories of New Farm State School*, 2001, p. 16.
6. George Cowin IV, Talk, 1998.
7. By 1953, Charles Hope Cold Flame Refrigerators were found in over 100,000 households. His motor-body business (including body-work for Brisbane City Council buses) was also prospering.
8. Oral History: Beattie Dawson, 2007.
9. Oral History: Fred Matthews, 1974.

St Michael & All Angels' Church

New Farm's Anglican Parish...

The parish of St Michael and All Angels was established in 1889 and the current church is the third on the site. — *Photo : G. Benjamin*

T HE HISTORY OF the parish begins in 1889 when the Rev. Manley Power, Vicar of Christ Church, Milton, was asked by Bishop Webber to explore the possibilities of building up a congregation at New Farm, which had until then, formed part of the Parish of Holy Trinity, Fortitude Valley. A portion of farming land was purchased in Brunswick Street for £2,500 and on 6 June 1890, the first meeting of Church of England residents was held at the home of Mr A.V. Drury who afterwards became the first Churchwarden.

Albert Victor Drury occupied a pivotal position in the government service, being the Clerk of the Executive Council, and was possibly living at the time in *Cairnsville* in Balfour Street, virtually across the road from his brother, the banker Edward Drury, whose large home *Hawstead* on Bowen Terrace overlooked the river. A.V. Drury "enjoyed the friendship of governors, premiers and many ministers of the Crown, and moved with them in the highest stratum of colonial society."[1]

Arrangements were made for the erection of a building to serve as a church, school and hall. The building was completed in November 1890 — but regrettably burned to the ground almost at once. A similar building was erected for £860 and dedicated by Archbishop Webber on 19 March 1891.

Rev. Manley Power resigned from the parish in April 1893 and returned to England. The following years saw two short incumbencies, the Rev. A.R. Rivers (1893-1894) and the Rev. F. Anstruther Cardew (1895).

Rev. Arthur Richard Rivers and his brother Godfrey Rivers had travelled to Australia from Devon. Godfrey became a prominent artist in Brisbane who supported the establishment of the Queensland National Art Gallery, and during one period he resided in Moreton Street.[2] His painting of Sir Samuel Griffith hangs in the Supreme Court of Queensland.

Rev. Frederic Anstruther Cardew was ordained in London in 1892 and came out to St Michael's three years later.[3] After a short tenure, he went to Charleville as the only priest in a territory so vast that it included Birdsville and Sturt's Stony Desert. In 1897 he returned to All Saints' on Wickham Terrace.

On 7 July 1895 the Rev. Walter Thompson took up the first part of an incumbency that would last over 40 years. In 1889 he left for England to study for his B.A. and returned to New Farm in 1901. The intervening years were guided by the Rev. J. Auchinleck Ross (1898) and the Rev. T.L. Jenkyn (1899-1901).

The original St Michael and All Angels' church dating from 1891 was re-located to 20 Balfour Street and positioned on top of the hall which had been built after WWII. Named *Friendship House*, it accommodated several non-government organizations as well as an amateur theatre group before being sold in 2001.
— *Photo: Deirdre Fox*

During the second part of Rev. Walter Thompson's incumbency (1901-1941), the parish hall and rectory were built, and the construction of a permanent brick church was first mooted. Plans were drawn up and appeals launched in 1923, however the vision gradually faded and the schemes dwindled away. After the elapse of another 34 years, the hope of a permanent church was fulfilled with Archbishop Reginald Halse laying the foundation stone of the present church in 1957.

Mrs Arden (nee Le Brocq) well remembered the Rector:

> CANON THOMPSON HAD *several daughters and a son. He was a very tall, gaunt man and wore a little velvet jacket and a cap around the house. His wife Mary was the step-daughter of the Toowoomba poet George Essex Evans.[4] The church organised picnics in New Farm Park. We'd have a mug around our neck and a handkerchief pinned on with a safety pin. We went to Sunday School and Evensong.[5]*

> CANON THOMPSON ORGANISED *a busy church. When it came to Confirmation Classes, we had about 30-40 boys and girls in the club, and of course, there was always a party happening…[6]*

During the pre-war years, most of New Farm's church communities enjoyed wide social participation:

> CHURCHES WERE INVOLVED *in sporting fixtures. St Michael and All Angels had a tennis and cricket team that would compete with other churches in the district. There were oodles of tennis courts and cricket grounds in New Farm. The young people of St Michael's were very active. We enjoyed picnics and boat trips. Large*

numbers attended church, confirmation classes and Sunday School. It was an important part of the New Farm community. [7]

The Rev. E.H. Smithy became Rector in 1942. Utilizing his many talents, he was able to consolidate the life of the parish and pave the way for the coming in 1945 of the very enthusiastic Rev. Cecil Brook.

During Rev. Brook's ministry, additional property was purchased at 20 Balfour Street. In 1954 the 63 year old wooden church was moved 150 feet to its new location to make way for a modern brick church. The old weatherboard structure was used as a parish hall and it sat upon a newly-constructed brick Sunday School. A newspaper article pictured the operation under the heading, "Church is getting a move on." Rev. Cecil Brook's unexpected death in 1955 was a great blow and was felt by all parishioners with the poignancy of a personal loss.

The new church was consecrated by Archbishop Felix Arnott on 8 December 1974.[8] The late 1980s and early 1990s saw great changes in New Farm in the form of urban renewal, but despite these changes, low cost housing remains, as do numerous hostels, nursing homes and welfare services. The old church hall in Balfour Street, known as *Friendship House* provided office accommodation for several non-government organizations on its upper level and at one time, the lower floor was leased to an amateur theatre group named Nash. The building was sold in 2001 and became a private residence.

Born just around the corner from Saint Michael and All Angels' Church and raised nearby not many doors along Brunswick Street, was a young parishioner named Keith Rayner who was later to bring great credit to the Anglican Church of Australia.

Incumbents at St Michael & All Angels, New Farm:

1893	Rev. Manley Power
1893-94	Rev. A.R. Rivers
1895	Rev. F. Anstruther Cardew
1895-98	Rev. Walter Thompson
1898	Rev. J. Auchinleck Ross
1899-1901	Rev. T.J. Jenkyn
1901-1941	Rev. Walter Thompson
1942-45	Rev. E.H. Smith
1945-55	Rev. Cecil Brook
1955-59	Rev. C.W. Smythe
1959-1968	Rev. Des Williams
1968-85	Rev. Ken Lashford
1985-90	Rev. Bill Carter
1990-99	Rev. Jack Phillips
2000-	Rev. Olaf Anderson

Notes

1. J. T. Maher, 'Drury, Albert Victor (1837-1907)', *Australian Dictionary of Biography, Volume 4,* Melbourne University Press, 1972, p. 104.
2. Jean Stewart, *The Life and Times of Dr Brockway and The Brockway Cup,* J. and D. Stewart, Kenmore, 2007, page 154.
3. Rev. Cardew resided at *St Clair* on James Street during his incumbency.
4. George Essex Evans (1863-1909) emigrated to Queensland from England in 1881. Described as an "all-round and highly respected man of letters," he was best known for his poem, *The Women of the West* (1902).
5. Oral History: Joy Arden (nee Le Brocq), 1997
6. Oral History: Ivy Henderson, 1992
7. Oral History: Arch Trail, 2002
8. The bell that hangs in St Michael and All Angels' Church was donated by Mr Sargeant of Heal Street. Manufactured in the 1890s, the bell had been used by the New Farm Volunteer Fire Brigade until 1923.

Convict Connections

Links with Australia's colonial past...

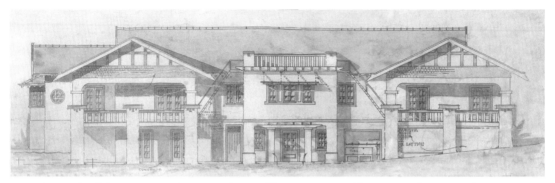

A.V. Dodwell's home in Moray Street was designed by prominent Rockhampton architect Roy Chipps in the late 20s early 30s. *Linden* had four bedrooms, drawing and billiard rooms, and incorporated a viewing deck overlooking the river, according to the rear elevation *(shown above)*. Two maids' rooms were on the lower level. The wide front steps featured a raised step so as to make it easy to alight from motor cars which in the 30s sat high. The home was demolished around 1980 and only a portion of the front fence remains at 119 Moray Street, in front of the home units named *Lindenlea*.
— *Photo: Anne Clarke*

H AVING ON YOUR property an old well, reputed to date from convict days, is a fact made more notable if you name your home *Denbigh*. Living on the corner of Merthyr Road and Mark Street, James Charles Hassall, named 17th out of 24 "Representative Business Men of Brisbane" during Queensland's 50th Jubilee in 1909,[1] had an ancestral link with the earliest days of Australia's convict origins.

J.C. Hassall was the grandson of the Reverend Thomas Hassall (1794-1868) who had opened the first Sunday School in Australia and had endeavoured to better conditions for convicts. Known as the 'galloping parson', the Reverend Hassall conducted a bush ministry from his property *Denbigh* near Cobbity in NSW. In 1822, he married the daughter of the Reverend Samuel Marsden, dubbed the 'flogging parson', who arrived in 1794 as assistant to the chaplain of the New South Wales convict settlement.

James Charles Hassall had yet another historic connection, since his mother Frances (Dixon), was a niece of John Oxley and had been brought up by the Oxleys after she had lost her parents at a young age.

New Farm proved attractive to several other members of this family, and a niece and nephew of James Hassall were two of the locality's well-known citizens.

Sir Edwin Marsden Tooth (1886-1957), son of Mr Hassall's sister, Emily Isabella, lived for a period in Bowen Terrace.

After seeing the potential of the motor industry on a visit to the United States in 1919 following his war service, he formed Austral Motors in 1924 which operated workshops in the block between Sydney and Welsby Streets. In the 1950s he established Farsley Motors named after the Yorkshire birthplace of his famous forebear, the Reverend Samuel Marsden.

Sir Edwin's sister, Elsie Hassall Tooth, married Alexander Vaughan Dodwell another leading figure in the motor trade in Brisbane. Before 1931, they built *Linden* in Moray Street beside Dodwell Lane and though the house was demolished in 1980 to make way for apartments, it was much admired by those who used to attend the St Michael and All Angels' parish fete, often held in its grounds:

> ONE OF THE nicest homes in New Farm was Dodwell's. The fence is still there. To approach the house, you would go around this beautiful garden on a circular driveway. The steps must have been fourteen feet wide. The front was stucco and there was a beautiful verandah. It was so impressive with those wide steps. I was never inside the house, and it was a shame to see it pulled down.[2]

* * *

JAMES CHARLES HASSALL'S wife Sarah (nee Coxen) had her own story to tell. Her father, Henry William Coxen (1823-1915) had been one of the best-known and most prosperous of Queensland pastoralists, despite the handicap of having his right hand rendered almost useless in a gunshot accident in his school days in England.

Sarah's brother Henry Coxen lived in Abbott Street, just a matter of a couple of backyards away, before moving to the other end of Mark Street.

Linden's wide lawn was the venue for the annual fete of St Michael and All Angels' parish. — *Photo: Anne Clarke*

The fire at Rosenfeld's timber yard on 18 February 1931. The house to the right is likely to be the Dodwell residence *Linden* on Moray Street. — *Photo: Courier Mail, 19 February 1931, page 14.*

Notes

1. Supplement to *The Queenslander,* Jubilee issue, 7 August 1909.
2. Oral History: Bryan Oxlade, 2008.

8

New Farm Private School

Miss Stevenson's emphasis on Elementary Decency

THE DEATH OF Miss Jeannette Stevenson at the age of 89 in July 1965 heralded the end of the New Farm Private School, an institution that she had established almost 70 years before. Some of Brisbane's top doctors, solicitors and business men had been pupils and three

"Stevenson Private School at Kilbowie, New Farm ca. 1904", so says the caption. This is likely to be *Alroy*, the Moray Street home of the Roebuck sisters in the 1890s, from which the Misses Roberts conducted their school, next door to the Stevenson property. This may also be the house contained within the modernised exterior of 174 Moray Street.
— *Image: John Oxley Library, 24147*

generations of many well-known Brisbane families had been educated by the three Miss Stevensons at this tiny establishment, just one of several local private schools.

Jeannette (sometimes Janet), Eleanor and Jeannie were the younger daughters of the 12 children (ten survived) of building contractor William Stevenson and his wife Margaret (nee Crompton). The Stevensons were early residents of New Farm, the land having been bought in 1866 two years after the birth of their first child. By 1888 the *Post Office Directory* showed their address as *Kilbowie*.

In a *Courier Mail* interview in 1960, Jeannette the eldest of the Misses Stevensons, explained that she always wanted to be a teacher. She had received a sound education at Miss Gilder's High School which later became Miss Moseley's located in the All Saints' Schoolroom on Wickham Terrace. Miss Stevenson's father "built her the schoolhouse she wanted and she opened for business in 'about' 1900." [1]

The actual opening date of Miss Stevenson's school is uncertain although a critical event would have been her father's death in 1900.

* * *

IT IS CLEAR that the Stevenson School was not the only one in Moray Street, considering this notice in the *Brisbane Courier:* "The Misses Roberts' Private School, Moray Street, New Farm (opposite Sir S.W. Griffith's) will OPEN on Monday 4th February 1895." [2] There could not be a more prestigious spot for a private school than opposite the entrance to *Merthyr* home of Sir Samuel Walker Griffith. This was indeed the 'smarter end of New Farm'.

A Scottish Presbyterian minister named Rev. Walter Roberts, his wife Christina, daughters Margaret and Christina, and son James Cockburn Roberts arrived in Queensland just before 1882. They purchased two adjoining blocks on the south-west corner of Abbott Street and Merthyr Road. Margaret and Christina were undoubtedly the two 'Misses Roberts' who had the use of a house in Moray Street from which to provide schooling. In 1895 they would have been aged 22 and 18 respectively.[3]

The actual school building is likely to have been Eliza and Margaret Roebuck's double-chimneyed brick cottage

Kilbowie at 23 Abbott Street, with two great Bunya pines in the front yard, was the Stevenson family's substantial dwelling. Likely to have been constructed by Mr. William Stevenson, a builder, the house was still standing in August 1961and has been replaced by a block of flats. — *Image: John Oxley Library, 16270*

with verandahs on three sides which is pictured in a photo labelled "Stevenson Private School at Kilbowie, New Farm ca. 1904."[4] The elderly Roebuck spinster sisters were also Scottish and may have helped with the Roberts' school. Indeed assistance may have also been forthcoming from the Misses Stevenson, particularly since their largely vacant adjoining block would have been a useful playground for pupils.[5]

In 1902 Rev. Roberts died, followed by his wife in 1904. That year Margaret Roberts married barrister Prescot Fewings and she moved to Torwood. Later her sister and brother, now a solicitor, also moved away from New Farm.

What became of their school? It seems probable that Miss Jeannette Stevenson assumed charge of the educational role that the Roberts' sisters relinquished. Rather than continue using the Roebucks' brick cottage (which may still be in existence today under the modernised exterior of 174 Moray Street), William Stevenson, before his death, possibly erected the two wooden school buildings on his own land.

* * *

By 1902[6] when her School was certainly in operation, Jeannette Stevenson was 25 years old and according to her later report, she was initially assisted by her sister Eleanor (then 23) until her death in 1942, when their younger sister Jeannie aged almost 60 joined the staff. Writing in 1960, Arthur Richards described their school as "a quiet little oasis where nothing has changed":

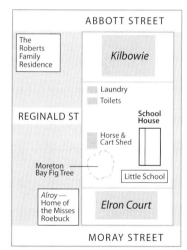

Reginald Street provided the main access to the New Farm Private School. The Infants' School, a tennis court and a large camphor laurel tree occupied the Moray Street frontage before *Elron Court* was built in the 1940s. The school shared a boundary with *Archibald House*.
— *Diagram: G. Benjamin*

THE SCHOOLHOUSE CONTAINS a single classroom, maybe 30 by 15 feet, with a long trestle table running the length of the room. This table occupies the centre of the floor. Miss Jeannette Stevenson sits at the head of it and the scholars sit on either side, away to the other end of the room. Behind Miss Stevenson, as she sits, is the blackboard. To her left is the piano. Before each pupil is the little personal pile of the scholar's tools-of-trade...[7]

The Stevensons' New Farm Private School was located within a block which ran from Moray to Abbott Street, thus creating cul-de-sacs in both Reginald and Herbert Streets. Despite surrounding land being progressively subdivided for housing lots, the Stevenson property remained intact.

Kilbowie, the family dwelling, was a high-set wooden house on the Abbott Street frontage and students from that street remember a pathway past the house to the school. Mrs Joy Arden (nee Le Brocq) who grew up in historic *Cairnsville* in Balfour Street attended the New Farm Private School, as did her son:

New Farm Private School pupils, pictured ca. 1963 with Miss Jeannie Stevenson, include Belle Davis, and (from left) Venero Armanno (who became a novelist and university lecturer), Roger Absalom (a vet), Arthur Davis (mechanic), Duncan Davis (wool classer) and the last boy is unknown. By July 1965 both Stevenson sisters had passed on, bringing to an end the school of almost 70 years. — *Photo: Isabelle Davis.*

I WAS THERE for six or seven years in the 1920s. There were only two classrooms. In the morning before Assembly, we'd do dumbbells (exercises), march around the table singing the ABC (Miss Stevenson played the piano), then we'd sing it backwards. The teachers did fairly well because when I left and went to a public school, I passed the Scholarship Public Examination. Of the Stevensons, there were three sisters who didn't marry, a brother and a brother's daughter.

When my son attended in the 1940s and 50s, Stevensons' school was a bit old-fashioned. The children took cut lunches and had to eat them in a tin shed which was hot. My son didn't like the ants. The classrooms were not quite up to it and there were paintings by the children and old photographs on the wall.[8]

Many other New Farm residents started their educational life at the Stevenson school in the 1930s. These included Cath Bishop (nee Carey) and Isabelle Davis (nee Taylor) from Abbott Street. Isabelle's uncle also attended the school as did her own children. Judith Lieberman, newly arrived from New South Wales in 1939, recorded her impression of Miss Jeannette Stevenson:

SHE WAS STERN looking with a stern manner but the two other ladies were very kind. I wrote on a slate but I don't remember doing a great deal of schoolwork. Our time seemed to be filled with knitting and crocheting for the war effort. The school itself was quite wild looking and overgrown with vines, while the big house at the end of the path had a ramshackle look … [9]

Little more than a block away on the corner of Sydney and Moray Streets was a school run by the McKenzie sisters. It was attended by local residents Bryan Oxlade and Russell Stevens as preschoolers in the 1930s.[10] Ivy Henderson (writing of the 1920s) also remarked about the McKenzies:

MUM DIDN'T KNOW much about New Farm or where the New Farm State School was, so she bundled us all up to Miss McKenzie's School. They were very happy to see us all and it wasn't until Mum received the bill at the end of the quarter that she thought, "What's this? You don't have to pay for school!"

She looked at her bill for the six of us then sent us all up to New Farm State School.[11]

Ivy Henderson ended up sending her own three daughters to Miss Stevenson's school "down near where the Carramar corner is." Her daughters went there until the age of 12 before going to the State School for Scholarship.

In 1939 the Moray Street portion of the Stevenson's land, on which there had been a grass tennis court, was sold so that a block of flats called *Elron Court* could be built. The Infants School was shifted to a new position and an easement preserved pupils' access from Moray Street. Miss Stevenson apparently followed a perennial curriculum consisting of the

The New Farm Private School's Prospectus. — *Kindly supplied by Isabelle Davis.*

The New Farm Private School.

MORAY STREET, NEW FARM,

(Opposite "MERTHYR.")

Conducted by
Miss Jeannette Stevenson
and
Miss Eleanor Stevenson.

'Phone: Central, 4476.

The Curriculum includes the following branches of Education—

ENGLISH.

HISTORY (Ancient and Modern).

GEOGRAPHY.

ARITHMETIC (including Mensuration).

FRENCH.

DRAWING.

GEOLOGY.

MUSIC (Theory and Practical).

PAINTING.

NEEDLEWORK (Plain and Fancy).

Music, Painting, and Advanced Drawing Extra.

Certificates from
TRINITY COLLEGE, LONDON.
and SYDNEY UNIVERSITY.

SPECIAL KINDERGARTEN ROOM.

FEES:

PER QUARTER
PAYABLE IN ADVANCE.

Higher School	-	£2 2s.
Middle ,,	-	£1 10s.
Lower ,,	-	£1 5s.
Kindergarten	-	£1 1s.

R. G. GILLIES & CO. LTD. PRINTERS.

elements of English and French grammar and literature, arithmetic, painting, music and social studies. She also advocated 'Elementary Decency' in an effort to stamp out juvenile snobbery, intolerance, deceit and disobedience.[12] All students were drilled in the school's motto, "Where there's a will, there's a way."

The three Stevenson sisters remained unmarried and were assisted by their niece Annie "Biddy" Wallace (b. 1898), daughter of their eldest sister Annie. Following the deaths of Jeannie (aged 75) in April 1964 and Jeannette (aged 89) in July 1965, Biddy hoped to continue the school but it could not be sustained without its founder.

The Stevenson contribution to New Farm is noteworthy for another reason. A 1965 newspaper article stated, "The longest tenure of land in New Farm is believed to belong to Miss Jeannette Stephenson's family." The article remarked that her father had bought the property more than 100 years before. In what could be a fitting epitaph to the sisters' educational achievement, the writer added, "At the bottom of the picturesque garden is to be found the New Farm Private School, a piece of Victoriana, which Miss Jeannette began more than 70 years ago." [13]

Notes

1. Arthur Richards, "A Little School that Time Forgot", *Courier Mail*, 27 June 1960, p. 2.
2. *Brisbane Courier*, 23 January 1895.
3. When the Misses Roberts advertised the re-opening of their school in 1896, the *Brisbane Courier* notice of 27 January 1896 stated that the school was in Moray Street, but added, "Apply *Ranza*, Merthyr Road." Presumably, *Ranza* was the Roberts' family home on the corner of Abbott Street and Merthyr Road.
4. John Oxley Library, image no. 24147. According to *New Farm Timeline* (researched and compiled by Helen Bennett & John Schiavo), Brisbane History Group Inc., April 1999, the house named *Alroy* was built for E.N. Marks and designed by John Hall & Sons in 1888.
5. The *Post Office Directories* for 1893 and 1901 show *Alroy* at 174 Moray Street to be occupied by Eliza and later Margaret Roebuck. Aged around 57 and 60 respectively in 1900, they were daughters of Captain GD Roebuck of the British East India Company and Henrietta (Andrew), a couple who married in Edinburgh in 1830. The girls were born in Calcutta and later lived with their Edinburgh grandmother. They came to Australia after 1881 and Eliza purchased the block at 174 Moray Street in 1892.
6. 1902 *Post Office Directory* stated, 'Stevenson, Miss Jeannette—Private School.'
7. Richards, *op. cit.*
8. Oral History: Joy Arden, 1997.
9. Oral History: Judith Benjamin (nee Lieberman), 2008.
10. There are few details of the McKenzie School. The 1907 *Post Office Directory* shows Miss Emma McKenzie, "Private School", on Merthyr Road between Bowen Terrace and Watson Street (northside), at the same address as Mrs Emma McKenzie of *Athelstane*. By the 1925 *Electoral Roll*, there are two teachers in Moray Street named McKenzie — Emma (jun.) and Louisa. Also listed is Louisa Hannah McKenzie, of Sydney and Moray Streets. In the *Courier Mail* of 24 January 1934 on page 3, the following notice appeared: "Miss McKenzie's School and Kindergarten, Moray & Sydney Streets, New Farm, 1st term, Tuesday 30 January 1934." In the 1936 *Electoral Roll*, Emma and Louisa continue to be listed, along with Edith Wilson McKenzie (YWCA, Bowen Terrace, New Farm—school teacher.)
11. Oral History: Ivy Henderson, 1992.
12. Richards, *op. cit.*
13. *The Telegraph*, 6 March 1965.

Some Early Industries

...now almost forgotten

Matthews's Nursery is likely to have taken over part of the old convict farm. The sketch accompanying the sale notice showed a large asparagus bed on the Brunswick Street frontage, along with rose beds and a fernery on the Bowen Terrace boundary. 39 blocks were for sale on 26 January 1901, "close to the proposed recreational reserve," said the advertising. It was not until 1913 that New Farm Park was established. — *Estate Plan: State Library of Qld.*

A N EARLY NEW Farm enterprises was Henry Matthews' Queensland Nursery begun in the late 1870s. It was on a block bounded by Brunswick Street and Bowen Terrace, and the tracks later known as Merthyr Road and Sydney Street.[1]

Henry had followed a circuitous route to New Farm. Born in England in 1829, he came to Australia in 1849 pursuing gold both at Canoona near Rockhampton and in New South Wales. Both adventures left him "rich in experience but poor in fortune." Instead he turned to the botanical wealth that lay in the soil, discovering his talent as a nurseryman. Henry had been in charge of Guilfoyle and Sons' Nursery in Sydney, setting up near Mrs Macquarie's Chair close to the Sydney Opera House. He later came to Brisbane, and as manager, worked for A J Hockings' nursery at Montague Road, West End. Next he was employed at the Brisbane Botanical Gardens under the first curator Walter Hill, who was credited with the introduction of the mango, papaw, ginger, poinciana and jacaranda to Queensland around 1864.

It was after this that Henry established, on a plot of around five acres of low-lying ground, the first nursery in New Farm. He resided in Bowen Terrace in a home that was still standing in 1974. His eldest son Richard lived in a small wooden cottage on the Merthyr Road frontage.

This nursery continued until around the turn of the century. On Saturday 26th January 1901, *Matthews's Nursery Estate* comprised of "39 large residence sites", was auctioned. Four years later, the estate plan for *Turner's Paddock* referred to this locality as "late Matthews' Nursery, now densely populated." Henry's son Samuel Costin Matthews (1862-1936) followed him into the nursery business establishing Rosenholme Nursery in Annie Street after the 1893 flood.

> MY FATHER SOON *won silver cups donated by the Queensland Horticultural Society in 1889 for roses and a special award for the Best Collection Cut Flowers. He was a great friend of Mr Walter Hill, the first curator of the Brisbane Botanical Gardens. The Lagerstroemia Matthews, the pink variety, was propagated by him as also was a variety of poinsettia.[2]*

The Rosenholme Nursery was a Sunday morning meeting place for many locals who came to buy flowers to place on graves, which was the practice then. Dr T. P. Lucas, the naturalist of Papaw Ointment fame, was a regular visitor seeking Mr Matthews' opinion on matters of their mutual botanical interest.

> ONE YEAR, THERE *was a great interest in growing giant chrysanthemum blooms for showing, and father would allocate areas of his nursery for his friends who would attend their plants on their chosen section. Another time, there were six hives of bees, one of which was Italian.[3] These bees disliked people who handled horses and Mr Tom Bowers,[4] a friend, who drove a horse and dray for the City Council, would be chased by them the full length of the nursery. It was quite an event when father decided to rob the beehives for honey and everyone was instructed to stay in the house to avoid being stung, until he had finished his operation.[5]*

Samuel Matthews designed and landscaped the surroundings for the Mater Hospital in 1912. This nursery appears to have benefited from a perennial water supply nearby, as Fred Matthews explains:

> THE ROADS OUTSIDE *Brisbane City were unsealed and council men were continuously filling in the ruts caused by traffic and rain showers. Half way up Annie Street towards Brunswick Street, there was always grass on the road due to a perpetual spring there. Inside the fence of a house owned by the Fawcett family,[6] there remained a well, and my father told me it was the only local water supply available during the 1892 drought, and people came from all around to draw their water from here. The well was never empty.*

There were many small businesses in New Farm, an example being that cabinet maker Benjamin Winston. There was a showroom on Brunswick Street, and the factory was near the corner of James and Browne Streets. He was in operation from at least 1903, and several of his sons followed him into the business.

Another of Samuel's sons showed a different talent. Electrician Ernest Matthews (b. 1891) was awarded First Order of Merit for his fire alarm at the Brisbane RNA Exhibition in 1911. He also patented the Matthews Automatic Fire Protection System. In 1916 he occupied a factory at 77 Annie Street (close to the family home at No. 57). By 1923 the company was registered and the manufacture and installation of thermal fire detection systems began. John Edward Hinton, first superintendant of the Brisbane Fire Brigade, encouraged Ernest in the development of his fire alarm patents. Ernest designed the first type of street fire alarm box, a 'Break-the-Glass and Push-the-Button' device. After 1974 the factory moved to Helen Street, Newstead and Ernest's brother, Fred Matthews, was managing director.

Mr Ernest Costin Matthews at the 1913 RNA Exhibition in Brisbane. He founded Matthews Fire Alarm in 1923 and the devices were later manufactured at 77 Annie Street. Matthews' Nursery may have supplied the shrubbery. — *Photo: Matthews Fire Alarms, Brisbane.*

* * *

THE SHOWROOM OF Edmund Rosenstengel (1887-1962) at 524 Brunswick Street in an old picture theatre not far from *Avalon* left a respectful impression on many New Farm dwellers. His furniture-making was distinguished by the use of Queensland timbers, particularly maple and silky oak, together with elaborate carving and marquetry inlay. As Grahame Miller explained:

A general view of lounge and dining room furniture at the Rosenstengel showroom at 524 Brunswick Street. — *State Library of Queensland, Image 141030.*

I KNEW SOMEONE at Rosenstengel's making handmade reproduction antique furniture. There were no nails or screws because everything was hand-dowelled. They had a window display that wasn't changed in 35 years. One window had a beautiful bedroom suite and the other was a dining suite, all carved with acorns and embellishments. Sometimes their furniture comes up at auction and it's worth thousands of dollars.[7]

Edmund Rosenstengel learned cabinet-making in Toowoomba and worked overseas in several countries before opening in Brisbane in 1922. He lived at 72 Harcourt Street and his dedication to quality was forthright, as Bryan Oxlade learned:

Rosenstengel's furniture shop on Brunswick Street was on the crest of the hill on the right. I was told that a representative said to Mr Rosenstengel, "I compliment you on your tradesmen."

"Tradesmen!" *he replied indignantly. "I don't employ tradesmen. I employ craftsmen!"*[8]

* * *

When digging in the grounds of his home on the corner of Hazelwood and Sydney Streets, a resident found little wooden toys. These were the last remnants of a largely forgotten but once flourishing business in the area. Sutton's Toy Factory made a full range of wooden toys including rocking horses, trains and pull carts.[9]

For those with the eyes to see, the clue is in the gable. This used to be the abode of Mr Sutton whose dexterity with wood earned him a flourishing toy business. — Photo: G. Benjamin

The factory was all corrugated iron. The windows were even corrugated iron. They used to lift the windows up and prop them open with a bit of timber. It must have been hot! Mr Sutton wore gray working clothes and he used to live a few doors from my home. On his old house in Mountford Road, the gable reads "Nottus" or "Sutton" backwards.[10]

* * *

There was another timber business nearby on Brunswick Street which was entered from Elystan Road. The Fooks owned two houses and ran a sawmill and joinery operation in a corrugated iron shed on the blocks behind the houses. Big logs were brought in by truck.[11]

On Oxlade Drive during the 20s and 30s from almost opposite 123 Oxlade Drive, an engineer named Sidney Dyne, ran Dyne's Wire Works which was particularly popular with local boys scouting for material to use on their contraptions.

The boys also liked to forage in the scrap metal piles looking for ball bearings for their slingshots or other interesting items.[12]

Notes

1. According to *Electoral Rolls*, in 1876 Henry Matthews was a gardener of Ann Street, Valley; by 1878-9, he was a nurseryman of Brunswick Street, New Farm and Ann Street, Valley.
2. Oral History: Fred Matthews, 1974.
3. Most likely 'Italian bees' rather than an Italian's hive. According to Eva Crane, *The World History of Beekeeping and Honey Hunting*, Taylor & Francis, 1999, Italian queen bees were imported into Queensland in 1880. "None had such a permanent or important effect on world beekeeping as the Italian." (p. 370-71)
4. 1905 *Electoral Roll*, a drayman of 90 Annie Street.
5. Matthews, *op. cit.*
6. An appropriately named family, on the 1913 *Electoral Roll* at 37 Annie Street.
7. Oral History: Grahame Miller, 1993
8. Oral History: Bryan Oxlade, 2008
9. Oral History: Russell Stevens, 1992-94
10. Oxlade, *op. cit.*
11. Oral History: Brian Hjelm, 2008; Oxlade, *ibid.*
12. Hjelm, *ibid.*

Old teachers never die...

New Farm State School's first year attendance in 1901, taken on the Heal Street side of the school. — *Photo: George Cowin*

WHEN THE LONG-AWAITED New Farm State School opened on Monday 21 January 1901, the Head Teacher Arthur Outridge no doubt thought that even if a few more than the anticipated 332 scholars arrived, they could be easily accommodated. The school building had been designed to house 392 pupils in three classrooms sized 12m x 7.3m which would hold two classes each.

One can only guess at Mr Outridge's dismay when enrolments on the first day totalled 582! Two days later when the total had climbed to 621, he felt compelled to write to the Department of Public Instruction asking for additional furniture and permission to hold classes under the school. So began the scourge of overcrowding that was to plague NFSS for almost the next 50 years.

* * *

WITH THE OPENING of CSR in 1893 and other industries soon following, the increasing numbers of workers living in the area and raising young families, added urgency to the need for a local school. The only alternatives were that the children either walk or travel to the Fortitude Valley School, Leichhardt Street School (later Brisbane Central), St. Patrick's in the Valley or the Stevensons' New Farm Private School in Moray Street.

On 3 February 1899 the New Farm State School Building Committee convened its first meeting under the chairmanship of Thomas Welsby. Influential in business and politics Mr Welsby resided close by at *Amity*, the home by the river that he built in 1892 which still stands at the end of Welsby Street. Other members of the School Building Committee included: P. Angus, J. Clark,[1] C. Cohen, W. Cowin, A Dougan,

E. Garnett, W. Jary, T. McMinn, W. Marchant,[2] J.W. Massey, T. Murfin, W. Scott and W.M. Thompson.[3]

Thomas Welsby arranged the acquisition of the land bounded by James, Heal and Annie Streets at a reasonable cost to the government and when building plans were approved and outlays tallied, the total was £3,571/5/-. One-sixth £634 was to be met by the local community. This was achieved, the last £100 being guaranteed by Mr Welsby and Alderman Thompson.

The building was ready for the 1901 school intake and officiating at the opening was New Farm's leading citizen Sir Samuel Griffith MLA.

The Departmental response to the unprecedented influx of new students was that pupils were "leaving other good schools to crowd into this fine new school," but nevertheless permission was granted to Mr Outridge to use space under the school for classrooms, but only on a temporary basis. This situation which was to continue until 1939.

The Head Teacher was forced to face the compounding problems of there being too few toilets, the prospect of average classes of 40-50 students and sometimes 80 pupils, plus dust and dirt coming down from above to the under-school rooms, particularly on windy days,

This framed memento was presented to Thomas Welsby on 19 December 1900 in gratitude for forming the Building Committee which raised the required local contribution of £634. — *Photo: George Cowin*

Amity was built for Thomas Welsby in 1892 and was named after the ship which brought the first soldiers and convicts to Moreton Bay in 1824. Welsby lived here until his death in 1941, the Royal Australian Navy occupied it during World War II, then it was owned by CSR until 1980. It still stands today. — *Photo: G. Benjamin*

all of which gave rise to this pithy evaluation by Brian Penton, a pupil around 1914 who took up a career in writing:

> (NFSS WAS ...) *an underfunded and overcrowded school built on a rocky outcrop, where almost half the children were taught in open classrooms underneath the buildings, exposed to the westerlies in winter and the dust from the floors overhead all year round.*[4]

Margaret Gilmour who started school in the 1920s expressed just how it felt for a young newcomer:

New Farm State School in 1995. The building on the right had more storeys added. — *Photo: Betty Smith.*

I WAS IN Prep One with young Miss Mills. There were long desks with slate holes to put your slate in and long forms so that you could rest your back on the desk behind. There were 70 children in that class. I was just five and a half, and to be put into a class of 70 was overwhelming.[5]

In August 1917 there was an epidemic of diptheria and the Health Officer who visited the school reported that crowding was severe, with 928 on the roll. Mr Cunningham, the second Head Teacher, negotiated unsuccessfully with the Department for glass windows in the new annexe instead of blinds. There were other causes for concern such as the playing area which was small, rough and rocky.

When the road cutting below the school in James Street was excavated around 1930 to allow the sewerage to be put through New Farm, the blasting meant that many rock particles were thrown onto the school grounds and surrounding houses, even though matting was used. As a result some windows were broken.

It took until 1939 for a top storey to be added to two wings thereby providing five extra classrooms. By 1962 the enrolment was 589, not far below the total for the opening week in 1901. The next major milestone was the opening of the swimming pool in October 1966. Now in its 107th year, there are many examples of NFSS's having taught several generations of the same family. Forebears of both the Garnett and Cowin families were on the 1899 Foundation Committee followed by three generations of scholars in each case.

The current enrolment is just above 300. It would come as a shock to current students to know that once upon a time, their school had just one building which housed more than twice the current enrolment.

Fred Matthews, who attended during 1909-1917, had clear recollections that hark back to a time when New Farm parents' occupations might have included bootmaker, farmer, tailor, blacksmith, saddler, sawyer, coachman, wharfinger, bill sticker, tinsmith, tobacco twister, bacon curer, lightkeeper, grazier, cornfactor, oysterman, manager of Turkish baths, mercer, hawker, coppersmith, clicker, drayman, paper bag maker, gold miner, fireman on a steamer, seamstress, letter carrier, pearl sheller, cooper, washerwoman, saw sharpener, tallowman or wharf lumper.

THE SCHOOL HOURS were 9:30am to 12:30pm, then 2-4pm. The one and a half hours for lunch gave us time to play cricket over the hill in what was known as

Howards Hollow — that is except when the gypsies camped there each year. During their stay scholars would remain in the school grounds because of the fear of being kidnapped by them...

Fred recorded a remarkable occurrence:

IN FOURTH GRADE I was taught by Mrs Mulligan and during an electrical storm, lightning struck a tall pine tree at St Clair School and a fireball entered our classroom, floated around, then went out of a window to explode over Heal Street.

Such phenomena must not have been unknown in New Farm since Isabelle Davis recalls that a teacher at the New Farm Private School had a profound fear of thunderstorms: "She must have once been in a shocking electrical storm because she used to turn off every bit of electricity when a storm was forecast."

"I say and I do," said the motto on a version of the school badge which reflected the reality of being so close to major military activity during World War II. The badge was possibly inspired by the Headmaster Pat Currie (1884-1949) who served in both world wars and retired as headmaster in December 1948.
— *Courtesy of Robert Blaikie*

In more recent times appreciation for the work of New Farm State School remains positive. Former pupil and past headmaster Allan Faragher considered that the ethnic diversity was a delightful education in itself, while Barbara Millward, a teacher-aide during the 70s and 80s, remarked: "Being a multicultural school made us unique. We may not have had the most modern of facilities but we turned out some outstanding citizens."[6]

A regular New Farm State School event was the annual fancy dress ball held in the old Rivoli picture theatre and elsewhere.

The fancy dress ball, usually held at the Rivoli Theatre, was a highlight of the school year and provided the opportunity for a child's (or their parent's) alter ego to have a night out. — *Photo: Robert Blaikie*

When very young, Ken Rayner won a prize dressed as a butcher's delivery boy pulling a tricycle on which was a butter box, painted in the blue of the Rayner truck and with the Rayner name on it. On top was a butcher's wicker basket containing a long string of sausages. "Nutsy", a tough footballer, was given the job of looking after Ken and protecting the sausages. On another occasion, Ken was John Bull; Sam was Uncle Sam several times; Madge was at various times an advertisement for Shell, a tennis player and, in her last year, a beau in the Regency dance, "The Gavotte". [7]

While schools are principally about students, it is worth remembering that those who assume the responsibility for the smooth running of a school often privately endure a personal cost. For instance John Skirving Cunningham, who was appointed as the second Head Teacher in 1909, was remembered by Marjorie Fischle (nee Thompson) as "wearing a little embroidered cap and using the cane," while Fred Matthews regarded him as "a strict one for discipline who tempered it with kindness." His daughter Miss Jean Cunningham was also a teacher at the school and was well liked.

The Cunninghams lived at 75 Moreton Street having shifted down from previous posts in North Queensland. Despite Mr Cunningham's difficulties in seeking better conditions for New Farm school, he clearly inspired sound instruction since, of the 1917 Scholarship class, all passed, with two students gaining third and fifth places in Queensland.

Mr Cunningham's son Cyril, a bank clerk, enlisted in the AIF in 1917 and his death 20 months later in France took its toll on the family. Mrs Mary Cunningham died in December 1920 and less than three months later she was followed by their 27 year old daughter Vera.

In a heartfelt letter written in 1922 to Army headquarters Mr Cunningham apologized for not completing a form relating to his son's death, and wrote, "I lost my wife and daughter recently, both practically the result of his death, and the filling up of the paper brought everything back." To compound the tragedy, he was forced to request a second commemorative scroll for Cyril since, "unfortunately my house was burned down and I lost mine." Mr Cunningham finished his term at NFSS at the end of 1923 but there was still more scope for teaching and apparently a local need for personalised instruction...

75 Moreton Street, the home of retired New Farm State School Head Teacher Mr Cunningham and his daughter Jean, also a teacher. Classes were provided underneath the house in the 1920s.
— Photo: G. Benjamin

A Mr Cunningham owned a house in Moreton Street and he had a room built underneath and used it as a school for boys. Around 11-12 boys attended. He was a retired teacher.[8]

This would have been conveniently located for brothers Allan and Ron Grant of Bowen Terrace during the later 1920s. Since educators rarely retire from providing instruction when the need exists, perhaps it was a collaborative effort by father and daughter, although it was known as 'Miss Cunningham's School for Boys.' John Cunningham died in 1936 aged 80.

Notes

1. The 'J. Clark' on the committee was possibly James Clark, the 'Pearl-King'. In 1915, Clark's son James Colin, married Tom Welsby's daughter, Marion.
2. Ellen and William Marchant, a paper merchant, lived at Annie Street, Kingsholme. Their school-age sons Henry and William would have benefitted from the new school close by.
3. George Cowin's plaque of 19 December 1900 shows four different names: A. Davidson, A. Bell, Jos. Bell and D. Tweedie. There were possibly some substitutions.
4. Patrick Buckridge's talk given to the New Farm Historical Society on 24 May 2008 entitled, "Home of the 'Nice People': Brian Penton's Vision of New Farm in the Late Nineteenth Century."
5. Oral History: Margaret Gilmour, 2007.
6. *Memories of New Farm State School*, 2001, pp 36 and 48 respectively.
7. Sam Rayner, *Sid & Gladys Rayner of New Farm, Brisbane & Their Ancestors*. 1992. p. 6.10.
8. Oral History: Ron Grant, 2002.

Left: Grade IIB, in February 1937. *Below:* Grade VA in 1940. — *Class photos kindly supplied by Robert Blaikie.*

11

St Clair School, James Street

Miss Annie Midgley's educational establishment

Cairncross House on James Street was built ca. 1865 and was known as *St Clair House* by 1882. Built as a grand residence, the home had also been used as an orphanage school and hospital before Annie Midgley established her school here in 1905, an enterprise that was to run for 38 years — *Photo: John Schiavo, 1997*

W ITH THE RECENTLY-OPENED New Farm State School increasingly overcrowded, the way lay open for competent teachers to take private pupils. Within a stone's throw of the State School lived the Midgley family, including the talented Ann. Since the family home named *St Clair* had once served as a school and later a hospital, it lent itself perfectly to becoming Miss Midgley's educational establishment which she opened in 1905.

Ann (b. 1866), known as Annie, was the eldest daughter of James and Elizabeth Midgley who rented *St Clair*, the handsome eight-roomed stone house at 135 James Street (then No. 235), having moved there from South Brisbane in 1903. Of the eight grown children in the household, Annie and Violet were artists, Madeline was a teacher, Harry a brushmaker and Richard a timber salesman.

Annie well merited the description 'artist'. Her 1899 painting *The Departure of the First Queensland Contingent to South Africa* found its way into the Colonial Collection of the Australian War Memorial in Canberra. Interest in military matters was uppermost in the Midgley family and all of Annie's brothers joined the Queensland Defence Force. Stephen — later Lieut-Col Midgley CMG DSO — was in an army contingent during the 1891 Shearers' Strike, fought in the Boer War in South Africa with Breaker Morant, and distinguished himself both at Gallipoli and in France.[1] Frank served in Africa and Harry also served at Gallipoli.

*The Departure of the First Queensland Contingent to South Afric*a painted in oil by Annie Midgley in 1899. When purchased by the Australian War Memorial in 1996 for its Colonial Collection, nothing was known of the artist. Soon after, a chance meeting between the AWM's art curator and the grandson (also Stephen) of Annie Midgley's brother Stephen, resulted in the painting's provenance coming to light — *Reproduced by permission of the AWM.*

According to Midgley family recollections, Annie was "ambidextrous and could instruct two pupils at the one time and write with both hands simultaneously. She painted in oils and water colours, modelled plaster busts, and after injuring her hand or developing arthritis, she took up wood carving as a therapy."

Miss Midgley's school, 'for boarding and day scholars, Music and public exams', is also remembered as a family enterprise. Since her brothers and sisters continued to live either at *St Clair* or close by, her nieces and nephews shared in the duties of running a school.

A charming vignette of life at *St Clair* during the late 20s and early 30s was provided by Thomas Love, a great-nephew of Miss Midgley, reminiscing about his boyhood there:

Annie Midgley's brother, Captain Stephen Midgley, at the Zulu War 1906. The photo was taken by Ivor Thord-Gray (1878-1964), a Swedish adventurer and soldier. — *Photo: Stephen Midgley, Canberra*

> *IN THE DRAWING room were many paintings by Ann, one of which was an oil of a troopship leaving Brisbane for the Boer War, no doubt just like 'Maori King' in which her two brothers Frank and Stephen travelled to South Africa.*
>
> *This room also contained a good deal of furniture which had been carved by Ann. A short distance down the hall to the right was the music room. On a pedestal outside the door was a plaster head of Stephen, also by Ann.*
>
> *In the music room hung a very realistic charcoal and chalk drawing of the head of a horse, apparently during a war action, showing great fear in its eyes and biting on the bit. Ann was obviously influenced by the family's army associations and her brothers' war service.*
>
> *Down a short flight of stairs was another small hallway which, to the left, led to the front door and the classroom, and to the right, the dining room and kitchen. The kitchen and dining room had that smell peculiar to schools, institutions and the like. Through the kitchen was the pantry and a passage where, among other things, Indian clubs and dumb-bells were stored.*
>
> *Outside this area was a toilet, and in a cage was a once-white sulphur-crested cockatoo which had lost almost all of its feathers except the sulphur crest. It talked quite well but its most frequent remark was, "Get your strap, Cockie." In the yard there were outbuildings and a fowl run. There was also an emu which was confined*

Miss Anne Midgley ca. 1922 holding her nephew Hamar, son of Stephen Midgley, pictured at top. In 1984, Hamar Midgley received the Order of Australia Medal for his studies of native freshwater fish. — *Photo: Stephen Midgley, Canberra*

to a certain area. This emu laid eggs quite regularly and these were given to anyone who asked for them.[2] There was also a pet koala in the early days.

Alongside the main building was the tennis court which had orange and purple bougainvillea growing over the enclosing wire mesh. In later days, two houses were built on the land once occupied by the tennis court and the land surrounding it. The sleeping quarters were on the upper floor.

On Sundays all pupils were marched to church services at the Holy Trinity Church in the Valley or to St John's Cathedral. All the family attended church at least two or three times each Sunday. On Sunday night was high tea usually consisting of boiled eggs. Each had their personal ring on their serviettes which were kept in a rack.

Ann and Madeline every night went from dormitory to dormitory after prayers, at lights out, and all would join in singing the hymn, "I have Promised to Serve Thee to the End." Mrs Brown was one of the professional teachers at the school.[3]

The land upon which *St Clair* stood was made available at auction in 1853 and in 1862, a large portion on the corner of James and Terrace Streets was acquired by Elizabeth Cairncross. The sizeable stone residence built in1865 became known as *Cairncross House*. It attracted the attention of Mother Vincent Whitty for the purpose of establishing the Roman Catholic Orphan School. It housed 47 children by 1867 and was the forerunner of Nudgee Orphanage.

Among subsequent owners of *St Clair House* (as it was advertised in an 1882 auction) was Sir Arthur Hunter Palmer, Premier of Queensland during 1870-74. When the Hunter Palmer family eventually subdivided the property, Annie Midgley took the opportunity in 1925 to purchase the house and a portion totalling around

Madeline Midgley (right) holding her niece Florence ("Sonnie") photographed in December 1912. There are 27 children pictured, along with two young women (top LHS) in front of *St Clair*. — *Photo: NFDHS.*

70 perches. That year only three of the family were listed as living at *St Clair* — Annie and Madeline (teachers), and Maude (who had joined an Anglican order of nuns and subsequently left). Next door on the corner of Terrace and James Street was Richard, still a timber salesman. Annie and Madeline continued to teach into the next decade and were joined by their niece Florence (Sonnie) Midgley who taught music.

Joan Kopelke attended *St Clair's* from around 1927 until 1930:

> I DO NOT remember much about St Clair's. I started school here as there were only a few private schools and the State School. An older girl, Drell Shields, would walk me there. I always said that the Midgley sisters were two old maids but when you are only six, everyone else is old. I can remember concerts in the Holy Trinity Church Hall and the Midgleys would stand in the wings and say, "Louder, louder," all the time we were singing. When I went to the convent, it was "Softly, softly…"[4]

While the sisters certainly taught young children, *St Clair* apparently also took in orphans and wards of the state as boarders, with the government paying for their upkeep.

> IT WAS A funny school. Mum decided she wanted us not to go to the State School but to be little ladies so we went to St Clair's. Most of the children came from the country and they were boarders in dormitories. There were two young teachers, just girls, who could never have coped with boys.[5]

In 1931, 11 year old Leona Ross boarded at *St Clair*:

> AT CHRISTMAS-TIME ALL the children left at the school received a gift, usually a book which the Midgley sisters may have paid for out of their own money. After marching back from the Christmas Day service at the Holy Trinity Church, the children would all sing songs and hold their books above their heads.[6]

Leona told her daughter Pat Smith that these were "the best and happiest memories from her childhood, and that the children loved the Midgley sisters."

Miss Annie Midgley is said to have always been meticulously dressed, with high collars buttoned up to the neck, dresses below the ankles and wearing laced boots. It was a 'uniform' that she continued up until her death in September 1943, aged 77. The property was conveyed to her sister Madeline, passing out of the family in 1951. The building was converted to flats and painted pink, becoming known locally as the 'Pink Flats.'

Notes

1. At Gallipoli Midgley wore "a piece of black felt shaped like a cat, tucked into his uniform. He believed it brought him good luck after a black cat had jumped onto his chest one night in Africa, forewarning him of a Zulu attack." John Hamilton, *Gallipoli Sniper: The Life of Billy Sing*. Sydney, Pan Macmillan, 2008.
2. Living in a Terrace Street property near *St Clair*, Florence O'Brien remembered two emus at St Clair that were very tame. See Oral History: Florence O'Brien, 2008.
3. Thomas Clyde Love (b. 1923), a great-nephew of Ann Midgley, recorded his recollections in 1982 which are part of the Family Records of the Midgley Family.
4. Oral History: Joan Kopelke, 2008.
5. Oral History: Dorothy Messinbird, 1992.
6. E-mail, 25 September 2008, from Pat Smith (daughter of Leona Ross).

12

New Farm Park

A venerable riverside sanctuary...

Parasols, umbrellas and canvas awnings were needed for shade in the very early days of New Farm Park. This scene dates from 1915 soon after the opening of the Park's band rotunda. — *Source unknown.*

Now 95 YEARS old, New Farm Park is regarded as a 'city icon.' In 2004 in support of its entry on the Queensland Heritage Register, an editorial lauded the Park's "practicality and ease of purpose", and the fact that since its inception it had been "at the centre of Brisbane's social and recreational development." [1] The scene had looked quite different in the very early days, as there had been a racetrack nearby but further to the north-east:

> BEAUTIFUL NEW FARM Park was a most dismal looking place, mostly covered in clumps of thorn bushes. A dirty muddy creek meandered across them to the junction of Brunswick Street and Merthyr Road and emptied into the river near the Powerhouse. The rose garden was a big shallow swamp and there was another ti-tree swamp between Merthyr Road and the New Farm Bowling Green. There was also a chain of swamps running from the back of the Sugar Refinery (before it was built) and ending in a bull-rush swamp at the foot of Kingsholme. [2]

A long-time local resident recalled that the location was "rather primitive" in the early days, [3] while Arch Trail explained that it was an asset to the nearby dairy:

> BEFORE THE PARK was developed by the Council, cows were grazed on the land and were taken across the road to the back of a house on the corner of Elystan Road and Brunswick Street. This house fronted Elystan Road and the milking shed was on the side fence on the yard of 1001 Brunswick Street. This operation ceased when the area was subdivided. [4]

IN A LETTER to the editor of the *Brisbane Courier* in 1884, Nehemiah Bartley pointed out that there was 'not one square inch of public land reserved for health, air, shade and recreation' for the growing population of Fortitude Valley, Teneriffe and the New Farm peninsula. In suggesting that the government buy 30-40 acres of riverfront land and plant it with shade trees, he was prefiguring the locality's iconic centrepiece. [5]

In 1913 the Brisbane Municipal Council purchased, from the Australian Bank of Commerce, 37 acres (15 ha) for a park costing £25,800. Soon after, a layout was designed which included a ring road, and there were substantial plantings of jacarandas, poincianas, bougainvilleas and roses, under the supervision of Mr Henry Moore. A band rotunda was built in 1915 followed by a refreshment kiosk.

Football and cricket ovals, croquet lawns and tennis courts were all established in 1917, but because of the Great War the official opening by the Governor was postponed until 19 July 1919. In 1922 'war trophies' of a German Albatross aeroplane and a 5.9 inch howitzer gun were added, later to be removed in 1931 and 1955 respectively.

A 1925 proposal for open air swimming baths was not completed. Basketball courts and change rooms were opened in 1938 and a playground was added in 1955.

From the 1950s the Park's rose gardens were redeveloped and expanded with many new varieties. At one stage the Park claimed to have 12,000 rose bushes representing 250 cultivated varieties.[6] It seems that ash from the nearby Powerhouse had much to do with the quality of blooms:

> AROUND 1936-37, I was on relief work in the Park. When the City Electric Light Powerhouse was operating the ashes were brought around. They opened up trenches with gangs. There would be a gang of us unemployed — about a dozen

New Farm Park ca. 1937, with its elaborate garden design. The rotunda (bottom left) and kiosk (top right) are clearly visible, as are Coronet Court and the Bowls Club on Brunswick Street which runs across the top left hand corner. — *Image: John Oxley Library, 34000*

young fellas — and we'd dig out this trench and the soil went up onto the rose (gardens. Trucks from the Powerhouse would fill those trenches up with ashes. Later on after the ashes had set and the grass had grown, they'd open up in between the ashes and take that remaining soil. They had gorgeous roses there then.[7]

New Farm Park had the benefit of an impressive sports oval near the corner of Brunswick and Sydney Streets, ringed by a low wire fence with white painted posts and rails. Cricket was played here in the summer, and goal posts were put up in the winter for rugby league.

LARGE WHITE PAINTED sight screens for cricket were at each end, and athletics and baseball competitions also took place there. A two-storey change room was at the street corner and it had a verandah on the upper level with space for the sporting officials. Another single storey change room was built at the other end.[8]

The parochialism of some football matches in the Park in the 1930s was recalled by John Rosenskjar whose relatives lived just across the road. "On the Saturday afternoon there were fairly wild sorts of football teams. Sometimes the visitors used to get pelted home with bricks…"[9]

* * *

AFTER THE 1974 flood deposited a layer of chemically charged silt over the entire gardens, extensive replanting took place. In recent years the band rotunda has been restored to its original form and is a very popular venue for weddings. The kiosk was destroyed by fire in 2002. The children's playground has enjoyed several redevelopments, though two historic steamrollers were removed in 1995 because they did not meet Australian Standards in playground equipment.

In recent years many of New Farm Park's grand jacaranda trees have suffered or been lost because of decreased rainfall. Others have been fenced off, pending reports by tree surgeons. This is in stark contrast with the impressive jacaranda blooms of a decade ago. In 1997 in Grafton, New South Wales, also famous for its jacarandas, postcards were on sale locally showing their own purple tree-lined avenues. It came to light however, that the photo on the postcard was actually of New Farm Park![10]

According to a resident who had lived across from the Park for 50 years, there was always a deep gully that was sure to flood into the river after any decent rain.[11] This is close to where the Brisbane City Council library was opened in 1975. In 1987 New Farm Park enjoyed some expansion when it gained an extra 2.57 hectares from land unused by the Powerhouse.

In 1979 the Park was chosen as a fitting spot for the installation of a clock and time capsule by Rotary International near the Brunswick Street entrance, while 1995 marked the unveiling of a sculptural monument of the terrain of Sabah outlining the route of the infamous Sandakan death marches of World War II.

A 1962 newspaper article described New Farm Park as "a mecca for gardeners, band lovers and sportsmen."[12] These days, it is still a mecca — and as New Farm becomes increasingly urbanised, the suburb's iconic recreational sanctuary is appreciated more than ever.

New Farm Park ca. 1925. The river is at the top and Merthyr Road runs across the bottom of the picture. The entrance to the Park was off Brunswick Street adjacent to the present day New Farm Bowls Club. On the upper left is the CSR Refinery. The empty ground on the corner of Welsby, Sydney and Lamington Streets was awaiting the construction of Austral Motors' workshops. Coronet Court and the Powerhouse were yet to be built. — *Image: John Oxley Library, 168678*

Notes

1. *Courier Mail*, Brisbane, 8 December 2004.
2. Stephen Wellstood Jack, *S.W. Jack's Cutting Book No. 2*, pp 28-29. Unidentified newspaper cutting, post-1928.
3. Oral History: Fred Matthews, 1974.
4. Oral History: Arch Trail, 2002.
5. *Brisbane Courier*, 29 October 1884.
6. Unidentified newspaper article, "New Farm Park — A Blooming Asset", ca. 1998; another report in *The Telegraph*, 6 March 1965 mentions 40,000 rose trees of 300 different varieties.
7. Oral History: Harry Barker, 1992.
8. Oral History: Brian Hjelm, 2008.
9. Oral History: John Rosenskjar, 2008.
10. *Grafton Daily Examiner*, 25 May 1997.
11. Alison Hamer of Sydney Street, interviewed by Robert Ferguson, in *New Farm Oral History Group Interviews 1992-1994*, New Farm Library; Brisbane City Council; New Farm & Districts Historical Society.
12. *The Telegraph*, Brisbane, 19 July 1962.

13 Rayner's Butcher Shop

Building a business... and an apartment block

R AYNER'S SHOP AND name endure to this day in the Merthyr Village shopping precinct. The establishment of the butcher shop there in 1925 was to meet the need posed by the increasing residential development in the lower-lying areas of Brunswick Street.

Sidney Rayner already had some acquaintance with the butcher's trade

Sid Rayner (right) standing outside the butcher shop at 770 Brunswick Street (corner of Browne Street) around 1920-1925. The Rayners lived in a house attached to the rear of the shop until 1930. — *Photo: Sam Rayner.*

when he emigrated from Lancashire in 1909 as a 22 year old. By 1912 he was a partner in a butcher shop in Milton Road, Auchenflower but war service intervened. By 1920 Sid was back in the trade, this time at 770 Brunswick Street (corner with Browne Street).

Now married to Gladys (Whittick), the couple juggled the business with parenthood since their dwelling was attached to the shop which dated from 1888. Stables with feed boxes and two cart sheds ran the whole length of the property's back fence, so earlier owners may have employed horse and cart deliveries to customers, though in Sid's time this was probably achieved by using a boy on a bicycle.

An early picture of this part of New Farm is provided by Sam Rayner's compilation of family history:

IN 1876 THERE were occupied houses on Brunswick Street only to Arthur Street on the north side and to Kent Street on the south side. By 1888 there was a butcher's shop at 770 Brunswick Street but only a few other houses on the eastern side of Browne Street. "Browne's Paddock" and a Chinese garden occupied the flat land at the bottom of Browne Street and this stretched to the Brisbane River. Nearby in Brunswick Street (beside the later site of Hamel) was the Acme general store, later occupied by R.O. Sands. In 1890 there were no homes on either side of Brunswick Street between Merthyr Road and the river. [1]

In 1925 a butcher's shop was erected at 882 Brunswick Street and by 1931 this was owned by Sid Rayner (no longer in partnership) in his own right.

In 1928 Sid Rayner bought a block of land on the opposite corner of Brunswick and Browne Streets. It had been vacant for some time, the house having been destroyed by fire. In 1930 he built his new home there. *Hamel* was a stucco-covered brick building, with the family home on the top floor and two flats below. As far as modern brick, multi-

Sid Rayner kept the butcher shop at 882 Brunswick Street (shown under construction in 1925) until 1956. His son Ken and daughter-in-law Fay took it over, and when Ken died in 1965, Fay continued until 1990. The butcher shop continues to trade, its current owner being Mike Carroll who began part-time work for Rayners in 1975. — *Photo: Sam Rayner.*

storey flats were concerned, it was thought to be only the second block built in New Farm. *Avalon*, for instance, was completed in 1929 on the Harcourt Street corner.

In naming the flats *Hamel*, Sid wished to commemorate the brilliantly successful WWI battle near the village of Le Hamel, five km north east of Villers-Bretonneux in northern France, in which he participated as signaller with the 43rd Battalion AIF.

The battle began at 3am on 4 July 1918 and Sid began the advance, equipped with his signalling gear (which included a lamp and rockets) along with his rifle,

Hamel, named after the WWI battle in which Sid Rayner fought, was built in 1930 on the corner of Browne and Brunswick Streets. It was one of New Farm's earliest multi-storey flat developments. The Rayners occupied the top floor, while two other flats were let out. Sid Rayner — *Photo: G. Benjamin*

100 rounds of ammunition, an extra day's food and reserve rations, a ground sheet, three sandbags and an entrenching tool. As the forward bombardment progressed, Sid's job was to look back to battalion HQ for a flickering lamp that might be sending new instructions. In addition, he stood ready to take written messages from an experienced sergeant, that needed to be sent back. The advance was so rapid that there was little need for messages until they could report that their objective had been reached. This was fortunate because the smoke and dust made it difficult to read the lamps, and some messages had to be sent half a dozen times. After the battle Sid was busy laying telephone lines back to battalion HQ. No wonder the memory of that overwhelming success deserved such public recognition.

* * *

JUST HOW WELCOME was the Rayner's new home can be gauged by what life had been like across the road in the 1920s:

Sid and Gladys Rayner pictured in 1970 with their son Keith, then Bishop of Wangaratta. — *Photo: Sam Rayner.*

> AT FIRST COOKING was done on a wood-burning stove but in April 1922 a gas stove was installed. The children slept on the open back verandah. When it rained, ill-fitting canvas blinds were lowered and gave some protection. Saturday night was bath night. Hot water was ladled from the wood-fired copper (used for boiling clothes) into the bath in the little bathroom under the house.
>
> As the wind whistled through the room in winter, baths were not popular. The dirty bath water ran into the backyard. Concrete stepping stones led to the outhouse in the backyard, but after the suburb was sewered in the mid-20s, a lavatory was built under the house. On Monday mornings, Gladys Rayner was helped with the washing by Mrs Kirkwood (paying her the equivalent of 50c). Taking clothes from the boiler to the blue tub and the rinsing tub and then hanging them out on the clothes line was heavy work, and the help was much appreciated — until the first electric washing machine was purchased a decade later.[2]

The Rayner family history provides yet another vignette of daily life in Brunswick Street in the 20s:

> SHOPPING WAS CONVENIENT for Gladys in the 20s; if meat was needed, the butcher could be sent the few metres upstairs to get it; a well-stocked grocer's shop was only 50m away and later the children, who were given a cone of boiled lollies with the weekly order on Mondays, could do the shopping; a fruit shop was little further away; the milkman ladled fresh (untreated) milk into a jug twice each day — a boon when there were babies' bottles to be made up; the iceman kept the small ice chest replenished daily, and in winter he brought clothes props to hold up the lines on which washing dried in the back yard; the baker delivered fresh bread

daily, the fish came around on Friday and some other days; and there were other vendors with their horse-drawn carts which left manure for the children to put on the garden. Patient old horses, such as those of the milkman, almost seemed to know where to stop and when to move on. Three large drapery stores in the Valley could be quickly reached with two trams every 10 minutes, for a cost of a 1 cent concession ticket.

If some New Farm families disapproved of the cinema, not so for the Rayner children. With the Astor (later the Village Twin) just up the street, the children were taken on Wednesday evenings and sometimes on Saturdays. One night the family returned to find the house robbed, the likely suspects being sailors from overseas ships at New Farm wharf. After two burglaries, Sid gained police permission to own an automatic hand gun. He carried this on Saturday mornings when the change he carried would have made robbery profitable and when there were few people about.[3]

The four children — Sam, Madge, Ken and Keith — were born at Nurse Austin's Maternity Hospital on the corner of Bowen Terrace and Barker Street and attended New Farm State School.

In the late 20s, Rayner's was a source of income for enterprising local lads.

Ken Rayner (pictured) continued the Rayner family business, assisted by his wife Fay. This photo dates from around 1954 in the Merthyr Road shop (site of the current New Farm Cake Shop as per below). Those were the days when sides of meat were on display around the shop. — *Photo: Fay Rayner.*

I USED TO save all the newspapers and sell them to Rayner's to wrap the meat. If you even thought of wrapping meat in newspapers today, you'd probably get prosecuted. Mr Rayner's son Keith later became an Anglican Archbishop. The Rayners were very genial. Everyone knew New Farm as pretty genial.[4]

Sid soon leased a second shop "Merthyr Butchery" nearby at 81 Merthyr Road.

There used to be an old general store on the corner but it was replaced in the 1940s by the Tedman's Building (still standing), modern shops with flats above.

Sid's other real estate acquisitions included an old house and butcher shop at 670 Brunswick Street for which he received a good offer from an oil company. He sold it and a garage was built. Sid was good friends with George Cowin of Cowin Transport whose father (also George) had purchased a one acre (0.4 ha.) orchard between Villiers and Browne Streets in 1893.[5]

Sid's son Ken trained as a butcher after leaving the army in 1946. By the 1950s, Ken and his wife Fay (who had boarded at *GFS House* while studying to become a domestic science teacher) gradually took over more of the management of the two shops. Another generation of Rayners, Ken and Fay's sons Mark and Rod, would clean the cold rooms on Saturday mornings for their pocket money before they started high school. When Ken died in 1965 of wounds arising from the war, Fay stepped into the breech and continued to manage the two Rayner shops until 1990.

Sidney and Gladys' youngest son Keith was ordained an Anglican priest in 1953. He served in Queensland before becoming Bishop of Wangaratta, then Archbishop of Adelaide. From 1990, he was Archbishop of Melbourne and Primate of the Anglican Church of Australia. His 1963 PhD thesis was *The History of the Church of England in Queensland* and he was honoured with an Order of Australia in 1977.

Notwithstanding his later illustrious career, Keith was remembered by at least one former New Farm State School student:

> KEITH RAYNER ATTENDED *one of the Fancy Dress Balls as a caveman and carried the most 'gi-normous' bone you could imagine (obviously from an extinct dinosaur). It clearly came from the butcher shop…*[6]

Many graduates of the University of Queensland will recall the name on the bottom of most official correspondence, "S.A. Rayner, Registrar." A teacher before his war service, Sam Rayner graduated to the position of University Registrar and went on to become President of the Executive, Australian Council for Educational Research.

Sid and Gladys' daughter Madge was a member of many New Farm voluntary organisations before serving in the WRANS as a leading coder. After the war she married Jim Liley who had grown up in Hazelwood Road.

Sid Rayner and his wife Gladys retired to *Wirrina* on the corner of Langshaw and Brunswick Streets. From here, they enjoyed a panoramic view of New Farm especially *Hamel* and Rayner's Butcher Shop.

Notes

1.   Rayner, Sam, *Sid & Gladys Rayner of New Farm, Brisbane & Their Ancestors*, 1992, p. 5.9.
2.   *ibid.,* p. 5.4.
3.   *ibid.,* p. 5.9.
4.   Oral History: John Rosenskjar, 2008.
5.   *op. cit.,* p. 6.10.
6.   Edith Sang nee Sams in *Memories of New Farm State School*, 2000. p. 21.

The Pearl-king's legacy, the sand pits and the League...

The intersection of Sargent Street and River Road (later Oxlade Drive) ca. 1901, showing the Brisbane River and homes on the far bank. — *Photo from the panorama hanging in the NFDHS office which was presented in 1981 by the Hon. Don Lane, Minister for Transport and Member for Merthyr.*

S HOULD IT BE named Oxlade Drive or Clark Drive? — This was the likely conundrum in the minds of some City of Brisbane Council officials in 1926. The issue seemed straightforward enough. James Clark's sizeable property extended right to the river's edge not far from New Farm Park. This meant that Geoffrey Street stopped abruptly at one side of his property, as did River Road on the other side. Resuming a portion of Clark's land would allow the urgently needed thoroughfare — but the risk of a serious difference of opinion as to what the new road would be called, among other things, was particularly high...

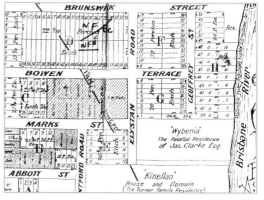

A portion of the Estate Map for *The Turner Estate, New Farm* (1901). Geoffrey Street (later Oxlade Drive) stopped at the boundary of James Clark's property *Wybenia*. By 1926, there were Council moves to resume land to put through the road.— *Estate Map, State Library of Queensland.*

James Clark the self-made man of wealth, and Allen Oxlade the long-serving Alderman, were almost neighbours in Elystan Road.[1] According to oral tradition in the Oxlade family once the resumption was confirmed in 1928, the two men though they had been friends, never spoke again.

By July 1933 both Allen Oxlade and James Clark had passed away. The 'Pearl King' may have outlived the Alderman by 15 months but the decision to attach the former's name to the new river road ensured that 'Oxlade' became part of New Farm history.[2]

* * *

FROM HUMBLE ORIGINS James Clark
(1857-1933) had made a fortune
from pearling in North Queensland,
giving rise to his being popularly
known locally as the 'Pearl King'.
Later he had interests in some of
Queensland's largest sheep stations.
He was a man who had negotiated
with governments all of his life
whether for pearling licences or on
behalf of powerful pastoral interests.
His New Farm property stretched

Wybenia, the residence of 'pearl-king' and grazier
James Clark. In 1983 Oxlade Drive was described as
'THE address in New Farm,' and it continues to be a
much-sought after location. — *Image: JOL 6944*

almost from Turner Avenue to Bowen Terrace and ran from Elystan Road down to
the river (near the present-day Riverside Centre).

Built in 1898 on high ground above the river, *Wybenia*, with its imported Spanish-
tiled roof was described as having beautiful grounds extending to the water's edge,
which were "rich in native trees and flowering shrubs, representing a collection of
tropical flora unequalled in any private garden in the State." [3]

* * *

ALLEN M. OXLADE was one of the sons of English immigrant George Oxlade (1848-
1910) who established in 1894 the firm of signwriters and decorators later known as
Oxlade Brothers Pty Ltd.[4] The convenience of New Farm to the Oxlade's Wickham
Street store meant that of the nine surviving children of George Oxlade, five chose to
live in New Farm very close to each other — as Bryan Oxlade, a grandson of George
Oxlade explained:

> WILLY LIVED IN *Bowen Terrace, Matt was in Hawthorne Road, Allen lived in
> Elystan Road, and Steve, my father, stayed in Moray Street. Of the girls, Rosa
> (Stanley) lived in River Road (later Oxlade Drive).*[5]

When Rosa Oxlade married William George Stanley in 1905 and they later built
on River Road (now 123 Oxlade Drive), this house was only the fourth in the area.

> THE TIMBER FOR *the house, hardwood weatherboards and Bunya Pine, came from
> Mt Tamborine. The timber was taken down to the Logan River, put on a paddle
> steamer, brought around Moreton Bay up the Brisbane River to the sand pits at
> New Farm on the Humpybong Reach, and carried up to the site. All around was
> originally cane fields. In the early days there was a creek running around the shop
> on the corner of Hazelwood Street and Oxlade Drive, along the drive and back into
> the lagoon between Sargent and Moray Streets. The road was dirt and we had a
> bridge over it in front of our place.*[6]

The childhood memories of Ivy Henderson (born ca 1906) who also lived in this
locality, add detail about the sandpit at the lower end of the New Farm peninsular:

When I was a child there were only dirt roads here, and down the end of Oxlade Drive on the riverside was what they called the sandpit. The drays used to come down to load up with their sand every weekday.

Just a bit further down from the sandpit was the dairy. We used to have to go to the gate and buy our milk every morning. As the cattle died, they buried them in the sandpit. We used to do a terrible thing. Well, my brothers were the leaders of it. We would dig the bones out, and with a go-kart that Dad made us, we'd wheel them down to the sugar refinery and get paid by the cartload. They used to measure them and give us so many shillings for them.[7] We had a ton of fun with the drays going down to get the sand because we used to know all of the drivers. We would come from school and meet them where the Village Twin is now, and get a ride home to Oxlade Drive in the dray. Every night after the last dray had gone through from getting its load of sand, we would put the chain across to stop anyone stealing the sand. There were as many as ten or twelve drays a day coming through. They would get beautiful sand from there.[8]

When *Doralma* was built by the Stanley family in River Road in 1909, it was only the fourth house in the area. Its River Road address became Oxlade Drive after 1928.
— *Photo: G. Benjamin*

The home at 261 Moray Street (now flats) where Bryan Oxlade, grandson of George Oxlade, was born. Bryan still lives in New Farm less than 200 metres away from this spot.
— *Photo: Bryan Oxlade*

As with most of the grand old homes of New Farm, *Wybenia* endured several decades of re-naming, re-purposing and internal re-arranging until it could be conscientiously demolished to make way for something considered far better. During World War II, *Wybenia* served as a WAAF hostel before being purchased in 1946 by the Methodist Church and renamed *Cooper House*.

It is worth noting that despite James Clark's passing, his activities and exploits seem to have caught the imagination of New Farm locals:

Clark's jetty was old and in a dilapidated condition with a corrugated iron shed somewhat the same. We used to fish off this jetty and catch bream and perch by using prawns for bait. Years before, the jetty and the slipway had been used for luggers belonging to "Clark, the Pearl King."[9]

When we were living in Sydney Street, my father and I would walk to the river and he'd point out a pearling lugger down from Thursday Island, and he told me stories about Clark. His residence was used in the war for a RAAF signals branch and barracks for WAAF personnel.[10]

In 1949 came a new phase of *Wybenia's* existence when the two-acre property with its grand residence was purchased for £11,075 by the Queensland Spastic Welfare League. This decision is considered to have secured the future of the League, thereby providing an inestimable resource for families who faced such dreadful situations as:

> AFTER MUCH DIFFICULTY *with feeding, the doctor at the Maternal and Child Welfare Centre near Brunswick Street Station told me to take our two year old son to the Spastic Centre at New Farm for their advice. I followed his suggestion, and the doctor at the Centre diagnosed our child as having cerebral palsy. This was a great shock to us as our second child was expected within a few weeks.[11]*

In 1957 gracious old *Wybenia* was remodelled and renamed *Harold Crawford House* after Dr Harold Crawford (1891-1958), the orthopaedic surgeon and the League's Patron who had proposed the inspiring vision for cerebral palsied children that "by proper care and attention, we can restore a portion of their birthright."

In November 1968 *Wybenia*, "the heart and soul of the League", was demolished to make way for the new *Harold Crawford House* which was opened in 1969. Now known as the Cerebral Palsy League of Queensland, the organisation retains a presence in Oxlade Drive though much of its original property, including the site of James Clark's palatial residence, has been sold for residential development.[12]

Notes

1. Allen M. Oxlade served as an Alderman on the Brisbane City Council (1916-1924) and Alderman for Merthyr Ward (1925-1931). On McKellar's *1917 Map of Brisbane*, 'Clarke Street' was the label on what became Elystan Road.
2. *City of Brisbane Council Minutes* for 4 May 1926 and 23 July 1928. Allen Oxlade was buried on 13/4/1932; James Clark was buried 10/7/1933.
3. "New Farm", in *The A and B Journal of Queensland*, 7 February 1924, p. 18. *Wybenia* was designed by Claude William Chambers (1861-1947) who, three years before in 1895, had built four houses in Moreton Street for G.C. Willcocks of *Wynberg*. They were later called *Doon, Garnock, Devon & Kent*. Chambers resided at Merthyr Road in 1913-14.
4. Oxlade Brothers Pty Ltd celebrated its centenary in 1994 and another generation is sustaining the business which continues to this day.
5. Oral History: Bryan Oxlade, 2008.
6. Stanley family records.
7. The animal bones were used in the refinery's carbon-filtration process. The bones were fired to make char which collected impurities from the sugar. These impurities were washed off so that the char could be recycled over and over. In the 80s, this process was superseded.
8. Oral History: Ivy Henderson, 1992.
9. Oxlade, *op. cit.*
10. Oral History: Arch Trail, 2002.
11. Vivienne Benjamin, *No More Tears*, Brisbane, 2005, p. 21. The 'child expected in a few weeks' was a co-compiler of this book.
12. In 1959 Ruth Neal began work in the Queensland Spastic Welfare League Post Office at New Farm and moved to Sevenoaks in 1974 to work as a clerk. Ruth helped to instigate a banking system for residents, was one of the first instructors of money management skills, and formed Crossroads at the complex. Despite a disability, Ruth completed 25 years of service at the QSWL. Ruth died in 2005 and a plaque commemorates her contribution at Sevenoaks. She was a cousin of Gloria, this book's co-compiler.

The Powerhouse

A generator of electricity, pollution and now creativity...

This photo's label reads, "New Farm, looking north from Hawthorne, showing Norris Point (1886)." On the left of the picture is the spot where the Powerstation now stands. The photo shows that this part of the river flat is occupied by a group of buildings, presumably the home or farm of the Norris family. Lightly wooded Teneriffe hill is in the background, as the river curves north. — *Source unknown*

WHILE THE NEW Farm Powerhouse has in part been preserved as a monument to Brisbane's technological progress in the interwar years, its closure in 1971 after 43 years of service, couldn't come quickly enough for most of New Farm's residents.

When the Powerhouse was constructed at Norris Point in 1926-28 by the newly formed Greater Metropolitan Brisbane Council to generate electricity for Brisbane's expanding tramway network, it was heralded as a major civic project along with other initiatives such as the Grey Street Bridge.

On start-up in June 1928, the plant supplied electricity for Brisbane's entire tramway system, as well as power and lighting loads for Ithaca, Toowong and Yeerongpilly. Designed by Roy Rusden Ogg, architect for the Brisbane City Council Tramways Department, the Powerhouse worked in conjunction with a series of Tramways substations. These were also designed by Ogg during 1927-30 and they converted the power for use by trams. This made possible the rapid expansion of the tramway system in subsequent years. The Powerhouse and substations all share characteristic features: the style of brickwork, elaborate cornices and careful detailing.

Siting the Powerhouse beside the river enabled water to be drawn for cooling, while coal was delivered by

View of the Powerhouse ca 1929, soon after its commissioning. — *Image: John Oxley Library 66421.*

rail. At the same time, being close to the city was ideal for supplying power to the tramway network. Along with the nearby sugar refinery, warehouses and wharves, the Powerhouse substantially complemented New Farm's riverside industrial and mercantile corridor.

The Powerhouse in 1942, showing men working on piles of coal. The soot that belched from its chimneys later inspired protests about pollution and health risks. — *Image: John Oxley Library 66435.*

The Powerhouse was built in four main stages, the final extension being in 1940. It operated at peak capacity in the post-war years and required additional railway and riverside access. In 1963 its operation passed from the Council to the control of the Southern Electrical Authority, which in 1977, became SEQEB (South East Queensland Electricity Board).

Fred Matthews could remember the spot in pre-Powerhouse days:

> THE MORE SOPHISTICATED *lads used to play 'Two-Up" in the bed of a dry creek near where the Powerhouse is today, that is, until disturbed by the local police sargeant. They would swim across the river and return again when he had left.[1]*

The stockpiles of coal were a tempting attraction for children — besides, a few pieces of coal could always be helpful at home:

> As KIDS WE *used to go along there and scavenge and you'd bring back the coal. We had a fuel stove and Mum used to wash with a copper. I've still got the copper under the house. It was great especially in the winter when you'd bring home a hatful of coal. The girls weren't supposed to do it, and the boys were supposed to do that — but it was a bit of fun for the girls to do it.[2]*

One of the by-products of the plant was ash and this was used extensively in New Farm Park, as well as to fill lower-lying parts of the suburb. Local policeman George Kopelke bought loads of ashes to build up the back yard of the family home in Lechmere Street. The wisdom of this was proven in the 1974 flood when no water entered their property. On the other hand, "The residents in the house behind (facing James Street) had to leave by boat," said his wife Joan.[3] Not only was the Powerhouse a significant local employer, but its activity was part of the suburb's daily cycle.

> WHEN THE POWERHOUSE *was going they used to work day and night. You always knew when it was change of shift because there'd be a lot of bicycles down James Street or Brunswick Street. In those days, there wasn't the traffic and there were more bicycles. I think they used to change shift at six o'clock in the mornings, about two or three o'clock in the afternoon, and then again about eleven at night.[4]*

Whatever the industrial advantages of building such a major power plant so close to the city, the dirt that it generated became a profound nuisance to locals, both in New Farm and across the river, and this was consistently remarked upon in people's reminiscences. Even allowing a child to crawl along the verandah floor of a New Farm house would ensure that it became dirtied with the same sooty grit that rotted the tin roofs by getting up under the overlap…

I LIVED UP the top end, the Valley end in Arthur Street. In those days, New Farm was always covered with smoke if the wind was blowing this way. Of course, women washing were always complaining about the Powerhouse so eventually they closed it down and it went out to Tennyson.[5]

WHEN THE WIND'S in the right direction, you get the smoke from the Powerhouse (in Browne Street). In lots of old homes around New Farm, you still get the soot out of the ceiling from that smoke. When the westerlies are blowing, with the old tongue and groove wood — this house is getting very old — then you get that black soot. I'd like to get someone up there to vacuum it out but he might come through the ceiling and then I'd have to have that replaced…[6]

Smoke pours from the New Farm Powerhouse in 1952, provoking much complaint from local residents. — *Image: John Oxley Library 66434*

A VERY SIGNIFICANT event was the closing of the Powerstation. The black soot (in Griffith Street) had been such a nuisance that the women were really delighted.[7]

'People power' played a significant role in achieving this result. According to Beattie Dawson, later Alderman for Merthyr Ward, the campaign had been waged since the 1950s:

THAT POWERHOUSE WOULDN'T be what it is today without people power. In the 1950s the emissions of coal dust from its silver and black-rimmed smoke stacks continually polluted the sky. There were no arrestors on the chimneys. The fallout blanketed New Farm and also nearby suburbs. At times it was like black rain, depositing ash on roofs, washing and curtains. My baby daughter had to go to the doctor because of dust in the eyes. The plant was belching up open cut Callide coal and the fire brigade would go down twice a day. Because they stoked the boilers to keep up the pressure, the dirt was just belching. It became so bad that a group of us held a meeting and in no time had Norman Park, Morningside and Hawthorne residents on side with us. They finally decided to close it down.[8]

In 1971 the Powerhouse ceased operation and was de-commissioned but remained in SEQEB hands until 1989. During that time the ground level in the area rose around two to three metres above its natural level as a result of fill being brought in from various SEQEB sites around Brisbane.

Even after the plant was closed, Beattie Dawson explained that community activists could not rest on their laurels since the site was being used to store dangerous waste:

> In 1980 we discovered that the Powerhouse was being used as a dumping ground for drums of a potentially dangerous chemical called pyrofil (polychlorinated biphenyl) which was said to be the cause of serious nervous disorders, stillbirths, miscarriages and lung cancer, so we put on another big protest. Eventually the offending chemicals were removed and the Powerhouse returned to its empty state.

1984 saw the partial demolition of the boiler house over safety concerns but it was claimed that there was never any intention to demolish the whole structure. Nevertheless, the caption under a photo of the Powerhouse in a 1978 newspaper read: "Brisbane's old power station is being pulled down to make way for a proposed freeway." [9]

The return of the site to the Brisbane City Council in 1989 was a mixed blessing. In its increasingly derelict post-operative state, the Powerhouse came to be described as a "long dead dinosaur and a shell of its former self," [10] an "albatross around the council's neck for more than a decade," [11] and seemed only fit for military exercises, film shoots or as a temporary refuge for homeless people. Nonetheless in the spirit of urban renewal, authorities felt inspired to find a fitting community use for what remained of this "dynamo of a bygone era." In 1995 the Council announced that a new stretch of parkland, overlooking the Bulimba reach of the river, was available for the public. This was land which had once been the Powerhouse's coal stockpiling area.

On 10 May 2000 the stage was set for the New Farm Powerhouse's next incarnation when the redeveloped 'Brisbane Powerhouse' was opened by the then Lord Mayor Jim Soorley. As a venue for a host of theatrical and performance activities, as well offering dining, gallery space, function rooms plus being a striking backdrop for regular farmers' markets, the Powerhouse has reclaimed its status as a prominent Brisbane landmark.

Notes

1. Oral History: Fred Matthews, 1974.
2. Oral History: Dorothy Messinbird, 1992.
3. Oral History: Joan Kopelke, 2008.
4. Oral History: Harry Barker, 1992.
5. *Ibid.*
6. Messinbird, *op. cit.*
7. Oral History: Judith Benjamin, 2008.
8. Oral History: Beattie Dawson, 2006; 2007.
9. *Inner City Times*, Brisbane, 3 August 1978.
10. *Urban Renewal,* Brisbane, Issue No. 13, August 1995.
11. *Northern News*, Brisbane, 23 Feb 1995.

The Brisbane Powerhouse's industrialesque setting has helped to magnify its impact as one of the city's creative hubs. — *Photo: G. Benjamin.*

Dr Windsor's home becomes Duchesne College...

On the front gate was a handsome brass plate announcing *Oakleigh*, the former home of Dr Harry Windsor and family. Set amid regal palm trees with mango trees at the back, *Oakleigh* was a substantial residence whose original architectural lines were obscured by closed-in verandahs and other modern accretions aimed to expand accommodation. — *Photo: Nanette Kay, Duchesne College.*

WHEN ARCHBISHOP DUHIG sought a post-war location for Duchesne College, *Oakleigh* at 52 Merthyr Road, a large rambling home on almost an acre, provided the perfect solution.

Duchesne, a residential university college for Catholic women, had been founded in 1937 in anticipation of one day becoming permanently established at the new St Lucia campus of the University of Queensland. Duchesne was first sited at Stuartholme School in Bardon but World War II intervened with American forces using it as a hospital.[1]

By 1947 Duchesne College was ready to resume and somewhere close to the University, which was then in George Street, was needed. *Oakleigh*, just a short tram ride to the city, would suit all requirements. Besides, since the College had been named after the inspirational Frenchwoman Rose Philippine Duchesne (1769-1852), a name that meant 'of the oak', the choice of *Oakleigh* was portentous.

Duchesne College was to take over the premises of the Union Jack Army Nurses Club, a legacy of wartime Brisbane which boasted a dining room that seated 40. Before this the property had been the home of Dr Harry J. Windsor (senior), his wife, a daughter and four sons, one of whom was Dr Harry Windsor (1914-1987) who became a foremost cardiothoracic surgeon, performed Australia's first heart transplant in 1968 and was a mentor to Dr Victor Chang.

A useful sketch of growing up at *Oakleigh* is offered by Dr Harry Windsor in his memoir *The Heart of a Surgeon* completed just before his death in 1987. One of his earliest memories as a five year old was being shown the red crosses on the front doors of some houses in Brisbane during the influenza pandemic of 1919. His clearest recollections were of the years after moving into the "rambling white and green two-storey wooden house":

> UNDER THE HOUSE was a large wood-heap to supply the stove and winter fires. Now and then, a rat — a problem around Brisbane in the early 1920s — would be seen in the wood-heap. One day Granfel (old Dr Windsor) announced, 'There's a sailor on a ship at New Farm wharf with the plague. The rat gang is coming!' The hunt was on. The gang arrived, cornered a rat in the wood-heap and killed it. Granfel said they would have it examined. Nobody got the plague; it was probably a false alarm. It was known that a few of the sailors and some of the ship's rats were from Manchurian ports where outbreaks of bubonic plague still occurred.[2]

Oakleigh's garden included a great variety of fruit trees as well as a large fenced area in which lived a cow and some chickens.

> INSPIRED BY BALLANTYNE'S "The Dog Crusoe", we children bestowed on this poor cow and its successors, the role of mustang and buffalo herd. Many were the blunt arrows that hit the cow. Sometimes she managed to get out of the back gate and then the hunt was on all over New Farm before she was brought back. The neighbours all knew the Windsors' cow and joined in. The cow kept us in milk, and the chickens kept us in eggs and Sunday dinners.

Young Harry Windsor's choice of medicine as a career was primarily influenced by his father whom he would accompany on his 'rounds in the sulky.' Some of these no doubt entailed visits to the home of the politician E.G. 'Red Ted' Theodore in Upper Bowen Terrace in the days when he was Premier (1919-1925) since Dr Windsor was the Theodore family doctor. Another great acquaintance of the Windsors was Archbishop James Duhig. "My father was his friend, confidante and medical advisor for 50 years," writes Harry Windsor:

> HIS WARMTH AND interest stimulated my visits to his home 'Wynberg.' There, amidst an unbelievable clutter of pictures and towers of books which occasionally avalanched from his desk, I would be encouraged by his words.[3]

Once the Windsors moved from New Farm to Gregory Terrace around 1928, the possibility that the Merthyr Road property might one day prove to be an advantageous acquisition for the church, had no doubt already occurred to Archbishop Duhig.[4]

* * *

DUCHESNE'S STAY IN New Farm was relatively short. In 1958 it moved to its current site among the other residential colleges at the University of Queensland's St Lucia campus. The College's 11 years at 52 Merthyr Road came to be known as the institution's "second era" (following the Stuartholme era, 1937-1942). Around 20 young women were accommodated in its first year, along with several Sisters of the Sacred Heart. While *Oakleigh* was recalled as a "gracious villa on high blocks with an extensive 'under-the-house' area," it became a particularly 'tight squeeze' to accommodate so many students amidst the post-war austerities of "double-decker beds and small rooms".

> THERE WAS THE two-storied verandahed extension to the old house, and the more recent army barracks-type hut plonked parallel to it where the students were housed, and the College dining room was in what must have been the "under the house" part of the old Queenslander. Upstairs there was a small study library in what would once have been the home's front room.[5]

The Principal of Duchesne at New Farm was Sister Joan Percy-Dove who was well degreed in English and History. Her insistence on formality and discipline inevitably brought forth exchanges that were recorded in College annals:

> MOTHER "PERC" LOOKED askance at some of the battered garments that appeared under gowns in chapel (sometimes with curlers under the trencher). "My dear," she asked in her quizzical way, "whatever is that?" "Sloppy Joes!" came the reply. "Well, my dear, I suggest you give it back to him..." [6]

The "redoubtable" Archbishop Duhig is remembered as personally bringing fish to the College every Friday and sitting at the dining room table talking to the girls as they finished breakfast.[7] There were also frequent visits from other well-wishers such as the Governor's wife, Lady Lavarack. The oaken theme was continued when a building, erected at the back of the main house, was christened *The Acorn*, and later an adjoining property was purchased on which *Little Oak* was built.

In retrospect, Duchesne's 'New Farm era' was seen as "twelve years of waiting" (for St Lucia to be ready) when the 20 'foundation stone' students of 'Phase 2,' enjoyed few of the mod cons of the future Duchesne. When Duchesne College left *Oakleigh* on 12 December 1958, this New Farm spot was destined for a new ecclesiastical phase with the Uniting Church of Australia.

Fete days, an Exhibition stall and card parties were all part of the hard work of fund-raising during Duchesne College's 12 years in New Farm.

Notes

1. Roger Marks, *Brisbane – WW2 v Now: No. 12: Nudgee Junior and Stuartholme*, RR & AJ Marks, Brisbane, 2006.
2. Harry Windsor, *The Heart of A Surgeon: The Memoirs of Harry Windsor,* University of NSW Press, 1987, p. 5.
3. *ibid.,* p. 19.
4. Once the Windsors had moved to Gregory Terrace, a resident of *Oakleigh* in the mid-1930s (per *Electoral Roll*) was salesman Herbert Leslie Tooth and his wife Audrey (Pratten). Herbert was a brother of Mrs Dodwell (nee Tooth) and Edwin Tooth. While at *Oakleigh*, Herbert Tooth was living just across Merthyr Road from the widow of his uncle James S. Hassall (1857-1934).
5. Kathleen McCarthy (Lynch) quoted in *Duchesne College 1937-1989*. Boolarong Publications, Bowen Hills, 1989, p. 26
6. *ibid.,* Marguerita Meredith, p. 25.
7. *ibid.,* Hazel Stuart, p. 25.

DUCHESNE COLLEGE

Fun and Games all the Afternoon for both Children and Grown-ups

at an attractive

Garden Party and Fete

Remember the date—

SATURDAY, 25TH OCTOBER,

Remember the place—

52 MERTHYR ROAD, NEW FARM,

New Farm Park tram — Stop 16.

Buy your Christmas Presents from us !

Art Union Prizes will be drawn at 3 p.m.

Punch and Judy :: Merry-Go-Round

Lucky Dips

Kingsholme Church

from Methodist in James Street, to Uniting in Merthyr Road...

Tᴴᴇ ɴᴀᴍᴇ Kɪɴɢꜱʜᴏʟᴍᴇ as a separate locality within New Farm would have disappeared far sooner, had it not been for Kingsholme Wesleyan Methodist Church on the corner of James and Annie Streets, a few doors above the 'Kingsholme Cash Store' of the 1890s.

Whether 'Kingsholme' was an anglicized form of the Swedish 'Kungsholm'[1] cannot be confirmed but *Kingsholme House*, adjacent

Kingsholme Methodist Church on the corner of James and Annie Street opened in 1927. Behind it in Annie Street is the hall. In 1981, the place of worship became St. Mary's Macedonian Orthodox Church. After the formation of the Uniting Church in 1977, the Kingsholme congregation joined with that of the Brunswick Street Methodist Church, and a new church was eventually built at Merthyr Road. — *Photo: Fred Matthews.*

to Hastings Street, lent its name to a housing estate advertised in October 1885. There was a horse-drawn bus service to 'Kingsholme' but when this was phased out in 1912, the locality name went into decline.[2]

The Kingsholme Methodist Church began in 1888.[3] Around 1908 the old Mission Hall from the corner of Browne and Hawthorne Streets was moved onto the land purchased from Mrs E. Garnett. First, however, the building had to be hauled up Hawthorne Street round into Annie Street. It was pulled by horses, with the men moving the rollers from the back to the front, all the way up the hill. Once installed, services were held at the Kingsholme Mission Hall at 7am every Sunday until a more permanent arrangement could be made.

One of this community's most remarkable gatherings was a memorial service for local grocer Private John Henry Butler, son of a Beeston Street saddler. J.H. Butler, elder brother of the community's long serving organist Eric Butler, was reported killed in action on the Western front in July 1916. The service took place on 27 August 1916 but it was not long before everyone joyfully learned that Private J.H. Butler was indeed alive and well. His Army record had been mixed up with that of Private H.J. Buckby of Charters Towers.

In the early 1920s Kingsholme shared a minister with Brunswick Street Primitive Methodist Church. If, for instance, he took the morning service at one church then a lay preacher would take the service at the other.

According to Dulcie Fleming (nee Twible b. 1914) of the Brunswick Street church, the need to remunerate the minister inspired a novel fund-raising initiative:

> WE REACHED THE stage where we couldn't pay our minister and we owed him quite a bit and he suggested we run a Queen Competition to raise money that was needed.
>
> Kingsholme, being the larger church, had two girls and we had one. Over three months we sold jams and cakes and so on. At a big crowning at the Rivoli Theatre, they announced how much had been raised. Our queen raised more than their two queens put together! This was such a success the minister (Rev. Frederick Malcolm) decided that we should have another one, and this time, build the hall. Well, I was the Queen the next year...[4]

On 4 December 1926, Dr Edwin Wesley Howard Fowles officiated at the placing of the foundation stone for a new Kingsholme Church on the corner of James and Annie Streets. It was opened and dedicated on 16 July 1927. The cost

Dr Fowles chose to *"place"* the foundation stone of the Kingsholme Methodist Church on 4 December 1926, rather than have the traditional wording relating to foundation stones used.
— *Photo: Merthyr Road Uniting Church.*

was £3,400, a debt discharged within six years, largely through the generosity of Dr Fowles and his wife Janet (nee Archibald). The organ was provided by Mrs Susan Lucas in memory of her distinguished husband, Dr Thomas Pennington Lucas (1843-1917) who pioneered the famous "Papaw Ointment."

In 1932 the Kingsholme Choir, making the most of the church's superior acoustics, was the first to broadcast over radio station 4BC. A key role was played by Eric Butler as organist from 1914 until his death in 1969.

In 1966 the Hall was extended and built in underneath, and was used for community activities such as the Kingsholme Indoor Bowls Club and playgroups. The upstairs hall was the first home for Noah's Ark Toy Library for children with special needs.

In 1976 the area under the church was converted into offices for the use of the Family Day Care program, which was then a very new concept in Queensland. Evening services continued at Kingsholme until the end of 1978, and from 1979 they were held at the recently-purchased property at Merthyr Road. In February 1981 the Kingsholme Methodist Church was sold to the Macedonian Orthodox Church and became known as St Mary's.

* * *

WHEN DUCHESNE COLLEGE left the big old Queenslander at 52 Merthyr Road at the end of 1958, the land was purchased by the Presbyterian Church of Queensland in 1959. Under the supervision of Rev. William Young of St Andrew's Presbyterian Church, Creek Street, a hostel for young men was instituted.

New buildings were erected including a manse for Mr Young, along with a dining hall, kitchen, recreation room and garages. From 1960 the large hostel kitchen, where breakfast and dinner were prepared each day for the residents, was an ideal place to prepare meals for the very first "Meals on Wheels" operation in Brisbane. Hostel cooks prepared the meals and a team of volunteers delivered them to folk in the community in need of such assistance.

New Farm's changing demographics meant a decline in the need for hostel accommodation and St Andrew's Hostel became uneconomic. It eventually closed and the property lay vacant. Unfortunately a fire damaged much of the original timber building.

By 1977 St. Andrew's Hostel was listed for sale and an offer of $165,000 had been refused. By the end of that year, it was sold for $63,000 to the Valley-New Farm Uniting Church Parish Mission which had been formed earlier that year when the Methodist and Presbyterian churches in the area united.

From early 1979, Uniting Church services were held in the recreation room at Merthyr Road while the dining room was extended into a hall. The former manse became the parish office and the office for the Family Day Care Scheme. The recreation room, at the back of the property, was used as a venue for playgroups for mothers with young children.[5]

By 1995 the original Brunswick Street Primitive Methodist Church, built in 1876 and designed by Brisbane architect Richard Gailey, had become Fusions Gallery. Redevelopment of the site in 2008 saw the building's beautiful architectural lines enhanced. — *Photo: Betty Smith*

Plans for a new Merthyr Road Uniting Church came to fruition on 26 March 1983, incorporating beautiful stained glass windows brought from the Brunswick Street Primitive Methodist Church.

* * *

ONE OF THE most interesting institutions in the Brunswick Street Methodist Church was the Fortitude Valley Penny Savings Bank. It was a monument to the patience, industry and business acumen of Mr H. Bennett. He noticed that the Sunday School scholars were leaving to join other Sunday Schools which had Penny Savings Banks attached to them. He decided to open a similar institution in connection with the Church, accepting small deposits of savings which the larger banks would not.

The first deposit was made on 3 October 1886 and the sum of £22/11/- was taken on the first evening. The bank soon won the confidence of the people in the district, and it was of invaluable assistance to the church because it supported every

venture of the people. It was largely due to the bank that the church building was maintained so well. The bank closed in 1993, having served the community for 107 years.

Stained glass windows from the Brunswick Street Primitive Methodist Church were incorporated into the Merthyr Road Uniting Church when it was opened in 1983 — *Watercolour by Gladys Blundell, courtesy of NFDHS.*

Notes

1. 'The name where you live — Kingsholme'. Newspaper article, NFDHS; date unknown.
2. Fred Matthews, who would have been 8 in 1912, remembers that a horse-drawn bus operated at Teneriffe and the terminus was in Annie Street near the New Farm State School. This bus route also went to Ropeworks (near Mowbray Park), another name long since forgotten. It was a reference to A. Forsyth & Co's. 'Kangaroo Rope Works' founded in 1876.
3. In November 1933, the community celebrated its 45th anniversary. *Courier Mail*, 4 November 1933, p. 17.
4. Oral History: Dulcie Fleming, 2007.
5. The former child care centre is now the New Farm office of *bric housing*, a community housing organisation providing accommodation for the homeless, or those at risk of being so. *bric's* New Farm office complements its other offices at Spring Hill and Sandgate.

Artistic, philanthropic and architectural themes...

Showing corresponding frontages on each side of George Street, this lithograph comes from the book *Sydney in 1848*, which Joseph Fowles (grandfather of Arthur Fowles of Abbott Street), illustrated and published.

SOME STREETS ARE notable for their homes' architectural exteriors, or for the noted people who dwelt there, or for the stories that the houses have to tell. Abbott Street seems to have a little of everything...

* * *

ON 8 NOVEMBER 1900, Arthur Edward Fowles (no relation to Dr Edwin Fowles) purchased four blocks of land, giving a double block frontage on both Abbott and Mark Streets. Soon after, Arthur, his wife Isabella and their two young children moved into their spacious new home christened *Yarrawonga*.[1]

Arthur Fowles was the son of renowned colonial artist Joseph Fowles (1820-1878) who made his reputation first as a marine artist then via his painstakingly illustrated streetscapes which he published as *Sydney in 1848* with the aim "to remove the erroneous and discreditable notions current in England concerning this City." Arthur's mother and the artist's second wife was Elizabeth Harris, a niece of Surgeon John Harris of Ultimo, one of Sydney's wealthier residents.

Originally a Sydney-sider, Arthur joined the Post-Master General's Department and worked in Townsville as a telegraphist before gaining his new position in Brisbane. Living in Abbott Street was convenient not only because it was within walking distance of the city for shift work, but also because the New Farm Private School was just across the road behind the Stevenson's house *Kilbowie*. Here, the Fowles' son Duncan began his education, joining children from some of Brisbane's leading families.

* * *

ARTHUR FOWLES' WIFE Isabella (Duncan) came from Glasgow and as the *Presbyterian Outlook* journal of 1937 put it, "this may account in some measure for her ability in handling financial affairs." It was said that in most public charity efforts,

A postcard image of *Glenugie* on Moray Street possibly ca. 1900. Later it was owned by the Archibald family before becoming a hostel for country girls operated by the Presbyterian and Methodist churches. As *Archibald House,* it still stands and is now privately owned. — *Photo: NFDHS.*

Mrs Fowles' appointment as treasurer was almost automatic.[2] Accordingly, she became one of the "best-known figures in social and charitable circles." It was almost inevitable therefore that she would become connected with the Archibalds of *Archibald House* at 186 Moray Street.

The rear of the two-storied timber house on Moray Street known as *Glenugie* later *Archibald House,* was clearly visible from the front steps of the Fowles' dwelling *Yarrawonga. Glenugie* was built around 1886-87 and had several owners before being purchased in 1902 by the Hon. John Archibald. Son of a Scottish coal-mine manager, John Archibald came to Queensland as an 18 year old and steadily prospered. He became a Member of the Legislative Council and proprietor of the Dominion Milling Co. Ltd. His sojourn in New Farm was short-lived however since he died in 1907. *Archibald House* remained the home of his widow until her demise in 1929.

One of the Archibald children, Amelia Eveline, married the investor Henry Robertson and by the mid-20s (her husband died in 1924), she was living a few doors from *Archibald House* having purchased the home built by the architect Robert Smith (Robin) Dods for himself and his wife in 1899.

On a block bounded by Sydney, Herbert and Abbott Streets, the house named *Harelvyn* (sometimes *Hareloyn*) incorporated features for which Dods was considered

The R. S. Dods home (1899) in Abbott Street (corner of Sydney and Herbert Streets) ca. 1906, which was later owned by Mrs Robertson (nee Archibald) before being replaced by a block of flats. Robin Dods also built the adjacent house (ca. 1900) on the right which still stands. On the left hand edge of the picture is the rear of *GFS House.*— *Photo: Robert Riddel.*[3]

one of Brisbane's best architects, that is, care with the home's orientation, generous
verandahs and doors, wide sheltering roof and the well-crafted use of timber. His
wife Mary (King) contributed an elaborate carving of their initials which she made
into moulds for the plaster ceilings. At the same time Dods built a house next door at
41 Abbott Street for his mother Elizabeth. In 1880 she had married the well-known
Brisbane surgeon, Dr Charles Ferdinand Marks.[4]

In 1932 the depressed market for home sales led to the decision to donate
Archibald House jointly to the Presbyterian and Methodist Churches as a hostel for
girls. A decade later the distinguished dwelling *Inglenook*, a few doors down Moray
Street on the corner with Sydney Street, was to be used for a similar purpose by the
Anglican Church when it became known as *GFS House*.[5]

Naturally the honorary
treasurership of *Archibald House*
fell to Mrs Isabella Fowles. As
a result, she worked closely
with Mrs Henry Robertson, the
former Miss Archibald, so as to
supervise the useful purpose
of the venerable family home.
In 1943 following the death of
Mrs Fowles, "one of Brisbane's
most notable patriotic and
philanthropic workers", her

Ladies on charity work in the late 30s-early 40s, including
(from left) Mrs J.C. Trotter, Mrs A.E. Fowles, unknown, and
Mrs Henry Robertson. — *Photo: Isabelle Davis (grand-daughter
of Mrs. Fowles.*

daughter Ruby Taylor (nee Fowles) succeeded to the position. In time, *her* daughter
Isabelle Davis (nee Taylor) continued the tradition and assisted with keeping the
hostel's books. Visits to the home of Mrs Henry Robertson (formerly the Dods'
house) were always a highlight, and visitors agreed that "the front lounge was as good
as a museum. The antiques must have been worth millions."

> SHE WOULD CONDUCT *Junior Red Cross meetings in her beautiful home with the
> assistance of Neta Watts (later Bradley). As children we'd play by the sundial in her
> front yard and refreshments would be served by Mrs Robertson's maid Katie.*[6]

Mrs Henry Robertson might well have been a millionaire but the end of this
particular episode of New Farm history was approaching. Just a year before her death
in 1969, Mrs Robertson's legacy of having founded the Junior Red Cross in the 1940s
was marked by a memorial drinking fountain in New Farm Park. Soon after her death,
her landmark residence was demolished and replaced by flats (though No. 41 Abbott
Street survives). *Archibald House* was spared this fate and it continued as a hostel for
young women until 1980 when it was sold and refurbished as a private home.

* * *

AFTER 70 YEARS in the same house, Isabelle Davis has a ready reservoir of
recollections about the comings and goings of Abbott Street. The next door

neighbour at No. 26, for instance, was once the public servant Henry Coxen.[7] About the same time that Isabelle's forebear Joseph Fowles stepped ashore in Sydney looking for work as an illustrator, Mr Coxen's father Henry William Coxen (1823-1915) was arriving in Tasmania as a 15 year old. He was in the company of his artistic aunt Elizabeth (Coxen) and her husband, the famous zoologist John Gould. The Gould couple later produced the remarkable publication *Birds of Australia*.

A later occupant of No. 26 was Miss Dora Birkbeck who taught art and had a studio in the city.

Some Abbott Street houses on narrow blocks were very close together, a circumstance that sometimes led to diverse consequences. Neighbourliness might mean, for instance, that a morning cup of tea be regularly handed through the kitchen window to an elderly neighbour. On the other hand, if the house next door were being put to less-than-respectable uses, innocently leaving a bedroom window open during the day for air, might mean being in very close proximity to a lady entertaining male customers in her adjacent bedroom next door. In the latter case, Robin Dods' architectural use of the 'blind bay window', which enabled views of the street or garden but not of the house next door, would have been a blessing.

In 1963, four year old Venero Armanno attended the New Farm Private School, almost within sight of where the Armanno family lived at No. 36 Merthyr Road on the corner with Abbott Street. Growing up amidst Abbott Street's attractive camphor laurel trees must have planted early literary seeds because many decades later, they flourished in a novel entitled *Firehead* (1999) in which Venero located the story's protagonist, Sam Capistrano, in a house on the very same spot. Its kitchen window was opposite the one next door (No. 34 on Merthyr Road) and was so close that the respective occupants could shake hands.[8]

While it's understandable that the novelist should locate Gabriella Zazo, Sam's spirited childhood sweetheart, in the house next door (No. 34 Merthyr Road), what is remarkable is that 50 years before, No. 34 was the boyhood home of Brian Con

Beside the camphor laurel trees on the corner of Abbott Street and Merthyr Road is the house where the Armanno family lived in the 1960s. The same house later featured in Venero Armanno's novel *Firehead*. Coincidentally, the house next door on the left was where another novelist, Brian Con Penton (1904-1951), spent part of his childhood around the time of World War I. — *Photo: G. Benjamin.*

Penton (1904-1951), newspaper editor, polemicist and novelist, who attended New Farm State School.

In his 1936 novel *Inheritors*, Penton also located his protagonist Derek Cabell and his daughter Harriet in New Farm:

> THEY LIVED IN *an old half-stone, half-timber house on the bank of the river at New Farm, with an army of servants… She was content to wander all day in the big garden, laid out half a century before by convict servants of the military officer who built the house, discovering the incredible beauty of magnolias, crepe myrtle, English violets, and the hyacinth which packed the river for miles after rain, to lie on the grassy bank, and watch ships come in with sides rusty from long voyages, to drive in the streets and see the traffic, three storey buildings, shop windows, crowds on the pavements, to admire from afar the men and women, more splendidly dressed than she could ever have imagined, driving and promenading in the cool of the afternoon.*[9]

Might this spot be a new 'literary corner' in New Farm?[10] To add to this possibility, the house just across the street at No. 25 Merthyr Road was once co-owned by Dr Edwin W.H. Fowles (1871-1945), barrister, politician and prolific writer. He wrote newspaper articles, published a Latin grammar textbook, produced a textbook on law, contributed to the *Queensland Readers* published by the Department of Public Instruction for use in state schools and edited a book of poetry.[11] He also wrote hymns and conducted the choir at Kingsholme Methodist Church.[12]

Dr Fowles was married to Janet, another daughter of the Hon. John Archibald. He was also family solicitor to Dr T. P. Lucas (1843-1917) who was so convinced of the healing effects of papaw that he established the 'papaw hospital' at *Vera*, diagonally opposite *GFS House* on Sydney and Moray Streets. In 1925, after the death of her husband and the sale of *Vera* to the Salvation Army, Mrs Susan Lucas moved only a block away. Her new residence, co-owned with Dr Fowles and now also named *Vera*,[13] was across Merthyr Road from the Penton-Armanno houses.

What of the perennial Abbott Street question, "who planted the beautiful camphor laurel trees?" A 1934 letter to the editor supplies the answer:

> ABOUT THE YEAR 1890, *Mr Kennedy of Abbott Street told the people then living in that street that he would plant shade trees along each side with the condition*

TRIBUTE PAID TO DR. FOWLES

"One of Queensland's most colourful personalities" is the tribute paid to the late Dr. E. W. H. Fowles, M.A., L.L.B., Litt.D., by a friend.

He writes: "The law, literature, Parliament, music, and education were among Dr. Fowles' pursuits.

"Graduating in arts and law at Melbourne University, he became a member of the Queensland Bar, where he practised for more than 40 years. He was the author of legal text books, and for 30 years conducted the examinations of candidates for the legal profession in Queensland.

"He was appointed a member of the Legislative Council in 1912, and recognised as one of the most perceptive and scintillating debaters. He was a foundation senator of the Queensland University. He compiled some of the text and reading books used in our Queensland schools.

"Music was one of his natural and best known interests. He was the outstanding hymnologist in the Methodist Church. He was a member of the Methodist Hymn Book Revision Committee, a composer, and choir conductor. Dr. Fowles was an active member and leader of the Methodist Church. Local preacher, youth leader, and choir conductor were among his roles, in addition to which he was a member of King's College Council

Married to Janet Archibald, Dr Edwin Fowles, barrister, talented scholar, writer and hymnologist, was described as "one of Queensland's most colourful personalties." His passing in December 1945 was lamented on page two of the *Courier Mail*, 12 January 1946.

that each householder watered those adjacent to their homes. This was done. They were carefully attended to, even during drought times, with the result that Abbott Street was pointed to with admiration...[14]

Dr Lucas purchased *Vera* on the corner of Sydney and Moray Streets in 1911, describing it as his 'Papaw Hospital'. In 1914 he wrote *The Most Wonderful Tree in the World: The Papaw*. The Papaw Ointment pioneered by Dr Lucas is still sold and the container depicts this house. The spot is now occupied by a unit block.[16] — *Photo: NFDHS.*

Perhaps Mr Kennedy had been inspired by the huge camphor laurel "probably the first of its kind in Australia" in the grounds of *Merthyr* nearby. It reportedly had a girth of 30 feet (9.1m) at the base and its branches reached out across the drive to a distance of 45 feet (13.7m).[15]

Notes

1. The Fowles' housing blocks were purchased from Mr D. Christison who had a tailoring business in Petrie Bight. Later Mr Christison's son Colin had the nearby corner shop on Merthyr Road.
2. According to the *Biographical Record of Queensland Women*, Webb, Elliot & Co., Brisbane, 1939, Isabella Fowles was a member or office bearer of 10 charitable organisations.
3. Robert Riddel, "RS (Robin) Dods 1868-1920. The Life and Work of a Significant Australian Architect." (Phd thesis, University of Qld, 2008). Image published in *The Builder* 3 February 1906; copy held in Lorimer Dods Collection, Dods Archive.
4. Joe Power had been born at 453 Bowen Terrace which had also been built by Robin Dods.
5. See John Mackenzie-Smith's *Caring For Young Women in War and Peace: A History of GFS House*, New Farm 1942-76, Brisbane, Qld, 2008.
6. Oral History: Isabelle Davis, 2008.
7. In 1937, the Coxens' daughter Maida married Harold Crawford, solicitor and Brisbane City Council Alderman for Merthyr Ward (1955-1973).
8. The family home on the corner of Abbott Street and Merthyr Road was close to Veny Armanno's heart. When discussing this coincidence by e-mail (August 2008), he wrote: "I must admit that even at the age of ten, when my father sold our house, I was thoroughly devastated. I think I always wanted to live there forever."
9. Brian Penton, *Inheritors,* Angus & Robertson, Sydney, 1936, p 191.
10. Other New Farm literary connections are discussed in: Todd Barr & Rodney Sullivan, *Words to Walk By: Exploring Literary Brisbane,* University of Queensland Press, St. Lucia, Qld. 2005. Walk 6.
11. *The Poems of Alfred Midgley*, Brisbane, Smith & Paterson, 1908.
12. J.C.H. Gill 'Fowles, Edwin Wesley Howard (1871-1945)', *Australian Dictionary of Biography,* Vol. 8, Melbourne University Press, 1981, pp 565-566.
13. The name 'Vera' appeared on the Brisbane City Council Sewerage Plan of 1925. Earlier residents of this house had been the Roberts family from ca. 1892.
14. *Courier Mail,* Saturday, 7 April 1934, p.12. Irishman William Kennedy, working first as a dairyman then as a gardener, lived next to 41 Abbott Street, the house built by Robin Dods for his mother.
15. Newspaper cutting of 23 October 1935, in *S.W. Jack's Cutting Book,* No. 9, p. 1.
16. Bill Metcalf, "Dr Thomas Pennington Lucas: Queensland Scientist, Author, Doctor, Dreamer and Inventor", in *Journal of the Royal Historical Society of Queensland*, Vol. 19(5), pp. 788-804, Royal Historical Society of Queensland, 2006.

19

A Bowen Terrace Stroll

An address fit for a Governor...

In the 1880s properties such as E.R. Drury's *Hawstead* and D.F. Roberts' *Ravenswood* extended from Bowen Terrace to the river's edge. Barker's Quarry (below present day Wilson's Outlook) is in the foreground, while at the far right is James Campbell's wharf next to his lime kilns site, adjacent to Julius Street. — *Image: State Library of Queensland, APO-026-0001-0005.*

T HE CLOSENESS TO Brisbane's town centre and the attractiveness of being able to overlook the river made Bowen Terrace especially appealing to the upper echelons of Brisbane society from the very start.

While Bowen Terrace clearly followed a natural track down towards the lower end of New Farm, in the early days it was just one of the localities on the peninsula around which settlement constellated, along with Kingsholme, Kinellan, Racecourse, Merthyr and Teneriffe.

Among those who found New Farm a particularly desirable locality were pastoralists from country Queensland and this is how Ron Grant was able to call *Wellington House* home. Built in the 1860s, *Wellington House* was a low set, wooden residence with wide verandahs front and back. It boasted two rotundas, 21 rooms, cedar interiors and accommodation for a maid. It was acquired by Alexander J.M. Terry, a wealthy grazier from north-western Queensland, as a wedding present for his daughter Clara, on the occasion of her marriage in 1911 to bank manager Francis Grant.

The scenario of a wealthy countryman establishing his daughter among the 'nice people' of New Farm was a theme depicted in *Inheritors*, the 1936 novel of Brian Con Penton (1904-1951) who spent part of his boyhood in Merthyr Road.

Ron Grant was born at home and raised in the same house in Bowen Terrace. The homing instinct has ensured that today he lives so close to his birthplace that he can overlook it from his kitchen window. His boyhood neighbours along the eastern side of Bowen Terrace, between Barker and Langshaw Streets, still come readily to mind.

Wellington House at 368 Upper Bowen Terrace was the residence of the Grant family from 1911 until 1948. Two wings ran towards the rear of the house from each side. These ended in a rotunda, making the most of the north-easterly aspect at the rear. — *Photo: Ron Grant.*

ON THE CORNER of Barker Street and Bowen Terrace was a private hospital run by Nurse Austin. Next door were the Powers,[1] and next door to that was 'Wellington House', the abode of the Grants. Then came 'Clinton' owned by Justice Hugh Macrossan, the Senior Puisne Judge of Queensland, then the Bevans, then the Steindls, then a little double-storied red brick house built on what was once Steindl's tennis court. The people

The former *Aurelia* Private Maternity Hospital on Upper Bowen Terrace ca. 1960. A woman hoses the garden and a boy waits for a tram on the Barker Street frontage. Later it became a guest house with four flats before being replaced by units. — *State Library of Queensland, 6668-0001-0014.*

who built this house won the casket that year. Lastly, there were the Tooths. Of this whole block, there are only two houses still standing, the Steindls and the red brick house. The rest are units, with the exception of the Tooth's home which is now a Telstra substation.[2]

Of the Grants' neighbours in the 1930s, Walter Bevan was an engineer/architect, Judge H.D. Macrossan was later briefly Chief Justice of the Supreme Court, Louis Steindl had a brewery business and (later Sir) Edwin Tooth started Austral Motors.

Along with his siblings, Ron was born at *Wellington House*, bearing out the observation of an elderly New Farm resident that those were the days when "babies were born at home rather than in hospitals." Two doors away at the *Aurelia* Private Maternity Hospital conducted by Nurse Mary J. Austin, ladies from the country were accommodated for childbirth. Gloria Grant's (no relation to Ron) mother travelled from Buderim in November 1929 to Nurse Austin's for the birth of her first child.

In keeping with the recurrent New Farm theme of large homes being turned to medical purposes, *Wellington House* was leased by Nurse Jane Ingram for five years while the Grants were living in regional Queensland in houses supplied by the bank. Later in 1939, Nurse Ingram bought *Bertholme* in Moray Street (now *The Moreton Club*) and converted it into a nursing home.

The properties facing Bowen Terrace ran through to Oxley Lane, the rear entrance providing the means by which groceries and vegetables, meat and milk were delivered by horse and dray. Being close to the Astor Theatre (now the Village Twin) had its advantages for the Grant children:

> THE ASTOR WAS owned by Mr Stevens who lived at Dutton Park. My brothers and I were able to watch the films from the back of the theatre in summer time, because they opened the doors into Oxley Lane and we lived so close.

* * *

AN EARLIER RESIDENT of 406 Bowen Terrace (ca. 1917-18) was Mrs Ellen Lawless of the family property *Booubyjan*, inland from Maryborough. She wished to be in town when her grandsons were on leave from the AIF. An indefatigable traveller, she is thought to have completed 16 sea trips between Australia and Europe during her life. In her diary, she wrote that she suffered some financial setback when her gas shares suddenly lost value because of the introduction of electricity.[3]

* * *

WITH THE ARRIVAL in Brisbane of around 100,000 American military personnel in 1942, many large New Farm homes were either requisitioned or used as billets for officers. *Wellington House* was no different:

> IN EARLY 1942, the Americans billeted three high ranking officers at our home. They installed telephones in each room and modern appliances throughout. I can remember Colonel Rathbone, and a Colonel Melinyk who was American Japanese. The latter used to disappear for 6 or 8 weeks at a time. His room was kept for him and after the war, he told us that during the times of his absence, he had been dropped into Japan by American submarines on intelligence work.
>
> By having high-ranking American officers staying with us, we came to know several officers from GHQ (General MacArthur's headquarters in the AMP Building in the city). Having three pretty sisters, many social events occurred at our home.
>
> Next door, Judge Macrossan's old home 'Clinton' was taken over by a Captain Teasley who was a full naval captain in charge of all American naval operations in the Brisbane area. They all, of course, joined us socially.
>
> My youngest sister Jeane married a U.S. naval lieutenant who returned to Australia in 1946 to marry her. She has had a wonderful life in Pasadena, California ever since. She is now known as "the little old lady from Pasadena", though she drives a Jaguar.
>
> At the end of the war, as the Americans pulled out, Dutch pilots moved into our home. Their duties were to fly prisoners out of Java and Sumatra back to Australia. One particular Dutch pilot flew into Batavia and rescued his sister from

the prison camp, brought her back to Brisbane, and one night at Wellington House, she told us the story of her four terrible years under Japanese rule.

Wellington House has been supplanted by *Amaroo Lodge*.

* * *

FOR THE MILITARY men billeted in Bowen Terrace in the 1940s who were fully engaged in trying to defeat Japan, it would have come as a surprise to learn that a remarkable piece of Japanese craftsmanship stood nearby on the corner with Langshaw Street.

Some long-time New Farm residents were aware that bookmaker George Maxted's house in the 1930s, with its chocolate-coloured roof tiles, was reputed to have been "brought from Japan and that it had no nails, having been constructed from Japanese joinery."[4] In fact the house dated from 1887 when it was imported from Japan by Southern District Court Judge George W. Paul who so liked the style of dwelling in which he stayed during a few months in Kobe in 1886, that he sought to recreate it in New Farm.

Sketches by the noted Brisbane "artist architect" G.H.M. Addison (1857-1922) of Judge Paul's Japanese House in Langshaw Street. *The Boomerang* newspaper considered the house to be an attempt to work out the problems of "climatic architecture", that is, the perennial problem of trying to make a Queenslander's home suitable for Queensland requirements. — *The Boomerang, 24 Dec 1887, p. 18.*

Originally from Penrith in New South Wales, George Paul had been a member of the English bar before returning to Australia in 1863. He worked in Queensland as a well-regarded criminal barrister before promotion to the bench of the District Court in 1871.

Considering that this oriental house would suit Brisbane's climate, he arranged for it to be fully manufactured in Japan then imported to Brisbane along with three Japanese carpenters and two plasterers.

Named *Yeddo* (the old name for Tokyo), the house was regarded as the first known piece of authentic Japanese architecture in Australia. In a detailed article with illustrations, *The Boomerang* commented, "The whole house is a perfect dream of Mikado-land where the harmony of decoration and the perfection of colour and outline is as perfect in its way as was that of the Greeks in theirs." [5]

The house was also furnished with an extensive collection of ceramics and other art treasures brought back from Japan.

A detailed description of the house appeared in a newspaper of January 1888 when it was listed for auction the following week, "by order of his Honour, Judge Paul". The prestige of its location was highlighted by reference to its being "surrounded by the residences of Sir S.W. Griffith, Messrs. G. Raff, J.D. Campbell and others."[6]

Judge Paul was still living in Langshaw Street in 1903 and died in 1909. The house eventually passed to George Maxted before becoming *Ruth Fairfax House* run by the Country Women's Association in 1948. In 1962 it was marked for demolition by a developer and at the eleventh hour, the structure was purchased for £600 by Dr Pam Markwell. She had it dismantled for transportation to North Queensland where it was re-assembled and continues as the 'Japanese house' at 5 Lynch Street, Ingham.

On the site of Judge Paul's house today stands the South Pacific Motel.

Notes

1. Josephine (nee Wilkinson) and Joe Power.
2. Oral History: Ron Grant, 2002.
3. Betty O'Connor of New Farm, is Ellen Lawless' great-great-granddaughter.
4. Oral History: Brian Bishop, 2007.
5. *The Boomerang,* Brisbane, 24 Dec 1887, p. 18. See also *The Brisbane Courier*, 12 December 1887.
6. *The Brisbane Courier*, Saturday 7 January 1888, p. 8, col. 3.

20

Wynberg

A residence for builders at heart...

FEW WOULD KNOW that the gracious residence at 790 Brunswick Street, behind the grand stone gateposts and beyond the circular driveway, is named after the South African town of Wynberg.

New Farm's *Wynberg* is the home of Brisbane's Archbishop John Bathersby AO, as it was for two of his predecessors, Francis Rush and James Duhig.

The land was once part of

Wynberg ca. 1928. The tower was added by Archbishop Duhig around 1927. — *Sketch by Vincent Sheldon in 1928, courtesy of Archdiocesan Archives.*

12 acres (4.86 ha) acquired by George Raff in 1854 for £63. John A. Abraham bought it in the 1860s, and in the 1880s, Charles Fisher, a wealthy retired squatter, built a fashionable residence.

In 1890, the property caught the eye of George Charles Willcocks who had acquired the reputation of being the colony's 'best contractor,' particularly in railway building. A Devonshire stonemason, G.C. Willcocks came to Queensland by a circuitous route. As a young man, he went to South Africa to seek his fortune, but discovered that his niche was not mining for diamonds but in engineering. The company he formed won the contract to duplicate the precipitous but scenic railway from Cape Town to Kalk Bay, and he made his base en-route at Wynberg (wine mountain). The project's success won him a reputation in railway contracting that eventually brought him to Brisbane.

Around 1896, G.C. Willcocks had the four identical residences built in Moreton Street for letting to affluent tenants. The roadway beside the closest house is today named Hazel Street, but in the photo ca. 1904, it was closed with a gate. — *Image: John Oxley Library, 141855.*

Naming his new house on Brunswick Street *Wynberg* (as he did his earlier Coorparoo home) was a reminder not only of a major professional milestone, but the town of Wynberg was where Willcocks met his wife-to-be Mary Ann Craig. She was a young widow stranded in South Africa by the untimely death of her husband, a Presbyterian missionary.

From 1885, Willcocks undertook many railway contracts for the Queensland Government. Several civil construction projects are also attributed to him, including the substantial retaining wall around All Hallows' School (which his daughters attended). With his interest in engineering, it was inevitable that he should turn his attention to re-modelling *Wynberg* to his taste, and this involved a new double-storied wing, marble fireplaces, red cedar trimmings, high patterned plaster ceilings, and the incorporation of his initials into an ornate stained glass window above the front door. The improved and enlarged residence, complete with ballroom, was complemented by a circular driveway, landscaped gardens and lawns, all of which made *Wynberg* the perfect setting for social events with the city's leading citizens among invitees.

Claude William Chambers was the architect involved in the improvements. In 1895, Willcocks had him design the four noteworthy identical residences around

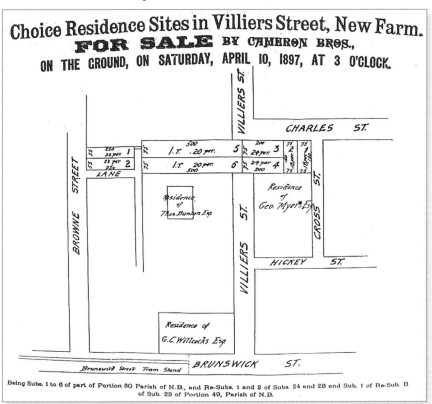

In addition to his purchase of *Wynberg* in 1890, G.C. Willcocks was still acquiring nearby properties in 1897. The tram stopped at his door and had not yet been extended down towards New Farm Park. In the vicinity of Thomas Bunton's house on Villiers Street, the Holy Spirit Church was completed in 1930. The Cowin family also bought sites in Villiers Street. — *1897 Estate Map, State Library of Queensland.*

the corner in Moreton Street (No. 28-44), intended as rental properties for affluent tenants. The birth of Hazel Willcocks in 1896 possibly inspired the naming of Hazel Street which ran beside these residences.[1] Willcocks is remembered by Fred Matthews as owning one of the first motor cars in New Farm, "a bright red Mercedes". Fred's father (Samuel C. Matthews) laid out the garden design for Mr Willcocks:

Archbishop James Duhig. — *Sketch by Vincent Sheldon, 1928.*

> IN THE SOUTH-WEST *corner, there is a lemon-scented gum tree from which we collected scented leaves to place in closed clothes-drawers for a sweet aroma.*[2]

John Rosenskjar (b. 1917), brought up at 902 Brunswick Street and later appointed as a priest to Holy Spirit parish, recalls:

> THE WILLCOCKS FAMILY *was still there when I was a child. Times were very simple in those days. I can remember the wedding of the daughter of the house. It was a night wedding, but pretty well the whole suburb was gathered outside the gates to see it going off.*[3]

Before G.C. Willcocks passed away in 1916, Archbishop James Duhig apparently contacted him with a view to purchasing *Wynberg*. Later an approach was made to his widow but she, being a strict Presbyterian who had viewed the marriage of her brother-in-law Richard Willcocks to a Catholic most unfavourably, was hardly disposed to such a sale. Indeed, it was said that in Methodist circles there was interest in securing *Wynberg* as a manse for their minister since it was close to both their Kingsholme and Brunswick Street churches.

In 1917, Archbishop Duhig visited *Wynberg* and made a personal offer to Mary Ann Willcocks the outcome of which was that the house 'changed denominations', the sale being effected in 1925. Archbishop James Duhig took up residence in 1927 and it was to be his home for the next 38 years. While his life has been well documented,[4] stories abound regarding his interaction with the citizens of New Farm. Young Harry Windsor, who was brought up on Merthyr Road, explained that one of the Archbishop's practices was to keep open house for an hour each morning when anyone could stroll in and talk to him. For this hour, he sat in a large, picture-lined reception room just inside the open front door.

> ONE MORNING AS *my father sat with him, a none-too-well-dressed character appeared, whereupon the Archbishop excused himself, saying: 'I must see that man. He's just out of gaol.'*[5]

Word had clearly got around that His Grace was susceptible to hard-luck stories and upon release, many dropped into *Wynberg* 'for a loan', the technical term for this manoeuvre being to 'go down and see Jimmy.' The Archbishop was also a substantial art patron and the fact that there were many paintings on the walls appealed to visitors of artistic temperament.

The ornate lobby at Wynberg. — *Sketch by Vincent Sheldon, 1928.*

VISITING ARCHBISHOP DUHIG on the way home from school was not an uncommon thing. The door was always open and if the Archbishop's purple biretta was on the back of the chair, then he was at home. We would ring the doorbell and the housekeeper would come and tell us that the Archbishop was not available. On hearing this from his study, Archbishop Duhig would come to greet us and invite us in for milk and fruit cake. The interior of Wynberg was quite grand with Baroque-style furniture and Tintoretto-esque paintings on the wall.[6]

When nominated for the episcopacy of Rockhampton in 1905, James Duhig was the youngest Roman Catholic bishop in the world. He was knighted in 1959 and died at *Wynberg* on 10 April 1965. His successor, Patrick O'Donnell, Archbishop from 1965 to 1973, chose not to live at *Wynberg*. Archbishop Francis Rush resumed the practice in 1973,[7] followed by the current Archbishop, John Bathersby, whose award of the Order of Australia in 2008 was for his efforts to bring churches together.[8]

Notes

1. G.C. Willcocks had stables on the upper side of Merthyr Road between Brunswick Street and Bowen Terrace, as per 1901 *POD*. The four houses in Moreton Street may have backed onto this land.
2. Oral History: Fred Matthews, 1974.
3. Oral History: John Rosenskjar, 2008. This may have been the 1919 wedding of Hazel Willcocks and Capt. Stanley J. Schooley, a beau who would have pleased the engineering heart of Hazel's father were he still alive. Capt. Schooley of the Royal Flying Corps was an engineer who had studied in the United States and served at Gallipoli. He was the son of Benjamin and Elizabeth Schooley who lived on the corner of Moray and Moreton Streets. According to *Jobson's Digest Year Book* (1929), B.L. Schooley was chairman of Intercolonial Boring Company Limited (IBC), established in Queensland in 1888 for oil exploration initially, later for water. IBC expanded into the manufacture of tools and products for industry, agriculture and mining. In 1952, R.J. Willcocks, son of G.C. Willcocks, was on the IBC Board with his brother-in-law, S.J. Schooley.
4. T.P. Boland, *James Duhig*, University of Queensland Press, St Lucia,1986.
5. Harry Windsor, *The Heart of A Surgeon, op. cit.*, p. 20.
6. Oral History: Leonard Brown, ca. 1994. See his essay in Ricardo Felipe (ed.) *Avalon: Art and Life of an Apartment Building.* Museum of Brisbane, Fortitude Valley, Qld. Vanity Publishing, 2005.
7. The co-compiler's first visit to *Wynberg* was in 1975, to explain to Archbishop Rush that after four years at Banyo Seminary, he had decided not to continue with training for the priesthood.
8. Additional material on G.C. Willcocks is at the Catholic Archdiocesan Archives in Brisbane, including Vincent Sheldon's Sketchbook on *Wynberg.*

An emblematic building signifying a uniting purpose...

"NEW CHURCH, VILLIERS Street," was the quaint address in 1925 for John and Marie Dempsey who, after caretaking *Wynberg* before Archbishop Duhig's arrival, had moved into the large house on Villiers Street once owned by the solicitor Thomas Bunton.

The back of this house became a temporary 'new church' and was used as a Mass centre for New Farm Catholics who had previously attended St Patrick's Church in Morgan Street, Fortitude Valley.

It was not until June 1927, under the administration of Father D.M. O'Keeffe, that the foundation stone of a new permanent structure was laid. Three years later, on 1 June 1930, His Excellency the Apostolic Delegate, Most Rev. B. Cattaneo, solemnly blessed and opened the new Church of the Holy Spirit in Villiers Street.

Designed by Jack Donoghue[1] and sited so prominently, the classical Italianate church with its landmark tower is one of New Farm's most emblematic structures.

The talents of several local artisans were drawn upon to embellish the building.[2] William Bustard (1894-1973) executed a magnificent mural painting of twelve angels and six cherubs, covering the semi-dome of the sanctuary. The cherubs were modelled on young children from the parish.

The twelve Stations of the Cross were designed by Miss Daphne Mayo (1895-1982) who was a student of artist Godfrey Rivers.

To celebrate the 50th anniversary of the Holy Spirit School, two former students, Brian O'Keefe and Alma McMahon (nee O'Dea), who were used as models for William Bustard's cherubs for the mural in the Holy Spirit Church, returned for the celebrations. The other cherubs were Vera and Leonard Dempsey, John Crowley and Joan Barrett.
— *Reproduced by kind permission.* "Mural depicts local children" by S. Nelson, *Courier Mail*, 1 May 1987.

CHILDHOOD residents of New Farm, Mr Brian O'Keefe and Mrs Alma McMahon, stand beneath the mural in the Holy Spirit church dome which depicts them as cherubs.

Mural depicts local children

THE last thing Brian O'Keefe ever thought he would be called was an angel.

But Mr O'Keefe is one of six former New Farm, Brisbane, residents to have been immortalised on the ceiling of the suburb's Holy Spirit church — as a cherub.

The church, which opened in 1930, features a large dome

According to local legend, the cherubs are Mr O'Keefe, Alma McMahon, the late John Crowley, Leonard Dempsey and his sister Vera, and Joan Barrett.

Mr O'Keefe and Mrs McMahon returned to the church yesterday to see the mural.

lescent home and Vera Dempsey is a nun in Sydney.

Miss Barrett died from lead poisoning in 1948 at the age of 23. She contracted the illness when she was 4, before she was painted as a cherub.

The cherubs were said to have been chosen by Mr Bustard for their "beautiful, chubby innocence".

HOW artist William Bustard painted Mr O'Keefe, left, and Mrs McMahon.

The school building was constructed in 1937, although the Sisters of Mercy had be-

For much of her life, she was one of Queensland's best known artists. The baptismal font of Celtic Gaelic design, was made from limestone originating in Waterford in Ireland. Columns of green and red marble from Connemara and Cork support the font. The total cost of the church with furnishings was £16,241/8/5.

* * *

ON MONDAY 7 July 1930, the Sisters of Mercy began Holy Spirit School using the previous Mass centre.[3] Every day the sisters travelled from All Hallows in a distinctive black bus. Sister Mary Benigna was the first principal, assisted by Sister Mary Paul and Sister Philomena. There were 79 pupils covering all classes.

The present school building was opened on 26 September 1937 with additions being made in 1959. Holy Spirit Hall was completed in 1966. When the Convent was opened on 30 August 1970, the nuns no longer had to travel to and from All Hallows each day. It replaced a house that had been occupied successively by Dr A.J. Morton, Dr Stoll and lastly the McGregor family. The Parish Centre opened on 16 March 1975.

The priests who have served the parish have included Fathers (later Monsignor) David Dee, Denis O'Rourke, Kevin Aspinall, Rollo Enright, John Nee, Kerry Ryan, Joe Duffy and Leo Coote. In 1956 another religious order came to New Farm, namely Our Lady's Nurses for the Poor (the Brown Sisters) and they are still at 407 Bowen Terrace.

The land purchased by Archbishop Duhig for the parish of New Farm extended from this home on the corner of Villiers and Brunswick Streets (facing Villiers), to just past the current school. — *From "75 Years of Memories: Church of the Holy Spirit," by Michael Kopelke.*

The Holy Spirit Church in Villiers Streets was completed in 1930. Its tower stands 38.7m tall.

The house where Mass had previously been held was taken over and opened as the Holy Spirit School. The initial enrolment over all classes was 79. Seven years later on 26 September 1937, the 'solid and handsome, two-storied' new school building was opened. — *Photos: Betty Smith; NFDHS.*

New Farm's various churches were once the focus of social and community activity to an extent not known today. At Holy Spirit Church for instance there were sodalities or confraternities, such as Holy Angels. "We'd attend Mass one Sunday per month wearing our veils and red cloaks," explained Joan Kopelke.

There were also Ladies of the Sacred Heart, the Grail Movement for Young Ladies, Children of Mary and the Holy Name Society, along with groups such as Young Christian Workers and the New Farm Catholic Youth Club.

In the 1970s after Vatican II, the focus shifted away from sodalities, and instead family members were encouraged to sit together at Mass.

Whatever the theological underpinnings of such societies, the Holy Spirit Church was likely to be the first port of call for young Catholics coming to New Farm for work or education. In 1948 for instance, a 26 year old lad from Rockhampton was assigned to attend a technician's course at the PMG Technical School on the corner of Sydney and Lamington Streets:

> AFTER CONTACTING THE Catholic parish at New Farm, shared accommodation was found for me at 32 Mark Street. On Sunday I attended Mass. The parish had a very active youth group which met in the adjacent school and organised football and cricket matches. I was a regular member of the choir and was delighted to be presented with a coffee set, when I returned to Rockhampton to get married the following year.[4]

As to the wider question of whether there were religious divisions in the community, Beattie Dawson put it succinctly:

> IT WAS VERY evident in my grandmother and the lady next door, because she was an Orange woman and Grandmother was Irish, but once Saint Patrick's Day was over, you couldn't wish for better people. They all had their little moments…[5]

With the influx of European immigrants after World War II, the Holy Spirit Parish played a far larger role than other local churches, in endeavouring to unite under one roof people from such disparate cultural and language backgrounds that they might not have otherwise associated with each other.

Notes

1. John (Jack) Patrick Donoghue (c1895-1960) also designed *Ravenswood* (1934), a unit block at 313 Bowen Terrace.
2. The stained glass windows were by Messrs. R.S. Exton & Co, and were possibly designed by Charles Lancaster (father-in-law of long-time New Farm resident Arch Trail) who supplied leadlighting for *Coronet Court* at 995 Brunswick Street.
3. *The Catholic Leader* of 17 July 1930 carried a full list of the names of all pupils of Holy Spirit School.
4. Oral History: Keith Benjamin, 2008.
5. Oral History: Beattie Dawson, 2007.

Horsepower... from racecourse to car assembly...

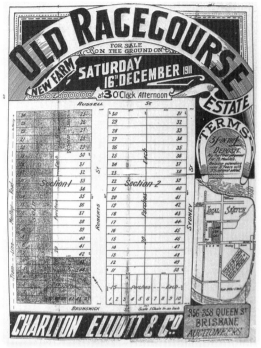

The 'Old Racecourse' was sufficiently part of collective memory to be used to promote this land sale in the vicinity of Roberts Street (later Welsby) and Russell Street (later Alford) in December 1911. — *Estate Plan: State Library of Queensland.*

Racecourse Road was the original name for the east-west track across New Farm (later Merthyr Road), clearly denoting what was to be found near its northern end.

With horsepower being one of the mainstays of the Moreton Bay settlement's economy, it was inevitable that riders and owners sought to compare the quality of their steeds and back them with a bet. A coterie of influential gentlemen, many of whom were pastoralists who owned land in New Farm, formed themselves into the Moreton Bay Jockey Club.

The first annual meetings were at Coopers Plains before the shift was made in 1846 to the low-lying portion of New Farm, corresponding to an area occupied today by *Cutters' Landing* and the old Powerhouse. The original course, which was a mile around, was pegged out by saplings on clay pans and quagmires. The meetings attracted crowds from all around Brisbane and Ipswich and as far away as Esk.[1] The first three-day meeting held during 26-28 May 1846, at the "new race-course at the new farm, North Brisbane," [2] was an exclusive event:

> The situation chosen for the 'circle' is a most enchanting spot, in close proximity to the river, giving the double advantage of land and water conveyance to the scene of revelry.[3]

One of the attendees at that 'rough ringed course on New Farm,' was most probably pastoralist and explorer Henry Stuart Russell (1818-1889)[4] who intimated that he could still see the boxes high up in the trees on the river bank, once occupied by sentries to guard against "pilferers of the golden cobs of the rich maize crops which once had decked that swampy bight in the penal period." By 1848 the race meetings were open to the public, becoming great social events especially for the 'turfites' (a term of the day), warranting extended newspaper coverage of the three-day carnival:

> THE GREATER PART of the assembled throng consisted of pedestrians who chose to make use of that far-famed animal known as Shanks' mare for the occasion. There was a goodly number of the fair sex dressed out in holiday attire, which, with the bright costumes of the gentleman-jockeys, gave a most animated appearance to the scene.[5]

Although the New Farm track ceased meetings early in the 1860s after a racing reserve was set aside at Eagle Farm, this part of New Farm continued to be referred to as the 'old racecourse'. During the speculative boom of the 1880s, new housing developments were subdivided but not necessarily built on. This included the *Russell Association Lands* auctioned in 1887, later advertised as the *Old Racecourse Estate* in 1888-89. In December 1911, house sites in Roberts (later Welsby) and Sydney Streets were listed for sale in an estate called the *Old Racecourse*.

* * *

RIGHT UP TO World War II, horses were central to life in New Farm. A long-time resident could reflect, "New Farm was always full of horses…"[6] as she recalled the fascination she had for them as an eight year old in 1941:

> ERNIE HAD A beautiful horse, and his dray was blue with red wheels. He'd go to the depot and fill up with hot bitumen, and his horse was trained to pull the dray to the next pothole, then whoa. Ernie's horse couldn't recognise the holes, but he recognised the sound — and he never had to be pulled on the reins.
>
> Ernie'd get home about 6 o'clock and it was a real thrill for us to watch when he brought the horse home. He'd drive it into the yard with a big mango tree, and it was our job to pick up the mangoes because they're no good for horses. Ernie cared for that horse the way people cared for their tools. The horse would be hosed, scraped, hoofs cleaned, tail and mane brushed, then Ernie would go under the house, cut up the lucerne and hay, mix it up and the horse would be fed. Only after all of this, would Ernie go upstairs and take his shoes off.

In the 1930s New Farm provided ample natural feed for horses, according to Harry Barker:

> I HAD ONLY the one horse. I used to take her around there near the sugar refinery and tether her, and she'd graze across in the park.[7]

Elsie Broadrick of Harcourt Street helped her husband on a local milk run and their two horses would take turns about to pull the cart:

> PSYCHO WAS VERY flighty. I think he was an old racehorse and he was a double for Bernborough, a beautiful red bay with black points. One night my husband tried to back him into the cart, but he took off as if he were going out of a barrier. He flew down the hill and luckily, a trammie caught him by the Bundy clock…[8]

If Psycho needed a run Elsie would ride him to Newmarket, but with the increasing traffic on the roads this was fraught with adventure. On the return journey, he bolted with her when a tram came behind them:

I PULLED HIM up by the time we got to the Women's Hospital. All he wanted to do was to dance his way home and get a feed. When we got down to that area, it was August just before Exhibition, and the trams used to run both ways up and down Gregory Terrace. I had to get him onto the footpath. He was very, very toey until the trams went past. A chap asked me, "Are you putting him in the Exhibition?"

Crossing the river in those days was managed on the vehicular ferry, the *Hetherington*. One of Elsie's horses couldn't be handled anywhere near water but it was different with Psycho. "You could manage him on the ferry, because the moment you put your foot in the stirrup, he was ready to go aboard. You should have seen his eyes looking over the river…" With horses having to share the road with an increasing number of motorists, collisions were inevitable. In the early thirties, drink driving was a peril to horses as well:

AT THREE O'CLOCK one morning Harry was delivering milk at the top of Harcourt Street and a drunk was coming the other way. The man's car slammed into the horse and killed it as it stood in the shafts. Harry had an awful job trying to get anything out of the man. He only managed about £30.[9]

Elsie Broadrick had a great affection for her equine charges. "I wish I'd written a book about all these horses," she said. "I had a Box Brownie but somehow I never got around to taking any pictures of them." Of course, some horses exhibited an intelligence which at times surpassed that of their masters:

Drayman Bill Gray retired at 65 in 1945. He worked the last dray for Cowin's Transport. Being a horseman, he could not learn to drive a truck in order to gain a licence. He moved steel plate from CSR wharf to storage within the Refinery, and did some short hauls of raw sugar from Macquarie Street to the Refinery. As with several other employees, he had been with the firm for 40 years. Pictured is the Cowin family residence in 40 Villiers Street. The house was eventually relocated to Fig Tree Pocket where it was restored and enlarged. — *Photo: George Cowin IV*

ONE MAN PULLED up with his dray every afternoon at the Queens Arms Hotel, and that horse got sick and tired of waiting. She would nay three times, and if he didn't come out she would trot off home. The owner's daughter would come out and say, "Mum, she's coming down the hill without Dad," to which Mother would reply, "Open the gate and put a feed bag on her." [10]

With wartime stringencies, horse-owners found it difficult to buy good quality chaff, plus blacksmiths who would shoe horses were moving out into the suburbs. During the 1940s the Broadricks ended an era when they bought a Morris Z utility.

* * *

THE REACTION PROVOKED by the shift from natural to motorized horsepower can be gleaned from "Spectator's" letter to the *Brisbane Courier* of 20 June 1905:

SIR, HOW MUCH longer will the authorities shut their eyes to the risk of citizens by motor cars being rushed furiously through our main streets at anything up to 20mph and cyclists scorching through the city at break-neck speed? … Why, Mr Editor, should these selfish people be allowed to take charge of our public streets to show off the speed they can get out of their machines at the imminent risk of less flighty citizens?

As much as young Fred Matthews enjoyed horse-drawn transport, he couldn't help but express the thrill of seeing the first cars:

IT WAS A luxury to have a ride in a motor car as there were very few of these. Mr Willcocks owned a Mercedes, and Mr Thompson Senior of Kingsholme, the father of Mr W. Thompson the founder of Annand and Thompson, drove a Studebaker. Most people travelled in horse-drawn wagonettes. Four-wheelers carried six people. Those who were able to yard a horse, owned a two-wheel sulky. Some of these were beautifully painted and varnished, and you'd ride with a rug over your knees. It was an experience to sit behind the horse jogging out in front. [11]

Les Dodwell was the son of Elsie (Tooth) and AV Dodwell, who was a prominent figure in Brisbane's early motor trade. As a young child, Les accompanied his parents on an epic motoring tour to Mt. Kosciusko. — *Photo: Anne Clarke.*

Dr Charles F. Marks, step-father of the architect Robin Dods who was building homes in Abbott Street around 1900, drove an 8 hp Rambler and was one of the first members of the new 'Automobile Club of Queensland.' Of the 11 cars that lined up at the Seaview Hotel at Sandgate for the first annual meeting and dinner of the Club on 7 July 1906, one was the Darracq of Alexander Vaughan Dodwell, soon to settle in Moray Street, New Farm. A.V. Dodwell had been a well known footballer and competitive cyclist, and in 1896, he opened Massey-Harris Co, a Brisbane branch of the Canada Cycle and Motor Car Co.[12] In September 1910, Mr Dodwell accompanied by his wife, their two children and nurse, joined Dr Brockway and

Austral Motors Pty Ltd's Assembly Works and Workshops on the corner of Welsby and Lamington Streets offered 41,000 sq ft (3,800 sqm) of floor space. A glance at the roof line profile of the Christian Life Centre in Sydney Street confirms that part of this original structure has been preserved. — *Photo: NFDHS.*

chauffeur in his new 16 hp Standard for quite a journey. They took 30 days to motor to Mt. Kosciusko and back, a distance of 2000 miles.[13]

With the advent of the motor car, sealing the roadways now became a priority.

The design of *Powerhouse Apartments* in Welsby Street pays deference to the spot's historical antecedents. — *Photo: G. Benjamin*

> IN THE 1940s, roads had been sealed in most of New Farm, however in some streets it consisted of a bitumen strip two cars wide up the middle. Kerbing was installed leaving a dirt area on either side of the bitumen and later this was sealed with a gravel and tar covering. Once all the roads were sealed, New Farm became more respectable. Some of the gravel used in the original bitumen had fool's gold in it. As kids, we used to dig it out and think we were rich.[14]

In 1923 George Cowin of Cowin Transport had a team of 36 draught horses stabled on the family property at 40 Villiers Street, but years earlier he had considered the possibility of motorizing his business. In 1917 he had purchased a solid-tyre petrol engine motor truck, an English "Belsize" with a chain drive to the back wheel.

> GEORGE COWIN I was the first Master Carrier to use a motorised transport vehicle in Brisbane. Over the next 20 years, solid-tyre petrol engine vehicles such as the Italian "O.M." and "Fiat", and the English "Dennis" and "Thornycroft" were used. Most were reconditioned ex-World War I vehicles sent to Australia to provide better means of cartage. In May 1938, the first pneumatic-tyred petrol engine "Dennis" truck was purchased.

* * *

IT IS REMARKABLE that near the site of New Farm's old racecourse, less than 70 years later modern horsepower was taking shape. In 1924 Austral Motors Pty.

Ltd. was established by Edwin Tooth of Bowen Terrace.[15] Initially referred to as Dodge Brothers because Dodge was the key agency, in 1928 the company expanded gaining the agency for Chrysler. Workshops were built on the corner of Sydney and Lamington Streets.

By 1933, Ed Tooth's firm was Queensland's largest motor business with its main showroom at Petrie Bight (now re-developed by All Hallows').[16]

During World War II Austral Motors assembled vehicles for military use, and locals can remember rows upon rows of utilities painted khaki parked on vacant land near Lamington Street. Into the 1950s, the assembly plant was employing 30-40 people. One such worker was Lew Hughes who

TEN YEARS OF GOODWILL

More than ten years ago, Austral Motors Pty. Limited (entirely a Queensland organisation) was appointed Sole Distributors by DODGE BROTHERS (Inc.) to control the destinies of **Dodge Brothers Motor Vehicles** in Queensland and the Northern Rivers of N.S.W.

Guided by the principles and policies of Dodge Brothers, marketing a product durable and dependable, constantly improving but never altering in fundamental ideals, Austral Motors Pty. Limited have justified the confidence reposed in them by more than **8,000 owners** of Dodge Brothers Motor Cars.

Today, **Queensland's largest Motor Business**, specialising solely in Motor Vehicles, is the home of Dodge Brothers Motor Cars in Brisbane, and the Queensland Distributors are justifiably proud of the monument erected to the power of an honest purpose.

And Now---

CHRYSLER MOTORS, in which Dodge Brothers is incorporated, has shewn their sustained confidence in extending to a Subsidiary Company of AUSTRAL MOTORS PTY. LIMITED the sole Representation for their entire lines including—
CHRYSLER, PLYMOUTH and DE SOTO Motor Cars.

Head Offices:
Adelaide and Boundary Streets, Brisbane.
45,000 Square Feet Floor Space.

Assembly Works and Workshops:
New Farm, Brisbane.
41,000 Square Feet Floor Space.

AUSTRAL MOTORS PTY. LIMITED
BRISBANE

In 1933 Austral Motors announced that after a decade of justifying the confidence of 8,000 owners of Dodge Brothers motor cars, they had gained the sole agency of Chrysler, Plymouth and De Soto brands. — *Courier Mail, 11 October 1933, p. 7.*

obtained a job at Sydney Street after working for a Chrysler firm in Breakfast Creek Road named Miracle Safety Wheels (the tyres did not come off if you suffered a puncture). According to Lew Hughes:

> THEY WERE ENGLISH cars — the Standard, Vanguard, 8-10 hp, little sedans but the Vanguard was a fairly big sedan. All the parts, chassis, wheels, bodies, etc. were assembled here and road tested for defects.
>
> Also Chrysler Corporation cars — Dodge, Willett and De Soto, Plymouth — which were made in South Australia, came up by road transport and we would check them before they went to the dealers. They were all the same car with different badges. There were three sorts of transmission: manual, 3-speed manual with overdrive and the most expensive was automatic. It was the same body with different transmissions.
>
> There was a park nearby where they did road tests with a steep short pinch and this bloke got at the bottom, revved it up as far as it would go and put on the brake. He got the sack. Sydney Street in those days was mainly residential. There were

only a couple of corner shops on the way from the Valley. If you wanted something like smokes, then you'd buy them before you got to work.[17]

Elaine Boyd grew up on top of one of New Farm's steepest hills, which had its attraction for the car industry in the 1930s:

> MY MOTHER WAS always complaining about Dodge Brothers testing their cars and trucks in front of our house, with the accompanying fumes and noise.[18]

The plant also serviced Dodge and Standard cars and trucks, as well as Ferguson Tractors. Austral Motors was a growing business, extending as far as Welsby Street. "As homes came up for sale, they were acquired and the business expanded." [19]

When Austral Motors eventually left, the premises had different uses including a soya milk factory and a carpet warehouse. The Christian Life Centre took over the building in 1984, and in 1998 it was renovated to house a printery, respite centre, worship services and the Harvest Rain Theatre. The modernisation project was funded by a part-sale of the site for redevelopment into warehouse apartments. The *Powerhouse Apartments* complex was the result, followed by *Powerhouse Terraces.*[20]

Notes

1. Judy Bell, 'New Farm: The Suburb and Its History'. (unpublished), 2003, p. 15.
2. *Maitland Mercury & Hunter General Advertiser,* 25 March 1846, p. 1.
3. *Sydney Morning Herald*, 27 May 1846.
4. *The Genesis of Queensland*, 1888, Turner & Henderson, Sydney, p. 882.
5. newspaper, NFDHS, unknown date.
6. Oral History: Dorothy Messinbird, 2002.
7. Oral History: Harry Barker, 1992.
8. Elsie Broadrick, *69 years in Harcourt Street : A Conversation with Elsie Broadrick, aged 96* — recorded by Gerard Benjamin. [Newstead, Qld.] 2008, p. 7
9. Broadrick, *ibid.,* p. 19.
10. Oral History: Beattie Dawson, 2007.
11. Oral History: Fred Matthews, 1974.
12. D.W. Martin *Cyclists, Doctors and Others: The Introduction of The Motor Car to Queensland.* Virginia, Qld: Church Archivists' Press, 2001, p. 19. The author explains that while Alexander Dodwell was a 'competitive cyclist', he had an enemy too. On one occasion in July 1893, just before a race at the Exhibition oval he found that both tyres on his bicycle had been slashed to pieces.
13. Jean Stewart, *The Life and Times of Dr Brockway,* J and D Stewart, Kenmore, 2007, pp 77-78.
14. George Cowin IV, paper, 1998.
15. Before enlisting in the AIF in World War I, Ed Tooth was a 'motor company manager' with Canada Cycle & Motor Agency of Creek Street, Brisbane, a firm managed by his brother-in-law A.V. Dodwell. Awarded a Military Cross, Lt. Edwin Tooth sought permission to return home via America so as to learn the latest about car engineering. In Brisbane, he resumed his employment at Canada Cycle, living at his parents' home, *Havrincourt* in Bowen Terrace.
16. *Courier Mail*, 11 October 1933, page 7 (display advert for Austral Motors.)
17. Oral History: Lew Hughes, 1997.
18. Elaine Boyd, "What New Farm Means to Me", letter, March 1992.
19. Oral History: Brian Hjelm, 2008.
20. "Vehicle Plant Makes Way for Residents", *Northern News*, 26 February 1998, page 28.

23

Shops and Businesses

...with deliveries by horse and bicycle...

Diagonally opposite the old Astor Theatre were the Brunswick Buildings built in 1889. This was the terminus of the horse-drawn tram service which had been operating from around 1885.
— *Photo: G. Benjamin.*

S ands the Grocer, across from the Astor Theatre (now the Village Twin) in Brunswick Street, made such an impression on youngsters in the 1920s that even the shop's aroma could be recalled:

> They mixed cinnamon *and spice into the sawdust on the floor and it smelt wonderful. Beer was 11 shillings a dozen, and the bottles were covered in straw jackets. If all the bottles were returned, you received one shilling deposit back. That grocery shop was a real family concern. They delivered our groceries in a basket on a horse and cart and asked, "What's for next week, Mrs Miller?" The kids received a little cornucopia of boiled lollies or some broken biscuits.[1]*

Reynah and Esther Sands' grocery store had been serving customers since at least 1912, next to where Sid Rayner built *Hamel* in 1930. Reynah Sands had earlier worked as a 'grocer's assistant' in the same location.[2] Home deliveries were the norm. "Hughie Gilmour came on Thursdays on horseback to collect mother's grocery order, and Barney Flannigan delivered it on Fridays, in a van drawn by a beautiful grey horse," recalled Fred Matthews.

> Like Garnett's store *Sands' Store generally gave credit to local people in hard times, all on a verbal arrangement. They must have had immense business good will, to the gratitude of the local residents.[3]*

Around the time of World War I when young Fred Matthews was looking for cycling experience, he developed a co-operative arrangement with Mr Sands:

ONE OF MY aims in life was to be able to ride a bicycle. Mr Sands had two of these for delivering small packages of groceries. He always had willing offers to do deliveries, because it gave us the most desirable opportunity to learn to ride. We soon became proficient and consequently, Mr Sands gave good service to his customers. This was a good indication of the times. Rather than asking for monetary reward, you would do things for people if you felt that something could be achieved for them by co-operating.[4]

Fred Matthews also recalled other local shops especially if a story was attached. There was Glover's Store in James Street near Kent Street, as well as the one in Merthyr Road near James Street ("one night there was a fire, and the daughter who was a scholar at New Farm State School had to jump out of the window to save her life.") There was an unusual event at Clark brothers' newsagency on the corner of Brunswick and Annie Streets in the 1920s:

ALONG BRUNSWICK STREET the electric trams passed their shop. One morning, Ray pulled up but the horse kept prancing. He jumped down to steady the horse then promptly jumped back again. The ground had become electrified through faulty insulation of the 500 volt tram wires.[5]

Youngsters could earn useful pocket money as 'paper boys' by delivering the *Brisbane Courier* in the mornings or the *Telegraph* in the afternoons. In earlier times this would have been done by a man driving a buggy:

OUR PAPERMAN USED to roll the newspapers up and bend them into a boomerang shape and shoot them into our yard. Sometimes he would even get them through the bay window…[6]

In the 1930s a shop on the Valley side of the Annie and Brunswick Street corner[7] was conducted by Misses Edith and Phyllis Day:

THEY WERE TWO elderly sisters who could have been twins. Both wore gold-rimmed spectacles. The wall telephone in the shop was installed at the standard height and being quite short in nature, the Misses Day had a special stool so that they could reach to crank the handle and make a call.[8]

A motor vehicle accident on the doorstep of Butler & Corkill's Cash and Carry Store in May 1935. On the corner of Merthyr Road and James Street, Butler & Corkill was considered the main competitor of Garnett's Store. On the adjacent corner was Cartwrights, the butcher. — *Photo: JOL 151096*

The main attraction at the shop on the Park side of the Brunswick Street and Merthyr Road intersection in the 1920s was a koala:

> MRS JESSIE GILL *kept the little shop on the corner with Merthyr Road. Her grown daughter was with her and she owned a koala bear. All the kids would turn up to nurse the koala. That old building is still there.*[9]

In Merthyr Road during the 1950s, next door to Rayner's second butcher shop, was Stewarts Grocers. Home deliveries cost one shilling, but orders over ten shillings were delivered free.[10]

Along the back lanes of the wealthier side of Brunswick Street as well as along the streets on its other side, home deliveries of milk, bread and ice came on a regular basis. Robert Blaikie remembers that a small van signed 'Ma's Cakes' arrived with wonderful cakes and pastries. The children called the vendor "Mr Ma."[11]

Though electricity came to New Farm around 1932-3, it was to be a long time before refrigeration was in every home. As a result, there was the need for ice deliveries from someone such as Mike Dwyer in Welsby Street who was a distributor for Trails Ice Works in The Valley.

> MIKE HAD A *truck with an insulated box on the rear. The boys picked up the block with large tongs and carried it into the homes, putting it in the ice chest. Sometimes, half a block was all that was required and they would need to break it up with an ice pick. It was heavy work, and it was disappointing to find a note at the back door saying that ice was not required that day. The deliveries continued into the 1960s as many furnished flats did not come equipped with a refrigerator.*[12]

* * *

MANY PEOPLE IN New Farm remember "the chemist shop that had been there for ages." They were thinking of the one on the corner of Brunswick Street and Merthyr Road, next to Rayner's butchers. Around 1934-35, Pauline Benjamin initiated the building of the shops and lived in the flat above with her sons, one of whom was Leslie, a pharmacist, who opened a chemist shop on the corner. A buzzer was

This building on the corner of Merthyr Road and Brunswick Street dates from 1933-34. The Benjamin family lived in the flats above and conducted the Chemist Shop until the 1960s when it became Sorbello's. — *Photo: G. Benjamin.*

installed so that people needing medication out of shop hours could call him in the flat above.

When the war came, Leslie's full-time duties with the Volunteer Defence Corps (VDC) meant that his brother Bertie, also a pharmacist, took over the running of the shop, meanwhile Jack (Leslie's stepson) was the shop's bicycle delivery boy. In the 1960s, Bertie moved to Sydney and the pharmacy was sold to Alf Sorbello.[13] Diagonally opposite was another of the earliest Italian businesses, Santo (Sam) Raiti's Four-Square store.

* * *

OF COURSE, THERE were always door-to-door traders and Beattie Dawson remembered one in particular:

> WE HAD A Chinese fruit man. He used to come around with the two baskets carried across his shoulders. He grew his own down at what we call Newstead but in those days, we called it Bulimba. [14]

> THERE WERE GYPSIES coming around selling clothes pegs whittled out of tree branches. The gypsies were from the park around the back of the sugar refinery and they wore flashy, bright clothes. The men repaired saucepans with Mendit soldered on. You had to be careful because they would offer to bless the money and you wouldn't get it back … [15]

Notes

1.   Oral History: Grahame Miller, 1992-94.
2.   R.O. Sands conducted the shop from 756 Brunswick Street. They continued to depend on ice when the trend was to convert to refrigeration.
3.   Oral History: Fred Matthews, 1974.
4.   Matthews, *ibid*.
5.   Raymond Clark was the newsagent at 720 Brunswick Street (1925 *Electoral Roll*).
6.   Maida Crawford, in "Old Farm", *New Farm News*, June-July 1994.
7.   During the 90s, the Brunswick 7 Day Medical Centre operated from here.
8.   Oral History: Leonard Brown, 1993. The Days' shop was at 720 Brunswick Street during the 1930s.
9.   Oral History: John Rosenskjar, 2008.
10. Oral History: Brian Hjelm, 2008.
11. Oral History: Robert Blaikie, 2008.
12. Hjelm, *op. cit*.
13. Oral History: Judith Benjamin, 2008.
14. Oral History: Beattie Dawson, 2007.
15. Miller, *op. cit*.

24

The Depression Years

I'll never forget my father getting a job...

Cairnsville at 41 Balfour Street in 1911, with members of the Le Brocq family in front of the home's open verandah. When Joy Arden (nee Le Brocq) returned to the house, the verandahs had been closed in to accommodate more relatives affected by the Depression. — *Image: John Oxley Library 21981*

IN THE DEPRESSION years, there were families who were so short of money that the only affordable socialising was calling on friends or welcoming visitors — yet even then, there were mothers who warned their children not to bring home school friends because there was not enough food to offer them anything.

When the Wall Street stock market crashed in October 1929 and share values plummeted, the price of Australia's wool and wheat exports slumped, governments cut back on spending and the economy suffered. People lost their jobs and some lost their homes. Door to door selling was one way of gaining some meagre cash and in addition there was relief work which offered a small government allowance.

Some pockets of New Farm felt the effects of the Depression right through the 1930s up until the start of World War II. Despite the fact that Cath Carey's father (from Abbott Street) had his own business in the motor trade in South Brisbane:

> ...THE DEPRESSION CAME and father was still paying an employee, but the bank foreclosed and he lost his business. He worked away from home for a time down south. Many of the houses were rented in those days. When the Depression really hit, people lost their houses and that was the day when the landlord moved in and bought them up. The people would tear their fences down to burn in their wood stoves.[1]

The government provided a small payment called "relief" for local roadwork and public projects. Relief work was carried out at various spots around New Farm including at the State School. Former pupils expressed their dismay not only about seeing men levelling the top playground using hand tools to remove the rock, but that some of the men were fathers of fellow students.[2] Often relief workers were professional men unused to hard physical labour.

Other former pupils remember that some children were poorly clothed and that during the really bad days, school friends took food from the rubbish bins.

> IT DIDN'T MATTER which side of Brunswick Street you came from; nothing was wasted and housewives prided themselves on their thriftiness. Bread was not thrown out; it was either dried in the oven and made into bread crumbs or used in bread and butter pudding. Bread and dripping wrapped in newspaper was not unusual for a school lunch in the Depression days and we more fortunate ones were often given extra to share with our friends.[3]

There was also relief work carried out at the Holy Spirit School:

> AT THE CONVENT, the tennis court was excavated with pick and shovel. The men on relief were always on the roads, chipping grass. There were multitudes of people working in the relief gangs, some of them local and others outsiders.[4]

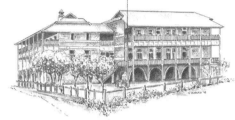

Those who were students at New Farm State School in the early 1930s still clearly remember details of the Depression years. — *Sketch: Courtesy of NFSS.*

Many people were "on the susso" or sustenance dole which consisted of food coupons for a cash value. This did not help towards rent, clothing or medicines, so a great burden was borne by churches and charities. The Depression affected all sectors of the community.

> MEN TRUDGED THE streets selling needles, cotton, matches, pegs and other small items. My mother nearly always gave them a cup of tea and a few biscuits which they would eat, sitting on the back steps. When she died in 1987, her drawers were still full of rusty needles and threads, more than she needed in a long lifetime.[5]

A boy growing up in Annie Street would witness similar scenes:

> TRADERS WOULD CALL from door to door. Local prawners would carry round and sell prawns for so much a pint. They'd cut clothes props out of the saplings in the bush, and come along and sell them for people to push up their washing line. It was a different world…[6]

At New Farm State School in the 1930s, textbooks and paper were extremely scarce. Notes were written on the blackboard before being transcribed by pupils into their exercise books. School reports sent home during this period were written on card about twice the size of today's credit cards.[7] Those businesses that survived had to take special measures. During 1931-34 Trails Ice Works Ltd operated at a loss and the directors agreed to a 25% reduction in salary.[8]

Joy Arden (le Brocq), who grew up in *Cairnsville* in the house at 41 Balfour Street that had been built by her grandfather, found an unexpected consequence of the economic downturn on returning to the house after living away in Clayfield:

IN THE DEPRESSION, everything was awful and houses needed painting. When we came back, they'd enclosed the verandahs and used up every bit of space to put up relatives.[9]

The Bavas family found that their James Street house, which had been rented out during the Depression years, had had its fence palings used to fuel the fire and the lead waterproof lining in the bathroom had been taken up and sold.[10]

The backyards of New Farm properties were put to good use and by the 40s, most properties had at least one mango tree or loquat tree:

SOME YARDS HAD fig, peach, persimmon, mulberry, orange, mandarin or lemon trees. In season there was always something hanging over a fence to sample (or thieve). Many vegetable plots abounded with lettuce, tomatoes and carrots.[11]

Some children in the 1930s resourcefully grew carrots, lettuce and radishes for sale so as to obtain some pocket money.[12] Beattie Dawson was a teenager in Annie Street when the Depression began to bite and recalled that the community feeling helped families to survive:

IN THOSE DAYS, everyone would share. I remember my grandmother would make a big tub of brawn and my cousin and I would have the job of picking out the bones. We'd go around to different ones and give people a basin. They were very good to my grandmother. I owe so much to the area.

There was a Sister Francis Mary from All Hallows' accompanied by another nun who would go around the streets helping the poor, many of them in boarding houses. Some men for whom liquor was their downfall lived in hovels. That was in the forties.[13]

Men without the fare who had 'jumped the rattler' would arrive at the Refinery on trains that had come from as far as Mackay. Beattie Dawson remembers that some people were sympathetic about their plight:

I REMEMBER MY uncle, who worked at the Dixon Street flock factory (just near the Refinery), helping one man. Many of those unfortunate men finally got dropsy. One Sunday morning soon after my uncle's wife had died, this man, in gratitude, had come to our house with a gorgeous bunch of roses that he'd picked from New Farm Park! My grandmother didn't know what to do, because while the flowers were for my uncle's wife who had died, they were really given to express the man's gratitude to my uncle. The flock factory used to chew up rags and make them into kapok. There was a similar place in James Street between Kent and Harcourt — Bakers flock factory.[14]

The man's gratitude was probably because sometimes the people from the trains would be stranded and would be walking around looking for something to eat. They'd be allowed to stay in the shed overnight then go on their way. They would get water and possibly have a shower with a hose.

Children growing up in the Depression suffered the privations of the times and witnessed the distress that their parents endured. Florence O'Brien (nee Charles) of

Terrace Street still recalls with feeling that her father would walk from New Farm to Ipswich looking for work. Luckily, the joyous moments were also remembered, such as this one in Browne Street:

> MUM HAD A hard time when the boys were young in the Depression. There was no money by the time we girls came along and were ready to go to school. I'll never forget my father getting a job. He was out of work for three or four years. He received a letter saying that he could start work on the Monday — and he danced around the kitchen. It was night-time and we were eating by the light of candles because we couldn't afford the electric light…[15]

It is sometimes remarked that a sure sign of the Depression years was that children often went without shoes. Those of that era reply however, that in Queensland's climate, going barefoot was what children preferred.

The skills of improvisation learned during the Depression years were to be a useful preparation for wartime in New Farm.

Notes

1.   Oral History: Cath Bishop (nee Carey), 2007.
2.   Norman Rogers and Donald B. MacDonald, in *Memories of New Farm State School*, 2001. p. 11.
3.   Velyian Todd (nee Macdonald) who attended NFSS during1934-1940, *ibid*., pp 11-12.
4.   Cath Bishop, *op. cit.*
5.   Velyian Todd, *op. cit.*
6.   Oral History: Brian Bishop, 2007.
7.   *MNFSS, op. cit.*, p. 52.
8.   Oral History: Arch Trail, 2002.
9.   Oral History: Joy Arden (nee Le Brocq), 1997.
10. Oral History: Jim Bavas, 2008.
11. Oral History: George Cowin, 2002.
12. Oral History: Bryan Oxlade, 2008.
13. Oral History: Beattie Dawson, 2007.
14. In the 1925 *Electoral Roll*, William Baker was a merchant of 111 Annie Street along with his son Samuel James Baker, a chairmaker, of the same address. By the 1936 *Roll*, Samuel James Baker was 'flockmaker' of 19 Beeston Street.
15. Oral History: Dorothy Messinbird, 1992.

A suburb on full alert...

Even after the war some signs remained. In June 1950, United States Army vehicles were still being warned to reduce speed in James Street adjacent to New Farm State School. — *Image: John Oxley Library, 83311.*

W HEN WAR BROKE out, New Farm residents felt particularly vulnerable with so many potential targets nearby: the Story Bridge, Powerhouse, the wharves and the sugar refinery, the large petrol storage area near the Wool Store, plus the oil and gas tanks nearby in Newstead. After the bombing of Darwin began in February 1942, the threat to Brisbane was real, and once the US Navy submarine base was established in April 1942 adjacent to Macquarie Street, the peril increased.

The war years had a significant effect on school life in New Farm. Though schools largely remained open, ranks of students were denuded when many women and children were evacuated to the country where the children's education was often continued via the Queensland Correspondence School.

There were troops camped in the grounds of the sugar refinery. Dodge Brothers (Austral Motors) were engaged in all types of military vehicle assembly, and they provided slit trenches for their employees on spare land in James Street near the corner of Merthyr Road. There were big movements of men and vehicles around New Farm State School. Disassembled aircraft were unloaded at the wharves and brought on trucks up James Street, and there was plenty of noise from American aircraft taking off from Eagle Farm in the direction of the suburb.

New Farm State School started the 1942 year some weeks late because of the need to dig slit trenches and install sand bag revetments parallel with the school's concrete retaining walls on two sides of the grounds.[1]

> JAMES STREET ROARED *with traffic. Many troops were transported and they would 'wolf whistle' the girls.*[2]

While the grown-ups were keenly aware of their vulnerability to a possible invasion, children mostly revelled in the excitement of such novel goings-on.

> OUR MOTHER BECAME *so concerned by the perceived threat to Brisbane posed by the Japanese that she decided to send us to a small Anglican boarding school,*

St Christopher's at Kenmore. This lasted no more than six months, because we were unhappy and threatened to run away.[3]

The tremendous influx of military personnel placed an enormous load on the public transport system, and as one observer reflected, "suddenly it was unusual to see people in civilian dress."

FROM A BOY'S point of view it was very exciting with lots of Americans around. American Army Officers moved into the house next door, baseball was played in the park and there were many trucks and vehicles on the local streets — and people everywhere![4]

There were many training activities, including night signalling which was readily visible to locals. There were also practice air-raid drills and search lights scanning the skies at night. When the air-raid sirens sounded, whether at home or at school, everyone would rush to the slit trenches in the yards of the houses or businesses. These were deep narrow trenches, which, if uncovered, would fill with water. Often a tin of water and some other supplies were stored close by.

AT HOME (IN Merthyr Road), our family had an air-raid shelter in the back garden complete with internal steps and a roof. It was a favourite place to play even though we weren't supposed to.[5]

Shop and house windows were criss-crossed with sticky tape in order to reduce injuries if the glass were splintered by a bomb blast. Wardens were appointed under the Air Raid Precautions (ARP) Scheme and they practised with the stirrup pump and had a bucket of sand to put out fires. Others joined the Volunteer Defence Corps (VDC).

IN 1943 NEW Farm State School was set up as the official First Aid Post for the district. A sand-bagged and blacked-out area under the Infant School was allocated for this. Regular first-aid and home nursing classes were held as well as air-raid drills and practice for emergency treatment of casualties.[6]

An unusual phenomenon of the times were internments. Individuals and families who had always been considered a familiar part of New Farm life "disappeared." If the breadwinner was interned then his family had to survive without his income. If the family were in business then the business was invariably lost.

A FRIEND OF ours, Gloria Torey, was missing from school one day and we thought she was ill. We learned later that the entire family had been interned for the duration of the war because she was part-Japanese.[7]

THE NAKASHIMAS HAD a laundry in Brunswick Street opposite the Police Station. They disappeared. They would have been scooped up, the same as the Kashiwagi Silk Store at Gipps Street in the Valley where we used to buy gut fishing lines.[8] *A lot of families disappeared off the map, never sighted again. The girls had attended our school. They were probably interned interstate. Lytton barracks was an interrogation centre.*[9]

After working as a tailoress all week plus seven hours on Saturdays, Florence Charles (nee O'Brien) played tennis with the T.C. Beirnes' Social Club, often at the Harcourt Street home of the Kashiwagi family, but then came the war and the Kashiwagis' internment.[10]

> I WAS SENT for a haircut and found the barber's shop ransacked. The Italian proprietor was gone. I think the authorities were looking for a hidden radio. The fish and chip shop near the Astor Theatre was run by an Italian family. After the father was interned, the business continued but faced hostility, so the women put up a Greek flag to protect themselves.[11]

The Evans Deakin shipyards at Kangaroo Point were working urgently to build vessels for war service. The noise was heard over most of New Farm but particularly in Griffith Street.

When Queensland's latest 10,000-ton merchant ship was launched today it became stuck on the slipway just as the stern reached the water. Despite the efforts of tugs and other attempts to dislodge her, she was still in this position when the crowd of about 3,000 spectators were asked to leave the yard.

> THE YARDS OPERATED day and night with much banging. The family had trouble getting to sleep. After a while they adjusted — and when the war ended and the shipyards returned to normal operations, it took them longer to adjust to the quiet…[12]

On 6 March 1943, Robert Blaikie and his brother Bruce peddled from Lower Bowen Terrace to the end of Merthyr Road to watch the *River Burdekin* being launched from Evans Deakin shipyards. The ship became stuck on the slipway, as reported in this newspaper (possibly *The Telegraph* of the same date.)
— Cutting: courtesy of Robert Blaikie.

The launch of a ship was always a sight to behold, especially if something went wrong…

> ONE SATURDAY MORNING, my brother Bruce and I rode our bikes to the end of Merthyr Road to watch the launch of a "River Class" freighter across at the shipyard. The vessel began its slide down the slip towards the river, but stopped halfway. Despite all of their efforts, the ship remained stuck. Over the next few days, it was pulled back up the ramp and this time the launch was successful.[13]

Because there were so many large naval vessels in port, the river became a 'stink hole' because of the amount of oil discharged into it.

> IF EVER I took my parents' dinghy onto the river, it was a real chore because when I had finished, I would have to upend the dinghy and remove the oil from the hull.[14]

Local businesses benefitted from the influx of so many military personnel:

> MY FATHER'S TAILORING business did well because he made clothes for the American soldiers. Sometimes he would bring soldiers home for a meal and I

particularly remember a Chinese gentleman named Mr. Chang. He and other US servicemen were kind enough to give my father American comic books for us children. With the outbreak of war, comics were no longer imported so this was a welcome gift indeed. I kept them for many years.[15]

There were several local organisations supporting the war effort and some offered hospitality to the soldiers and sailors who were a long way from home. At the Holy Spirit Parish for instance, dances were held and meals provided.

THERE WERE CATHOLIC youth group meetings and dances during the war, part of which was offering soldiers a meal for a shilling. We would wait on the tables. They would be offered fish, mutton or veal, and then the workers would have tomato on toast. After that, there were the dances. We danced the war away.[16]

Others helped by producing or supplying the very items that were needed in the physical struggle to protect Australia.

ON THE VERANDAH of our house (in Griffith Street), my mother erected two large poles and a cross bar, which were used to knit large camouflage nets. Two days per week she went to the city to pack parcels at the Australian Comforts Fund building for soldiers overseas. A government department named Manpower organized people to be billeted in private homes and I remember a lady from Warwick who had been brought to Brisbane to help address the labour shortage.[17]

Those who were performing essential work for the war effort found New Farm convenient, especially if on shift work. In 1944, a telephone technician, his wife who was a central telegraph operator, and their three year old child, moved to New Farm and became long-term residents at *Coronet Court* in Brunswick Street.[18]

Even relatively young people willingly contributed their skill so as to play their part on the road to victory. From late 1942, 16 year old Deirdre Fox was a mine watcher with the Civil Defence Organisation. On the night before, during and after the full moon, there was the chance that Japanese mines could be positioned in the Brisbane River either by submarine or aircraft. A group of young women had been trained to be watchers, working from a system of lookouts along the length of the Brisbane River. Some observation spots were concrete bunkers, while others were verandahs on homes overlooking the river.

TWO OF US were on watch at the same time. We went on duty at 8pm and finished at 6am, summer and winter. Everyone was transported to their homes after their night of duty. During the night, several exercises were planned so that we could practise. A launch, about the size of a cross-river ferry today, would go down and up the river. When we saw the launch showing the white, green and red lights on its beacon, we would map the location as well as send a message in Morse code by torch light. The results of these exercises were always examined at the next meeting of the Mine Watchers.[19]

QUEENSLAND
CIVIL DEFENCE ORGANISATION

Certificate

This is to Certify that

DEIRDRE LILIAN FOX

was enrolled as a member of the

MINE WATCHING ORGANISATION OF QUEENSLAND

and has loyally served in the Civil Defence Organisation of the
State in that capacity during a period of national emergency

This Certificate is issued in appreciation of
the services so rendered and as an expression
of the thanks of the Government of Queensland
for the voluntary assistance so generously given
in the interests of public safety and welfare

Thos. A. Foley
MINISTER FOR CIVIL DEFENCE
BRISBANE, APRIL 30, 1945

Q.C.D.O.

Deirdre Fox was presented with this certificate for her membership of the Mine Watching Organization
of Queensland during a period of "national emergency." It was signed by Thomas A. Foley, Minister for
Civil Defence, in Brisbane on 30 April 1945.

Other youngsters were encouraged to become collectors for War Savings Certificates. This was a government scheme to help pay for the war by borrowing surplus cash from the general public. Most people would not have the money for a full Certificate, so War Savings Stamps of various denominations were issued, and when the stamps filled the card, it could be exchanged for a Certificate. One Certificate was expected to mature from 16 shillings to £1 in seven years. By 1942 the sale of War Savings Certificates was a major source of government revenue, and Australians were strongly encouraged to invest during 'Victory Loan' drives.

> I BECAME A collector for this scheme and one afternoon a week after school, I would ride my bike around the streets that had been allocated to me, visiting individual houses to make collections. Julius Street off Moray Street was one of the streets assigned to me. It was a very short street. On a telegraph pole at the entrance to the street, I can remember nailing a sign saying, 'This is a War Savings Street.' This sign stayed there for some years after the war and I remember seeing it many times when I passed by. Now, it has long since gone…[20]

If 12 year old girls from Browne Street were kept close to the apron strings ("Mum was even more strict with us,"[21]), and those from Abbott Street were warned "*not* to go over to the other side of Brunswick Street," the 14 and 15 year olds — boys and girls — apparently suffered no such limitations, their bicycles symbolic of their freedom and mobility:

> AT TENERIFFE PARK we saw a lookout built high up in a pine tree and there were dummy anti-aircraft guns made from timber. Air-raid sirens were mounted atop strategically located power poles. Occasionally, we saw General MacArthur's amah taking his son Arthur for a visit to New Farm Park. Once we saw the General arriving at his headquarters in the AMP building at the corner of Queen and Edward Streets. Military police armed with sub-machine guns were protecting the General.[22]

New Farm kids such as Robert Blaikie rode their bicycles as far as Eagle Farm aerodrome, to find a peep hole in the galvanised iron perimeter fence in order to watch the line-up of American aircraft preparing for wartime operations in the north. Robert also used his bicycle for the more sobering part-time job of delivering telegrams, some of them clearly containing grave news.

Notwithstanding the seriousness of this era, wartime managed to produce some very unusual occurrences which were either puzzling, funny or scandalous, depending on one's viewpoint:

> WE THOUGHT ONE boy was incredibly lucky. He had a never-ending stream of American servicemen visiting his home, who were all uncles of his. It appears that his real father was absent from home and his mother just did her bit by entertaining all those uncles. The uncles gave him heaps of chewing gum, hats and badges. They were extremely generous in providing him with picture money, which meant that the boy was often at the pictures instead of being at home.

One Monday morning he told us about his incredible luck on the previous Saturday. Uncle Bud gave the boy something like ten shillings and suggested he spend it all by visiting picture theatres that day.

He told us he jumped onto the tram and went into the city. He went to one morning session, had lunch, then an afternoon session, then back to the fish shop in Brunswick Street before the evening session at the Astor began.

When he returned home at 10pm, Uncle Bud had left to fight the Japs. Our boy still had money left over to spend at the school shops. What luck to have a vast spread of uncles who were so generous! [23]

* * *

ONE OF THE legacies of so many military men coming to town was that some Brisbane women married American servicemen and went to live in the United States after the war. A number of the women and children returned to Brisbane and settled in New Farm, as it was one of the few places with accommodation for single parents. Leonard Brown remembers:

THE AMERICAN CHILDREN dressed 'very cool', had exotic names, and had a 'from someplace else' quality about them. Sometimes their Daddies would patch things up and they would return to the US, sorely missed by us. [24]

Notes

1. James Alexander Macdonald (1940-48) in *Memories of NFSS, op. cit.,* pp. 22-24.
2. Oral History: Jim Bavas, 2008, who grew up at 123 James Street.
3. Oral History: Robert Blaikie, 2008.
4. Blaikie, *ibid.*
5. Oral History: Judith Benjamin, 2008.
6. Edith Beryl Farne Sang (nee Sams) (1940-47) in *Memories, op. cit.,* p. 18-22.
7. Sang, *MNFSS, ibid.*
8. Mr T. Kashiwagi was a silk merchant and president of the Brisbane Friendly Society of Japanese. He had strongly protested against Japan's siege of Shanghai in 1937, but this did not stop his internment. See Kay Saunders in: Rod Fisher & Barry Shaw (editors), *Brisbane: The Ethnic Presence since the 1850s*, Brisbane History Group, 1993, p. 107.
9. Oral History: Brian Bishop, 2007.
10. Oral History: Florence O'Brien, 2008.
11. Bavas, *op. cit.*
12. Oral History: Jack Benjamin, 2008.
13. Blaikie, *op. cit.* 3,000 spectators were asked to leave Evans Deakin shipyard when the 10,000 ton (9070 tonne) *River Burdekin* became stuck on the slipway on 6 March 1943.
14. Jack Benjamin, *op. cit.*
15. Judith Benjamin, *op. cit.*
16. Oral History: Cath Bishop (nee Carey), 2007.
17. Jack Benjamin, *op. cit.*
18. Oral History: Brian Hjelm, 2008.
19. Deirdre Fox
20. Blaikie, *op. cit.*
21. Oral History: Dorothy Messinbird, 1992.
22. Blaikie, *op. cit.*
23. Macdonald, in *Memories, op. cit.*
24. Oral History: Leonard Brown, 1993.

A friendly invasion to thwart an enemy one...

Aerial view of the US Navy "Receiving Station with Bachelors Officers' Quarters and Dispensary" in New Farm during World War II. The photo shows New Farm Park (top), the Powerhouse (just off to the left), the sugar refinery (bottom front), with Lamington Street curving in from the bottom RHS. The 'white' buildings at the centre of the photo are the New Farm Naval Barracks in the block bounded by Lamington, Dixon and Richardson Streets. The latter street now approximates part of Hopetoun Way. — *Courtesy of New Farm Naval Barracks file at Queensland Maritime Museum.*

EVEN BEFORE THE Japanese attacked Pearl Harbour on 7 December 1941, a US Navy battle group visited Brisbane, making a great impression on New Farm's youngsters. In March 1941 the cruisers *USS Portland* and *USS Chicago*[1] tied up at Newstead, while the accompanying five destroyers berthed at New Farm Wharf. This was a goodwill mission and the crews marched through the streets of Brisbane.[2]

Less than four months after Pearl Harbour, the District Naval Officer in Brisbane received a letter dated 29 March 1942: "I am directed by the Naval Board to inform you that the United States Navy desires to base a submarine flotilla in Brisbane … due to arrive about 15 April 1942." That was indeed the day when the US Navy, represented by the submarine tender *USS Griffin* and her squadron of six submarines, tied up at New Farm Wharf.

The original base was to be at Pinkenba but an early American representative did not like that option so the day before the flotilla's expected arrival, they took over New Farm Wharf (Macquarie Street, adjacent to the riverfront between Hastings and Beeston Streets). Within a week of a marathon voyage from Panama to Brisbane via Bora Bora near Tahiti, the first boats were sent out on patrol, and these operations lasted until January 1945 with the base closing in March 1945.

* * *

WHILE THE SUBMARINE bases in Pearl Harbour and Fremantle were bigger than the Brisbane base in terms of the number of patrols undertaken, the busiest time at the New Farm Wharf was between October and December 1942 when the New Guinea and Guadalcanal campaigns were at their height.

In addition to the stores and workshops on the dedicated wharf area, the submarines were also maintained by the tenders *USS Griffin, USS Fulton* and *USS Sperry* which were completely filled with workshops covering every trade needed to keep submarines operational. A tender might have several submarines tied up alongside, with others berthed nearby.

At Christmas 1942, both *USS Fulton* and *USS Sperry* were in port, and a customary goodwill gesture was to host a Christmas party for local underprivileged children. The crews raised money so that each girl could receive a new dress, each boy a new suit, and all a new pair of shoes, plus other presents more welcomed by children such as cricket bats, etc. Despite the fact that Brisbane was suffering the rigours of wartime rationing, the Christmas meal for the children was a source of wonder in itself — with apples, tomato soup, sliced cheese, roast turkey, sliced ham, asparagus tips, porterhouse rolls and ice cream. A seven year old boy is said to have stated, "This is the first time I have ever tasted ice cream!"

By contrast, it is understandable that there were lapses of law and order, especially when it was traditional to have a big crew's party before a submarine went out on patrol. 'No alcohol at dances' was the law in Queensland, but somehow the police and American Navy officials in Brisbane agreed on an arrangement that there could be dancing *and drink*, provided that only the invited lady came with the sailor, and that police were in attendance. As it turned out, the police were not always admitted…

After visiting friends in Oxlade Drive one evening in 1944, noted Brisbane journalist and later war correspondent, Osmar White penned an article entitled "Rowdyism, Vice Mar City Nights", describing how an excess of money, alcohol and war-fever brought unseemly capers to the streets of New Farm.[3] In the same vein, Harcourt Street milkman Harry Broadrick encountered a novel request regarding his horse and cart:

> ONE DAY HE came out and found an American sitting there on the cart, and he had spilt whisky into some of the empty bottles. He said to my husband, "How much do you want for the gig, buddy?"[4]

* * *

"Post Office, Enlisted Mens' Barracks," says the caption in the US Navy Report on New Farm Naval Barracks. This spot appears to be at the end of Dixon Street with the perimeter fence separating the camp from the back of New Farm Park.

US Naval Headquarters, New Farm. The location is possibly the corner of Lamington and Sydney Streets with the overhead lines leading to the Powerhouse. The flag may be the one in front of the building pictured below. The corner building may have later become the PMG Technical School.

US Naval Headquarters, New Farm. The actual location is uncertain. The roadway on the right may be Lamington Street. The profile of the building on the left hand side resembles that of the Austral Motors Assembly Works (now *Powerhouse Apartments*) between Sydney and Welsby Streets. There were several spots in the vicinity of the sugar refinery where this building might have stood. — *All photos on this page: New Farm Naval Barracks Report, courtesy of Qld Maritime Museum.*

AUDREY ABRAHAMS (NEE Maloney) who grew up on the river next door to Tom Welsby's house *Amity*, had a dress circle view of the submarine base:

> *THERE WERE TIMES when I could come home from school and look out to the river to see a submarine with the stern on the surface and the bow underwater, and also the reverse. They were carrying out tests.*[5]

The memorial to submariners in Newstead Park was installed in 1995. It lists the US submarines that were based in Brisbane at New Farm Wharf, including six that were lost on patrol out of Brisbane, four of them with all hands. — *Photo: G. Benjamin*

A memorial in Newstead Park lists the US submarines that were based in Brisbane at New Farm Wharf. Some famous names appear among them. *USS Amberjack, USS Dace, USS Grampus, USS S39, USS Seawolf* and *USS Triton* were lost on patrol out of Brisbane, four with all hands (including the first listed with 73 on board). The loss of *USS Triton* continues to be a subject of controversy, as to whether it was sunk during March-April 1943 on patrol in the Admiralty Islands or by friendly fire in northern Moreton Bay.

USS Wahoo's new skipper Lt. Cdr. Dudley Morton gave a dramatic pep talk calculated to boost morale before casting off from the submarine base in early 1943:

USS Growler at the New Farm Submarine Base around 17 February 1943. The CSR Refinery is in the distance, while the Maloney Brothers' jetty and moorings are to the right. *USS Growler* limped back to Brisbane from the sea lanes near Rabaul, following action which involved its ramming a Japanese gunboat. Badly wounded by enemy gunfire, *Growler's* captain, still on the bridge, courageously ordered, "Take her down," so as to save his ship. Commander Gilmore was posthumously awarded the Medal of Honor. A new bow, replete with a metal kangaroo welded to each side, was constructed at Evans Deakin Shipyards in Brisbane. — *Courtesy of Qld Maritime Museum.*

Wahoo is expendable. We will take every reasonable precaution, but our mission is to sink enemy shipping… If anyone doesn't want to go along under these conditions, see the Yeoman. I am giving him verbal authority to transfer anyone who is not a volunteer. Nothing will ever be said about your remaining in Brisbane.

Understandably, no crewman elected to remain behind. Soon after this, *USS Growler* limped back to Brisbane with its bow extensively damaged after ramming a Japanese gunboat. Its commander had courageously given his life to save his ship. A new bow was fitted by Evans Deakin and the boat was nicknamed *Kangaroo Express*.

Apart from New Farm Wharf, there were several US Navy installations in New Farm. There were buildings in Sydney Street and various barracks in a camp bordered by Lamington, Dixon and Richardson Streets, backing onto New Farm Park.[6] Officers were either billeted or found accommodation in many of the large homes or apartment buildings in the suburb. When it came to relaxation facilities for US Navy commissioned officers, a spot was chosen in Oxlade Drive on the riverfront. The land was acquired from the Brisbane City Council, and a Mess was constructed, consisting of two 40' x 100' (12m x 30.5m) Stran-Steel (Quonset) buildings joined by a foyer constructed between the units.

The riverside land had previously been a rubbish dump,[7] so before building began, a considerable amount of fill was imported to bring the elevation of the property up to a more even grade. US Navy documents reported on the result:

The US Navy did an excellent job of landscaping and the US Navy Commissioned Officers' Mess was a Brisbane River showplace. There were so few places of entertainment in Brisbane for the Naval Officers that it was decided to construct the New Farm Mess.[8]

The original Quonset buildings are still at 50 Oxlade Drive as Riverside Receptions. Indeed, the two buildings of the adjoining Merthyr Bowls Club also may have been part of the USN Riverside Officers' Club.

New Farm was considered a great posting. The submarine base was at the New Farm Wharf tram terminus. The barracks were a short walk from both the New Farm Wharf and New Farm Park tram lines. Within 15 minutes the sailors could be in the centre of Brisbane. When submariners were paid on arriving back from patrol (they received 50% more than those serving on other ships), £5 was often their smallest denomination, causing headaches for the tram conductress!

The Riverside Centre on Oxlade Drive, once the US Navy Officers' Mess. The foyer joins the two original Quonset huts. — *Photo: G. Benjamin.*

Some New Farm citizens had reservations about the military installation being so close to their suburb.

> JACK BENJAMIN ATTENDED New Farm State School until his mother became concerned about the risk of bombs being dropped on the submarine base nearby and he was moved to Churchie (at Norman Park). His mother felt that this was far enough away to be safe.[9]

Robert Blaikie remembers seeing the masts of the submarine tenders from the verandah of his grandfather's house at 591 Lower Bowen Terrace. His curiosity to take a closer look at the base met with a sobering warning:

> WE ENJOYED SAILING as a sport and regularly sailed on the Milton, Bulimba and Hamilton Reaches of the Brisbane River in a 16' skiff. On one occasion, being boys, we sailed too close to the submarines in order to take a closer look, but were warned off by a rifle shot across the mast.[10]

The 'Yanks' were generally well-liked locally and appreciated the open-hearted hospitality shown them. H. Gray Forrest, ex-Chief Yeoman in the US Navy, addressed a letter to the editor of a Brisbane newspaper around 1970, expressing his regret at not being able to re-visit Brisbane for the 25th anniversary of his leaving Australia. "I may never see Australia again, which I hoped to do," he said, "however please rest assured that I still consider it my second home and always will."[11]

Notes

1. *USS Chicago* was the primary target during the attack of three Japanese midget submarines in Sydney Harbour on the night of 31 May-1 June 1942. A torpedo passed close to the cruiser and hit another vessel.
2. Oral History: Robert Blaikie, 2008; The five destroyers were *USS Downes, USS Reid, USS Conyingham, USS Cassin* and *USS Clark*.
3. "Rowdyism, Vice Mar City Nights," *Sunday Mail,* 13 February 1944, p. 4.
4. Elsie Broadrick, *op. cit.,* p. 17
5. Audrey Abrahams, *Brothers of Bribie Heritage,* Wavell Heights, 1999, p. 23. Next to Thomas Welsby's home *Amity* in Welsby Street, James Maloney built maisonettes, a depot and storage area on the riverfront, along with a jetty and moorings. In December 1936, Maloney Bros. began supplying shell grit from material they brought from the Pumicestone Passage. One of their boats *Kauri II* was requisitioned by the Navy in 1942. The same year, the Royal Australian Navy built a depot on their downriver side, later known as *HMAS Moreton*. James Maloney's daughter Audrey Abrahams (nee Maloney) recorded these details in *Brothers of Bribie Heritage* (1993). Audrey's maternal grandparents had lived in Florence Street, and her aunt Mrs Eileen O'Connor owned *Coronet Court* in Brunswick Street. The Maloney home and jetty were demolished and today *Freshwater* apartments occupy the spot.
6. "The old US Military Barracks which faced Dixon Street had been converted into housing commission flats. Braemar hot water systems were made in this building." (Brian Hjelm, 2008)
7. The spot was attractive to local boys. Bryan Oxlade explained, "We used to spend hours down there. I had a habit of bringing home things from the dump, just in case it could come in handy one day. Every few months, my father would put it all in the old Chev and take it back to the dump."
8. "US Naval Base," Navy 134; Section 10, Part B, Item 53. p. 89. Copy available from Queensland Maritime Museum.
9. Oral History: Judith Benjamin, 2008
10. Oral History: Robert Blaikie, 2008
11. "A Yank who'll never forget us", Letter to the Editor, unknown date.

The Jewish Community

Just a walk to the Synagogue on Saturday…

A HEBREW CONGREGATION HAD been founded in Brisbane in 1865 and the Synagogue in Margaret Street — designed by Arthur Morry though Andrea Stombuco also submitted plans — was consecrated in 1886.

In 1929-30, Rabbi Nathan Levine lived in Upper Bowen Terrace, a further indication of New Farm's significance for the Jewish community. Families could walk to the Synagogue on Saturdays, thereby keeping the faith that work is not done on the Sabbath (by themselves or by others such as tram or taxi drivers). When religious observance became less strict in the late 1960s and the 1970s, people followed the trend of moving to the newer suburbs.[1]

The Brisbane Synagogue ca. 1906 in Margaret Street was within easy walking distance for those of the Jewish community who lived in New Farm. It was completed in 1885 and consecrated on 18 July1886. — *JOL 145942.*

New Farm's popularity among those of the Jewish faith can be traced back to the previous century. Leopold Solomon Benjamin (d. 1916), financial manager of Benjamin Brothers Limited, General Merchants and Importers, bought a one and a half-acre site and built his residence *Inglenook* (now *GFS House*) on the corner of Moray and Sydney Streets around 1888. The choice of John Jacob Cohen as architect (he designed the Bellevue Hotel in George Street) was likely to have been influenced by their religious association.[2]

Further down Moray Street and several decades later, Blanche Norman along with her sister Marjory Pitt, recorded a vivid memory of growing up in New Farm.

My father was Louis Norman, a tailor's cutter. Born in England his family moved to South Africa where he met my mother. He obtained a job in Australia from South Africa and sailed over to it.

Mum was to follow to be married but they quietly went off to the registry office and got married before he left. When Mum arrived here, Dad had already made some Jewish friends and they were married again in a Jewish home. They lived in Bowen Terrace and then at 32 Moreton Street, one of a row of similar houses. Next, Dad built a home on the corner of Moray Street (with Mountford Road) on a very strange shaped piece of land. We lived there from the early 1920s. On the other side of the road there was a big empty area covered with water. Dad had many offers to buy that place. We lived there until 1924. As a child of five in 1920, I remember a dreadful hail storm that came and took our roof across the river to Norman Park.

There were many Jewish families around New Farm then. We used to walk to the Margaret Street Synagogue on Saturday mornings. In fact, the Rabbi even lived in Bowen Terrace. In 1925 we acquired a car, a second hand Durrant. Next we bought a new Overland 6, and they were imported in their own crates. Later, that crate became the garage, or the nucleus of the garage. Dad never drove. Mum drove as well as my eldest brother, but he was such a mad driver that our school friends were not allowed to get in with us. We used to drive to Redcliffe where we went every year for our holidays until I was quite a late teenager.

The Jewish in New Farm were very close then. It was always, 'Next year in Jerusalem'. That was their cry, 'Next year in Jerusalem.'[3]

"We supported all the local businesses if the service was good, plus the ones operated by Jewish families. These included a bootmaker in the shops on Merthyr Road, a dentist, and Meadow's Grocery Store on Merthyr Road towards the intersection with James Street," explained Judith Benjamin whose husband's family ran Benjamin's Chemist Shop.

Judith's mother, Mary Lieberman, was a member of the National Council for Jewish Women and she decided to open an Op Shop in what is now New Farm Village. The women ran the store so well that they were able to buy the building. Eventually the concept became more popular and the shop was sold. As well as assisting with running the shop, Judith was President of the Council for 14 years.

Jack Benjamin's father supported the Guardian Society which helped fund the passage of young Jewish men and teenage boys who needed a new start after the war.

AT TIMES WE would have a young person come to stay with us. I recall how disturbed some of these individuals were as a result of their experiences. The Society had a farm at Redland Bay and my sister Joyce taught English there.[4]

There were several waves of immigration that brought Jewish people to New Farm, including a pre-war influx from Nazi Germany and the annexed territories, followed by the great surge of emigres after the end of the war in Europe.

One young new Jewish arrival at New Farm State School was interviewed by the headmaster, who considerately pointed out that because of the boy's European name, it was likely to suffer instant schoolyard conversion to the local word 'loafer'.

Knowing that the family had already lost 40 relatives in Poland, the headmaster suggested this additional burden could easily be avoided by a name change. The lad went on to become a Wickham Terrace pharmacist, and the story of how Brian Lister gained his new name formed part of family folklore.[5]

Notes

1. Oral History: Judith Benjamin, 2008.
2. John Mackenzie-Smith, "GFS House, New Farm, 1829-1942". Paper given NFDHS. 2008.
3. Oral History: Ethel Blanche Norman (1915-2001) daughter of Louis Norman (1882-1930), 1992.
4. Oral History: Jack Benjamin, 2008.
5. Conversation with Joan Lister, 2008.

Despite the differences, it has all worked out alright...

Today, 73 Moray Street is the home of *The Moreton Club*. Once known as *Bertholme*, the dwelling was built by Andrea Stombuco in 1882-83 as a family home.
— *Photo: G. Benjamin*

EVEN BEFORE NEW Farm became "Little Italy" during the mid-1950s to the mid-1960s, the forerunner of Italian influence on the locality was the Florentine Andrea Giovanni Stombuco (1820-1907). After 25 years in the southern states, he travelled north to Queensland in 1875, ready to put his sculpting, masonry, building and architectural skills at the service of Bishop O'Quinn. While his architectural contribution to Brisbane is substantial, New Farm was where he designed two homes for himself: *Bertholme* (1882-83) in Moray Street (now *The Moreton Club*), and his later residence — when working with his son as 'A. Stombuco & Son' — *Briar House* (1888) at 15 Lechmere Street.

At the same time, countless Catholics from New Farm have encountered his craftsmanship in the designs of St. Patrick's Catholic Church in the Valley, St. Stephen's Cathedral, All Hallows' Convent and St. Joseph's College, Gregory Terrace.

By 1891, *Briar House* was sold and Stombuco, known as a man of 'fiery temper', left for Perth where he died in poverty in 1907.

* * *

THE MIGRATION OF Italians to Queensland dates from the expedition of 106 Tuscans who arrived on the barque *Indus* in 1877. This was followed in 1891 with the arrival of 335 'Piedmontese' on the *Jumna*, indentured to cut sugarcane — thus was laid the foundation of the substantial Italian contribution to the Queensland sugar industry. By 1933, Queensland had the largest number of Italian-born residents in Australia, numbering more than 8,300, testament to the success of the 'chain of migration' that continued from early arrivals. It was into this setting that there arrived a man who was to loom large among the Italian community of New Farm.

In 1930, Dr. Francesco Castellano (1899-1976) from Grumo Appula near Bari, settled in North Queensland. The son of a medical practitioner, he was appointed to an Italian community hospital at Ingham. By 1935, he was the sole Italian doctor in Cairns.

When World War II began, Dr. Castellano along with many others endured internment from June 1940 until December 1943, spending part of it at Gaythorne in Brisbane. It is generally agreed that this policy was more often to please public sentiment rather than counter any real security concern.

Following his release, the doctor began work in Brisbane and was on hand to witness the flood of post-war immigration. With the building boom of the 1950s, Brisbane became home to the majority of Queenslanders of Italian origin, many moving down from North Queensland. A great proportion lived in New Farm, so it is understandable why, for 20 years from around 1960, the Italian Consulate was located at Carramar Corner where Merthyr Road meets Moray Street.

The 'new Australians' faced barriers of ethnic intolerance that gradually receded with each decade. One solution was to form community associations along regional lines:

> THE MANY ITALIAN associations symbolized the reality of the early postwar immigrants who were not so much 'Italian', as Calabrian, Sicilian, Piedmontese, Abruzzese, Friulian or Sardinian.[1]

Dr. Castellano eventually established a practice at 303 Bowen Terrace. He was regarded as the 'dean' of many Italian communities and he strenuously promoted Italian culture, by supporting Italian bodies such as the Dante Alighieri Society, that spoke to the wider Australian community. His death in December 1976 at New Farm was much lamented.[2]

Italian immigrants were also able to count on the support of Archbishop James Duhig, a fact recognized by the gift of the striking fountain in the centre of *Wynberg's* circular driveway.

* * *

GIUSEPPE RINAUDO'S 1992 account of his life in New Farm typifies the experience of many Italians attracted to the locality from regional Queensland:

> I ORIGINALLY CAME from North Queensland. I met my wife who is from New Farm, and through her influence bought a house in New Farm and have been here for nearly 40 years.
>
> Soon after the war, people started coming down from the north and one of the early ones here was Dr. Francesco Castellano. He practised in Langshaw Street and from there he shifted to Bowen Terrace.
>
> Because he was a professional man and trusted, people would look around for a place to live close to him. The fact that New Farm was central and you could radiate to other suburbs for work, was why this suburb was very popular.
>
> Many people chose here because of the large blocks of land, but we only had a small 15.8 perch block. I enlarged the house so that it took up most of the land. It was on the corner of Villiers and Chambers Streets. Chambers Street is a dead end so the kids could go up and down it and have their own playground.
>
> Archbishop Duhig was one who pushed for migrants from Italy, Spain and other countries to Australia. He would encourage people to settle around

The gateposts of *Briar House* at 15 Lechmere Street, the dwelling designed by A. Stombuco & Sons in 1888, make a striking statement even before one examines the home's pleasing architectural lines. — *Photo: G. Benjamin*

here, including quite a lot of professional people. They believed that he was doing that because he wanted people to come to the area from Catholic countries. At that time we had about 10,000 Italians around Brisbane.

Among the Italian community, families did not visit each other very much. The New Farm community came from various sections of Italy, and different regions. You have the Sicilians, the Abruzzesi, the Piedmontesi and people from every other region — but while they were friends, they rarely visited each other.

On the other hand, from a religious point of view, there were activities such as dances in the parish or functions in town. There were specific Italian community dances at the Holy Spirit parish, and this was one of the reasons why the school built the hall at the back.

Eventually, as the Italians became more and more financial, they moved away because it became fashionable to buy a block of land at Aspley and places like that, and build their own houses in the style they liked—whereas here, they all had wooden buildings. Very few ever thought of taking away those wooden buildings and putting up their own houses here.

The local Italians worked mainly in factories such as Nanda Spaghetti, the Cannery and Marchant Brothers. Others were in construction and some of them are still living here. They were builders, and they worked from here and radiated to wherever they were working. Very few from here worked on farms.

The New Farm people mainly worked at CSR, and quite a lot were employed at the Brewery. Many worked at Coca Cola for about 30 years and left just recently. They remember when Coca Cola was a tiny factory,[3] and then it grew and grew, so the workers bought homes nearby.[4]

* * *

TWENTY-TWO YEARS AFTER arriving in New Farm from Italy in 1970, Signora Rena Ravalese explained how it felt trying to settle into very unfamiliar circumstances:

IN 1970, MY husband and I, with our two children, moved to New Farm, living first in my brother's flat. Next, we bought this house and have stayed here ever since. When I arrived there wasn't much here even in the main part of New Farm. There was the little chemist shop of Sorbello's, and we liked it here a lot. My children went to the Holy Spirit School.

When I arrived, my husband and I both worked at the hospital because my brothers had two convalescent homes. I worked in the laundry and my husband worked as a handyman.

I worked for 15 years until I went on the pension. The first years were horrible. Horrible! I found the house and everything fine, but my husband didn't like it because he's from the city of Napoli. My husband is Napolitano proper. He was born in the city and someone who was born in the city has no idea of what the country's like. He was a shoemaker and worked in Napoli for 25 years — always with shoes, but when he came here, he didn't have the language, and there wasn't the work, so my brothers kept him working with them. After a few changes of job, he started working at the hospital and stayed there until retirement.

This was just a small 'town' and there were lots of Italians at that time. That's why I found myself somewhere where people spoke Italian — but I didn't get to know too many of them because I was always working. For 15 years, I didn't have one day's holiday. I worked from morning until 9.30 or 10 at night because they gave me work to do on my own.

I was in the laundry working by myself. Next, I'd go to do the shopping and then I'd go home. This was a life that you don't like when you just arrive. When you can't understand anything, it's difficult. After a certain period of time, all immigrants see it's not like that. There are good things here too.[5]

* * *

BEATTIE DAWSON who was Alderman for Merthyr Ward during 1973-1976, was one of many who sought to help the newcomers settle into the suburb:

IN THE SIXTIES I was in the Good Neighbour Association, and would spend Saturdays and Sundays with lists of migrants who came each week. I would visit them and tell them where the schools were, where the church was, where transport was available, and so on.[6]

MY HUSBAND HELPED new migrants with their English, to read their mail and assist them with their income tax return. Our house was always full of people because everyone knew where to come for a meal and a chat.[7]

Of course the language barrier and cultural differences brought their own frustrations:

THE POWERHOUSE COULD possibly have become a sports oval. When I was Alderman, I negotiated with CSR for a sports field grandstand. It was all envisioned with an Italian group. The hard thing was that there were so many Italian dialects at that time. It was very hard for the Sicilians and those from the north of Italy to all know what you were planning. I asked one chap to try to interpret a brochure for me…[8]

There were visionaries among the Italian community who could see that the schools were the key to achieving better understanding between those of different nationalities. A 'first' was achieved at New Farm State School:

AN INNOVATION WAS the introduction of Italian language classes in the late 1970s. To facilitate the program, language books worth $1000 were donated by local Italian businessmen and the Italian Government. These were the first Italian classes conducted in a Queensland State Primary School.[9]

New Farm State School was considered to be "ahead of its time" with regard to 'multiculturalism',[10] and the result, from the pupils' point of view, was positive:

> WE MIGRATED TO *Australia from Sicily in 1954 and New Farm was our first home. I remember in particular the difference in the two cultures and the difficulty of being accepted — but it worked out alright.*[11]

* * *

NEW FARM HAS played its role in nurturing political aspirations in the hearts of several of its citizens. Teresa Gambaro, daughter of Dominic, one of the brothers who made the Gambaro name an institution in New Farm *and* in the Queensland food industry,[12] became a Federal Member of Parliament in 1996, and in 2007 was Assistant Minister for Immigration and Citizenship before the change of government.

In the arena of state politics, Grace Grace was elected in 2007 to the Queensland Parliament, and became one of the few if not the only Australian of Italian descent in the Queensland Legislative Assembly. This followed her being elected in 2000 to the General Secretaryship of the Queensland Council of Unions. She was the first woman to hold such a position in the Council's 115 year history. Both achievements give her pause for reflection:

> AS THE CHILD *of Italian migrants Salvatore and Concetta Farfaglia from Castiglione in Sicily who came to Spring Hill in the early 1950s, later moving to New Farm, I am intimately familiar with the sacrifices that migrants made and the hurdles they faced in coming to a new country. I have benefitted enormously from my parents' courage and hard work.*

The plaque outside *Casa Italia* in Gray Street, New Farm records the names of Italian immigrants to Queensland dating from 1921. The memorial was unveiled on 1 September 1984. — *Photo: G. Benjamin*

It is a great privilege to represent the community in which my parents chose to raise their family and in which I am raising mine. I have seen tremendous changes in New Farm over the years, with industry and its blue-collar workforce moving on, and the new generation of Italian Australians moving up the income and social scale. One thing never changes, however, and that is the strong sense of community that still captivates those who make New Farm home.

* * *

IN 1996, THOSE born in Italy made up the largest of all migrant groups in Australia, numbering 238,216. Only 7% of these were in Queensland—and almost half of these lived in Brisbane.[13] Despite these figures, Italian culture continues to enjoy a disproportionately strong influence on Australian society, and few places demonstrate this more remarkably than New Farm.

Whether it be the cafes, the restaurants, the family businesses, the cuisine, the fashion, the shoes, the boarding houses, the unit blocks, the soccer in New Farm Park, bocce, the Italian festival of St. Joseph which started in 1977 and by 1982 had become the biggest Italian Festival in Australia, the accent on working and the family, the Italian conversations in the street, the art and the politics — the Italian community continues to make an indelible mark on New Farm.

It's a story all of its own.

Notes

1. Jan Dickinson in Maximilian Brandle, editor, *Multicultural Queensland 2001: 100 years, 100 communities, A Century of Contributions*. Brisbane : Multicultural Affairs Queensland, Dept. of the Premier and Cabinet, 2001, p. 218.
2. Jan Dickinson described Dr. Castellano as, "an extraordinary figure, who, nearly 30 years after his death, continues to cast his benevolent shadow across all things Italian in this State." She recommends Enzo Palmieri's account of Dr Castellano's life in *Multicultural Queensland 1988*.
3. The Coca Cola bottling factory was located where the James Street Markets now stand.
4. Oral History: Giuseppe Rinaudo, 1992.
5. Oral History: Signora Rena Ravalese, 1992.
6. Oral History: Beattie Dawson, 2007.
7. Oral History: Florence O'Brien, 2008.
8. Beattie Dawson, *op. cit.*
9. Herb Huth (principal 1972-77) in *Memories of New Farm State School*, 2001, p. 40.
10. Melissa Griffiths (1976-1982) in *MNFSS, ibid.*, p. 39.
11. Charlie Cacciola (at school in 50s) in *MNFSS, ibid.*, p. 47.
12. Daryl Passmore, 'A family's heartbreak', *The Sunday Mail*, 15 August 2004.
13. Dickinson, *op. cit.*, p. 215.

The New Farm Neighbour Centre's inclusive role...

NEW FARM'S NEARNESS to the city and Fortitude Valley has made it particularly attractive for dwellers at both ends of the income scale, hence newspaper headlines such as "Where Posh and Poor Live Side by Side" might have rung true for many periods of the locality's past.

"New Farm is a place where the haves and the have-nots share the same corner of the world. If you've got money, you live up a garden path. If you don't, you've probably got a spot in some shady lane," explained a 1981 *Courier-Mail* article.[1]

For many, the 'shady lane' was a boarding house, the poor condition of one being lamented by a Browne Street resident:

> THE VERY LOW *cost flatettes next door are full of old aged pensioners who daren't complain because there's no other accommodation available. They are paying perhaps two-thirds of their income in board and lodgings, for shared accommodation. They dare not complain if the washing machine breaks down or if there's no hot water, and they have only one toilet between 5-6 people. They don't complain because they've no place to go.*[2]

Sometimes the 'shady lane' was just that — living rough — and by way of pithy illustration is this anonymous aboriginal man's testimony from the early 1990s (he chose to be known as 'Taipan'):[3]

> A DRONE IS *a person who sleeps "five star hotel". You know what a five star hotel is? The stars — you sleep out. I used to be a drone and work at the same time. You just camp out anywhere. I start camping out when I was only young, 19 year old. Didn't like to be caged up, see. Being used to jail, it was too much. Just get out in the open and I used to go and drink in the parks, buy a feed, cook it up just before the evening in the New Farm Park, before they even had these barbecues.*

The headline still holds true today. — *Nick Maher, "New Farm: Where Posh and Poor live side by side", Courier Mail, 24 July 1981. Reproduced with kind permission of the Courier Mail.*

That's back in '64 we were there, me and my friend Ronnie. He's dead now though. First thing in the morning, come out and see the coffee woman. Used to see her at the Gardens. You get a cup of coffee and a sandwich. I went to work then. That was the days when I was a drunk.

When I was going to work, I'd have half dozen big bottles before I start work in the morning —and at dinner time, smoko I'd have three pots, something to chew. Dinner time then I'd have eight pots beer, go back to work in the afternoon, knock off at 4 o'clock. I'd be in the pub then till closing time. I'd go home to bed but I always had a reviver. Same thing day after day.

George and me, we sat up here at the Lookout. This Lookout is my favourite drinking spot.[4] *The police know me. We sit up there and drink. That's where all the Murris come. We all get up there and drink, every day.*

Just come in here (139 Club)[5] *in the mornings. I got a towel and soap, have a shower here, have breakfast, then go. I give drinkin' away, see? No more drinkin' for me. New Farm and the Valley used to be popular with us 'cause the bus used to run straight through the Valley and it used to be good, shops everywhere, you know? There used to be a lot of pubs. That was back in '67.*

You couldn't walk down the street here or you'd be picked up. They'd be on the street, you know? On the game. It was parlours mostly. Brothels. Down Heal Street, Kent Street, and further up there, down around New Farm, way down the bottom end of Sydney Street, that was the king of the brothels. All them back streets, they were all call girls. Behind all that there, there was really bad men. This has been goin' on for years and years all around New Farm. Even further down there, Newstead. That used to be Chinatown, up near Cloudland.

There's a lot of things people don't know about, see? But they only got to live around New Farm, see? I know every street around here. When you drone, you get around. You know all your squats. You know the back streets. Every street. Where to go. How to get away.

That was my life story then for me. I got a flat now, I got my daughter with me now. Yair, that's it. Well, it's the only way to live now—but my opinion now of these young kids—they want to stay home 'cos it's no good for them. Stay home. Don't go on the street, 'cos once you're on there, it's a hard road. It's not all milk and honey there. You gotta battle for survival. You gotta know where to go.

* * *

WHEN PEOPLE FIND themselves unequal to the societal forces under which they labour, individuals will often appear prepared to champion the rights of the vulnerable and needy. One such local defender was James Gordon Fredericks. Born in 1921 Gordon came to Brisbane in 1951, working as a tram conductor and bookstore shop assistant, before becoming a state public servant. An avid reader with a sharp intellect, he was largely self-taught and fearlessly 'mounted his soapbox' to wage an untiring battle against what he considered were the inequalities of an often unfair world. At public meetings, Gordon was a formidable protagonist and it was considered inadvisable to interrupt one of his 'monologues'. Exponents of

Above: An unknown artist has captured Gordon Fredericks' passionate advocacy on social issues affecting New Farm.

Below: The upturned milk crate was Gordon Fredericks' signature soapbox, memorialised on the corner of Welsby and Brunswick Streets. Beginning with this quotation from George Bernard Shaw, "My life belongs to the community and as long as I live, it is my privilege to do for it whatever I can," the plaque continues, "In Memory of Gordon Fredericks (1921-1997), People before bricks and mortar." — *Photo: G. Benjamin*

urban renewal were left under no delusion about his position that 'planning is not about bricks and mortar — it is about people'. He was dedicated to the view that New Farm should remain a community where people from all walks of life could make a home.

Gordon lived in his beloved New Farm for 22 years, and in 1997, only weeks after shifting home, he passed away. Tributes flowed for his uniquely passionate advocacy. Councillor David Hinchliffe summed up the sentiments of many who knew this consummate 'little Aussie battler':

GORDON WAS ONE of the strongest and most vocal advocates for the voiceless of New Farm, the people who were on the margins of our community. Gordon was never reluctant to step forward and plead on their behalf. His voice may be lost in New Farm, but his message has been heard and he will be remembered.

Gordon Fredericks' enthusiasm enspirited many other people, and no doubt his influence was a contributing factor in the ultimate establishment of the New Farm Neighbourhood Centre Inc. Located first in Hawthorne Street and later at 967 Brunswick Street, the Centre continues to provide support on a range of housing, homelessness and community engagement issues.

In the early 1980s housing in New Farm was a key issue, since there were concerns about plans to resume Department of Transport houses where people were living on low incomes. Dorothy Messinbird expressed the feelings of many during the lead-up to this period:

IN 1974-75 WHEN Mr Hinze was alive, we were going to have a bridge across here.[6] That's why a lot of the bigger homes became so run down, because there was a period of about ten years when we didn't know whether the bridge was going ahead or not. At one stage, the only way you could sell was to the Main Roads Department.

I stayed on — but a lot changed hands then, because they couldn't stand it, since Main Roads might want the house next week. Main Roads rented the houses out, didn't spend money on them, they were never painted, the type of people renting got worse and worse, and the homes became more derelict.[7]

With the gentrification of New Farm gathering pace around the time of the 1982 Commonwealth Games, and the threat of yet more boarding houses closing, co-operative housing was seen as a worthy response. This, along with the converging desire of Lifeline to support a community development strategy in New Farm, culminated in the incorporation of the New Farm Neighbourhood Centre in 1986. With its aim to 'work with the community towards social justice, diversity and inclusion in Brisbane's inner city,' the NFNC has provided a first port of call for those directly affected by the shortage of low-cost housing or the closure of local boarding houses.[8] It has also offered substantial support for the rights of tenants in low-cost accommodation. In the early days, there was even a shop providing cheap second hand clothes, as well as a fruit and vegetable co-op.

Just across from New Farm Park, the New Farm Neighbourhood Centre at 967 Brunswick Street provides a congenial and energetic focus for community assistance and interaction. — *Photo: NFNC*

Occupying a typical New Farm wooden house (it was once high-set and located in Hawthorne Street before removal to the current site), the colourful Centre provides a congenial and energetic New Farm location for community interaction, where advice, learning and hospitality can be offered. The Neighbourhood Centre certainly enjoys support from many local organisations, but its unique contribution to New Farm's cohesive sense of community cannot be underestimated.[9]

Notes

1. Nick Maher, "New Farm: Where Posh and Poor live side by side", *Courier Mail,* 24 July 1981.
2. Oral History: Dorothy Messinbird, 1992.
3. Oral History: 'Taipan', 1992.
4. The Lookout — possibly adjacent to Wilson's Outlook Reserve on Bowen Terrace and Moray Street.
5. 139 Club Incorporated is a welfare centre for homeless people situated at 505 Brunswick Street, Fortitude Valley.
6. John Schiavo, "New Farm: A Study", *op. cit.,* "A freeway from Bowen Hills was planned to cut through the centre of New Farm to join a new bridge at the southern end of Sydney Street that then crossed the river to East Brisbane, as part of a 1965 Wilbur Smith & Associates'Transport Study." p. 42. In December 1989, New Farm residents were fighting a Brisbane Traffic Study proposal to build a four-lane freeway and river crossing from New Farm to Bulimba. *New Farm Newspaper*, Christmas 1989.
7. Messinbird, *op. cit.*
8. Boarding house closures continued each decade. A 1997 report, "Inner City Squeeze", claimed that 66% of boarding houses in Bowen Terrace/Lower Bowen Terrace had gone, while Merthyr Road had lost 44%, plus there was a 'high risk' that Brunswick Street boarding houses would be redeveloped. (*Northern News,* 20 March 1997, p. 3)
9. The Centre's property was previously owned by Mr Cochran, a school inspector (per Beattie Dawson, 2007).

Coolden in Brunswick Street

THE place to book your wedding reception…

Lola McCausland's 1949 portrait of Elsie Dunstan, who conducted Coolden Reception Lounge for almost 40 years.

A TYPICAL NEW FARM wedding in the mid-30s might well have been where Josephine Wilkinson of Maxwell Street married Joe Power of Bowen Terrace:

> THE WEDDING WAS at 3.30 p.m. at Holy Spirit Church which was quite new then. I wore pink. The dress was so pretty, people got a surprise because of the colour. It was a draped panne velvet gown and I had a large sheaf of pink roses. The head-dress was pink roses too and my sister Ruth who was my attendant wore a pink floral georgette. It was a small wedding, we had the reception at home, and McWhirters catered for the afternoon tea. They were well known for their catering and people always went to their store for morning and afternoon tea. McDonalds made my wedding cake and we had a week's honeymoon.[1]

Less than two decades later, New Farm's own venue for wedding receptions was so prominent that a newspaper story stated, "New Farm also boasts two bowling greens, the Riverside Ballroom and the Coolden reception lounge."[2]

> COOLDEN WAS THE place to have your wedding. If you wanted to be in the Women's Weekly or the Courier Mail social pages, you had your wedding at Coolden because Elsie would just ring up the press and notify them that they could come and take photographs at such-and-such a time.[3]

Elsie Dunstan's propulsion into business arose more from the necessity of being the mainstay of her family than by choice. By 1939 Elsie Bugden had married Tom Dunstan, son of the popular Gympie Labor MLA and newspaper owner Thomas Dunstan (1873-1954),[4] and the couple had moved to Brisbane. This was to help generate sufficient income to assist Elsie's unwell mother who had been left to raise Elsie's younger siblings. The hair-dressing salon in Queen Street that Elsie opened during the war years more than succeeded — and it was said that she didn't just support her family, she actually brought them into prosperity.

Soon after the birth of Elsie and Tom's son Bevan, concerns for her husband's health problems meant that she would have to be the mainstay of her own family also.

After the end of the war, the business shifted to the Valley where Elsie was doing two things at once, hairdressing and running receptions. Eventually, she concentrated on receptions. She bought a big old house in Brunswick Street that she converted into a private hotel, which accommodated some notable guests:

> THE VON TRAPPS (of 'Sound of Music' fame) stayed there while they were in Brisbane, and Maria used to write to Elsie all of the time, about the children and Elsie's child.[5]

The modern *Coolden* at 769 Brunswick Street. The name originated from a combination of 'Coolum', where Elsie used to holiday from Gympie, and the fact that she wanted her new home to be a 'cool den'. — *Photo: G. Benjamin*

After that, Elsie bought the adjoining property (on the corner with Langshaw Street) which was a double-story art-deco building, probably once a block of flats. She knocked out some walls so that it could become part of the private hotel. The two properties were eventually connected by the kitchen which was located between them. Eventually, the hotel was closed and by the early 60s, the property had been turned into a wedding reception centre named *Coolden*. Elsie and Tom lived on site in apartments which had been part of the private hotel.

AT ITS PEAK Elsie used to have nine receptions a weekend, starting on Friday night, with three and sometimes four on Saturday. Coolden had four rooms: the Ballroom, Ancestral Room and the Ballerina Room, plus the Bamboo Room for meetings and get-togethers. Coolden was very 1930-40s inside. Elsie never tried to change the feel of the era in which it was built, which gave it a sort of charm. Some things were changed to allow the business to run more efficiently but the character of both buildings was retained.[6]

Brisbane's other wedding reception venues included *29 Murray Street, Moomba* and *Wanganui Gardens*, but *Coolden* was the first choice for innumerable local weddings for almost 40 years. Elsie employed a large and varied staff, and while she didn't stop guests from having alcohol, she tightly controlled it at receptions. This did not stop the 'interesting weddings' that sometimes eventuated when inter-family antipathy surfaced, but the neighbours were rarely disturbed.

COOLDEN WAS JUST across Brunswick Street from Wynberg, Archbishop Duhig's residence. There was never any complaint from Wynberg but Elsie would send something over there regularly, being the good diplomat that she was, and she kept on very good terms with the Archbishop.[7]

Wedding menus invariably included prawns, so their homely preparation was a perennial part of the business:

MUCH TIME WAS spent peeling prawns because in those days, you couldn't get peeled prawns. Everyone wanted a seafood cocktail for the first course, so Bevan and his father would sit out in the courtyard under two big old mango trees and they'd peel prawns. They'd have to whistle because, as Elsie said, "If they are whistling then they can't eat the prawns."

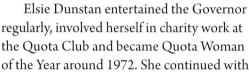

Above: A typical Coolden wedding: Sandy and Bevan Dunstan.

Left: Elsie Dunstan met a young Deirdre Fox (a current New Farm resident) at the Ann Street Church of Christ in the 1940s, and made her the gift of a notebook with four cake recipes that she had written out. It was Elsie's way of offering the young girl early culinary encouragement.

Elsie Dunstan entertained the Governor regularly, involved herself in charity work at the Quota Club and became Quota Woman of the Year around 1972. She continued with the business following the death of her husband in the late 70s, and was on the board of a Senior Citizens' association in her 80s.

Despite saying that if ever she retired from *Coolden* she would like to live at the Canberra Hotel, a Temperance establishment, Elsie Dunstan died in 1989. It was two days after she turned 83 and a day after she had supervised a reception. With Elsie's death, the business ceased and the property was eventually sold to a developer. Today a block of units on the site preserves the name *Coolden*.

Notes

1. Oral History: Josephine Power (nee Wilkinson), 1994.
2. *The Telegraph,* Brisbane, 19 July 1962.
3. Oral History: Sandy Dunstan, 2008.
4. I. G. Carnell, 'Dunstan, Thomas (1873-1954)', *Australian Dictionary of Biography, Volume 8,* Melbourne University Press, 1981, p. 381.
5. Sandy Dunstan, *op. cit.* This may have been 1956 when the Trapp Family Singers toured Australia, New Zealand and the South Pacific. Their Sydney host was the Apostolic Delegate, Archbishop Carboni, so perhaps Archbishop Duhig was connected with the Brisbane stay. Later in the fifties, Maria and her children did missionary work in New Guinea.
6. Dunstan, *ibid.*
7. Dunstan, *ibid.*

What a thrill for twopence...

Toastrack Tram No. 159, enroute from New Farm Wharf to Dutton Park along Merthyr Road around 1935, had at least three passengers on board. In the background is Hawthorne Street and the Merthyr Café. The Café still stands along with the houses in view, albeit with their verandahs closed in. — *Mitchell Library, State Library of NSW [BCP – 04952].*

A s MUCH AS some people enjoyed the brisk walk from New Farm to the city in the early days, the enthusiasm for a quicker form of transport spurred the provision of horse-drawn buses (or omnibuses). Among the earliest, from 1876, was the enterprise of John Chalk and family who operated 40 horse-drawn buses until the demise of the business around the time of the 1893 floods.

Other licensed omnibus proprietors provided services to New Farm including John McMaster and R. Jenkins. Donald Gemmell, earlier a "horse-drawn tram driver", became the licensed omnibus proprietor of the "New Farm Bus Co." from Roberts (now Welsby) Street during 1893-98. Later he kept a store in Merthyr Road on the corner with James Street. Nearby in 1901 from the corner of Merthyr Road and Gertrude Street, Henry Dean operated the Penny Bus Co.[1]

In 1885 the Metropolitan Tramway Investment Company commenced operation using horse-drawn trams and because there was the possibility of sufficiently strong patronage from middle-class residents, a line was extended to the terminus near the corner of Barker and Brunswick Streets, known later as the Astor Junction (after the Astor Theatre). Horse-drawn buses were clearly in service for some time following the introduction of trams, according to a longtime Llewellyn Street resident (born in 1899) who recalled:

> I REMEMBER TRAVELLING *home in the old horse bus. It was like one of those old matchbox trams, set on very low wheels and drawn by two light draught horses. The terminus was where the Astor Theatre now stands. Next came the trams. We had the cheapest service of all time. New Farm to North Quay cost twopence.*[2]

In 1897 the tramway system was electrified. The service came down Brunswick Street in 1905 when the lower end of Brunswick Street was opened up for sale. Later the service to New Farm extended via Barker and Moray Streets towards Merthyr Road. The trams reached New Farm Park in 1926. Bill Stanley, who grew up on River Road before it was Oxlade Drive, heard these stories from when the old tram terminus was at Moray Street at the Carramar Corner: "Mr Stanley used to cut a path with a scythe to get to the tram." A 1916 estate map for Lechmere Street shows a "proposed" tram line marked along James Street, but this was never built.

Those with an eye to mechanical detail couldn't help noticing the duties of the tramway motormen:

> IN THOSE EARLY *days, some of the trams were called 'toast racks' where the seats were fully across and the conductor walked along the running board to collect fares. Coming from the Valley and turning right at the Astor Theatre (at Barker Street), the driver had to get down and change the points with a small jemmy bar. There was a Bundy clock on the Astor corner where the conductor — when the tram was on the way to town — would alight, and turn a key in the clock, no doubt to register whether he was keeping to his timetable.*[3]

The tramway system was controlled by a series of private companies until 1923. As of 1 January 1926, the Greater Brisbane City Council took over the operation of the tramways network, extending and upgrading it.

New Farm tram-travellers never forgot the ritual of arrival at the Brunswick Street terminus when the conductor jumped down to retract the power pole at one end of the tram, and walked around to raise the other one, while the driver changed ends as well as the destination board. It was as familiar as the 'clickety-clack' sound of crossing the Brunswick Street-Merthyr Road intersection.

The spectacular fire at the Paddington tram depot in September 1962 destroying 20 percent of the Council's tram fleet, was the beginning of the end of tram-travelling in Brisbane. The last trip was taken on 13 April 1969.

Notes

1. Beryl Roberts, "Horse-drawn Buses and Cabs, New Farm". An address to NFDHS on 24 August 2002.
2. Timothy Scott, Queensland Registrar-General, had lived in *Rossmore*, his Llewellyn Street home since 1918, as reported in *The Telegraph*, 19 July 1962, p. 28.
3. Oral History: Bryan Oxlade, 2008.

...from single rooms to self-contained apartments...

Having lost his wife to Bright's Disease three years earlier and with his daughter at a convent and his youngest son at an uncle's, Michael McCann, along with his 14 year old son John, was trying to make headway in the world. The year was 1929 and father and son lived in New Farm 'between boarding houses', an experience recorded 60 years later by the son:

Looking like the ramparts of an art deco castle, the angular faces of Coronet Court continue to evoke the era of the 1930s-40s.
— *Photo: G. Benjamin*

> WE MOVED ABOUT *a bit, sometimes because the place was just a bit too crummy. Other times we just couldn't pay our board and we were asked, politely or otherwise, to move on. We were only really evicted once and it was like something out of Charles Dickens. It was about 8 o'clock at night, a wet drizzle was coming down outside and there was a knock at the door. It was our landlord. We often had landlords knocking on our door and it was usually about money. This fellow was a mean-looking, exasperated chap who ran this rundown collection of rented rooms in an old wooden house in Brunswick Street, New Farm.*
>
> *The conversation between him and Dad was depressingly familiar. He wanted our board money ... now, but when Dad presented the usual excuses and promises this fellow was intractable. He said tightly, "OK, pack your bags and get out. Now ... and I mean now!" He repeated this a couple of times to make sure we'd got the message. He was furious and he spoke loudly.*
>
> *Within 15 minutes we had packed our bits of luggage and were headed out into the drizzle. New Farm had boarding houses all over the place in those days. We found another one in the next street and after some urgent talk by Dad we were in out of the rain and had a bed for the night. I never kept an actual count but I reckon we would have checked in, and out, of about a dozen boarding houses in New Farm.*
>
> *It might sound depressing but looking back, I feel this was quite an invaluable experience. It helped me in my future life to place a high value on security and to take all possible steps to reduce the risk of this type of humiliation.*[1]

Countless others found themselves in similar (or worse) situations, adding to the pressure to squeeze more and more people into homes. Some remember back to the times in New Farm when whole extended families of three generations had to squeeze in together.[2]

Many helped out by taking in boarders and the council encouraged the break up of the big houses into flats and even medium-sized houses were turned into flats or boarding houses. The sign of the times said, "Single rooms to let."

Another solution was to build new multi-dwelling houses and so started the remarkable era of blocks of flats, of which New Farm is still amply filled. One of the first was *Avalon*, on the corner of Brunswick and Harcourt Streets, completed in December 1929 and officially described as:

> TWO-STOREY, RED-TILED ROOF and cream-coloured wall with roughcast render. It has an interwar, multi-styled exterior from Californian Bungalow to Old English and is of solid brick construction.[3]

Ricardo Felipe's superb compilation on *Avalon* explains not only the architectural character of this particular block of 26 flats (numbered A to Z, each with a bedroom, kitchen and bathroom), but its social setting ("located at the crossroads of sleeze and affluence"), as well as the creative offerings of the many artists who have at one time or another been Avaloners.

Hall & Prentice, the designers of *Avalon*, were also the architects for the Brisbane City Hall which was opened four months later. In his study of every nuance of *Avalon's* life and history, the editor of *Avalon: Art & Life of An Apartment Building* proposed a telling point:

> MEDIUM DENSITY, LOW-RENT apartment buildings such as Avalon, housing a variety of residents in a socially, ethnically and economically diverse neighbourhood, provide the inner city with its vibrant and stimulating character.[4]

One of the artworks depicted in the book consists of four columns of typewriting entitled, "All the Apartments in New Farm, 2001" by Greg Nelson (Flat J: 2001-03). The number of apartment blocks listed came to 179.[5]

* * *

FIRE PLAYED ITS part in clearing the way for new blocks of flats. Even *Avalon* owed its existence to a spectacular fire in 1928 that destroyed a 13-room boarding house, three and a half neighbouring houses, and damaged *The Laurels,* a neighbouring private hospital at 554 Brunswick Street.[6]

> I CAN REMEMBER the fire on the corner of Harcourt Street when I was coming home from school (Commercial High). The minister we had at that time, Mr. Kleindienst, lived at 89 Harcourt Street and he was a very sick man. They carried him across the street in case the fire reached the parsonage.[7]

In Julius Street following the conflagration that destroyed the Rosenfeld sawmill in February 1931, seven blocks of flats were built, offering in that short cul-de-sac a unique snapshot of a different era. Numerous blocks of flats around New Farm have

The faded facade of *Sherborne*, the peeling paint of its neighbour, and the sign saying "Serviced Rooms" encapsulates an aspect of New Farm's history. These buildings, on the corner of Merthyr Road and Gray Street, have been replaced by a modern apartment block. — *Photo: NFDHS*

arisen out of the ashes of large old homes.

* * *

FIFTEEN HUNDRED METRES along Brunswick Street towards New Farm Park and a world away, lay an apartment block completed four years after *Avalon. Coronet Court* is a striking and high-visibility example of the locality's rich collection of art deco

This nondescript flat dwelling in Annie Street near the intersection with Clay Street was typical of New Farm's phase of run-down economy accommodation. The recent redevelopment of this property has revealed a remarkably splendid residence of a bygone era. — *Photo: NFDHS.*

apartment buildings. Built by Max Strickland in 1933-34, its dramatic projecting angles served the very practical purpose of providing more light, and catching breezes and views for occupants of the nine flats.

The flats included rare innovations for the period, including a refrigeration installation operated from a multiple unit in the basement, with independent controls for each flat. This obviated the need for meat safes or ice boxes.[8]

Born in Germany and arriving in Melbourne by 1919 in his mid-twenties, Max Strickland found work as a draughtsman, started a plaster business called "Stucoid" and took out patents for designs. He moved to Brisbane with his wife Marie to assist with the decorative plastering work on the Regent Theatre. He met Charlie Lancaster, an artist trained in stained glass and leadlight when doing the leadlight for *Coronet Court.*[9] Lancaster's daughter Ailsa married Arch Trail, a long-time New Farm resident whose grandfather began Trails' Ice Works:

Just along Elystan Road from *Coronet Court* is *Elystan Court*, a block of flats with Tudoresque features, built in a period when the attention to detail extended to the typeface of its entrance-way leadlighting. — *Photos: G. Benjamin.*

> STRICKLAND WAS A bit of a mystery man. He came from Germany, said nothing about himself and his wife, and had no family. When we were married, he gave us a block of land at Auchenflower.[10]

Max Strickland also built 999 Brunswick Street, next to *Coronet Court* on the river side. Here he and his wife lived until their untimely deaths in the early fifties. In 1939 *Coronet Court* was bought by Thomas Maloney, one of whose sons operated a shell grit business on the river next to Thomas Welsby's house, *Amity*. On Thomas Maloney's death, the apartment building passed to his daughter Mrs. Eileen O'Connor and it has remained with that family ever since.

> ACCORDING TO AN Art Deco magazine, "Coronet Court is one of the grooviest addresses in town."[11]

In 1962 New Farm entered a new phase of apartment dwelling when the suburb's first high rise block of units, *Glenfalloch,* was built on the corner of Sydney Street and Oxlade Drive. Merthyr Bowls Club, which vacated this site, merged with the Limbless Soldiers Bowls Club on Oxlade Drive and the result was Merthyr Bowls Club as it is known today. *Glenfalloch* was quickly followed by *Gleneagles* and *Gemini Towers*. The momentum towards apartment-building continues, confirming New Farm as a haven for inner suburb dwellers.

Notes

1. John McCann, *How It Happened,* A personal memoir, 1993.
2. Oral History: Brian Hjelm, 2008.
3. Ricardo Felipe (ed.), *Avalon: Art & Life of An Apartment Building*, Museum of Brisbane, Fortitude Valley, Vanity Publishing, 2005, back cover.
4. ibid., p. 19.
5. ibid., p. 103.
6. Robert Riddel, "Avalon: A Brief History", in Ricardo, *ibid.,* p. 230.
7. Oral History: Dulcie Fleming (nee Twible), 2007. The clergyman was most likely Rev. William Christian Kleindienst (ca 1883-1958).
8. Nancy Weir & Tamsin O'Connor, "An Art Deco Marvel", *Village News*, New Farm, April 2008.
9. Charles Lancaster trained at the Melbourne Gallery Art School in stained glass and leadlight and was a traditional artist of the Heidelberg school, painting mainly in oils. In 1913, he moved from Melbourne to become leadlight and stained glass Manager of R.S. Extons. He was a camouflage artist in WW2, then draughtsman for the Queensland Irrigation Commission for 12 years. He retired in1956. He was a trustee of the Queensland Art Gallery 1945-51, Life Member and Past President of the Royal Queensland Art Society, and represented Queensland at British Empire exhibitions.
10. Oral History: Arch Trail, 2002.
11. Trail, *op. cit.*

A walk on the wild side...

Thomas McMahon's baker's cart of Terrace Street, as depicted by Gladys Blundell in her 1997 watercolour. Described as a 'master baker', Thos. McMahon operated from 35 Terrace Street and died in January 1934. — *Courtesy: NFDHS.*

C LAY STREET, RUNNING at right angles to Terrace Street, is a clue to an earlier usage of the area. Robert Scott established a pottery business during 1856 in Kent Street amidst half-cleared land in what was regarded as a remote part of Fortitude Valley.[1] This stimulated settlement along Kent, Clay and Terrace Streets, with small residential blocks for the working middle class.

By 1913 master baker Thomas McMahon had a business at 35 Terrace Street.[2] Further down the street at No. 186, during 1923-25 it was the home of widow Alice Walters and her three daughters, along with several boarders to help supplement the income. Two of Mrs Walters' daughters attended the nearby St Clair School for music and elocution training, and the three daughters later worked as seamstress, hairdresser and live-in house-keeper respectively.

186 Terrace Street (ca. 1923) was owned by Alice Walters, a widow who lived there with her three daughters, along with boarders. A later owner was Harry Broadrick, milk vendor of Harcourt Street, who sold it in 1955 to Florence O'Brien's parents. — *Photo: Deirdre Fox (grand-daughter of Alice Walters).*

* * *

FLORENCE O'BRIEN (NEE Charles) was born in England in 1922 and arrived as a five year old aboard *Osterley* at New Farm Wharf in 1927. She and her parents Elizabeth and Ernest[3] stayed with other members of the Charles' family already established nearby. This included Alex and May Charles who had the butcher shop where the Purple Olive restaurant is today in James Street (later purchasing the shop that is now Petersens' Butchers). From the late 50s, Lilly and Harold Charles had a shop on the corner with Harcourt Street.

Living at several different houses in Terrace Street including No. 147, Elizabeth, Ernest and their daughter Florence found it convenient for many reasons:

> THE DWYER FAMILY *had a milk run so it was very handy because we could get our milk from them. We had McMahon's bakery further up Terrace Street, so our bread was delivered to our door, and Dan Murphy's brother was our fruit man in those days. It was so much easier having everything delivered to the house.[4]*

The Bavas family lived at 123 James Street, on the corner of Terrace Street, with St Clair School in the background. Jim Bavas and his sister are pictured standing behind their parents, John and Helen. The Bavas family were next door neighbours of Florence O'Brien (nee Charles). John Bavas came to New Farm in the 1920s from Greece, via Egypt, the USA and Sydney. A trained confectionery maker, he began making Easter Eggs by joining two chocolate halves with a candy binding. The eggs were then decorated on top with flowers and wrapped in cellophane. Later, working from home with the whole family helping, John introduced Turkish Delight to Queensland. — *Photo and Oral History: Jim Bavas.*

After attending New Farm State School, Florence worked as a tailoress in Harcourt Street where the weekly wage was seven shillings and twopence. Next she worked in Wharf Street making American officers' uniforms. The hours were 7.30am-9pm Monday to Friday and 7.30am-3pm Saturday. Sunday was spent going to church before doing voluntary work for the war effort.

After the end of the war, at St. Michael and All Angels' Anglican Church, Florence married Gerald O'Brien who had served in New Guinea during the war as a linesman. They purchased a house at 158 Terrace Street in 1946, buying from a Jewish family named Glick for £809.

In 1955 Florence's parents purchased their own home at 186 Terrace Street which included a stable in the backyard. The vendor was Harry Broadrick, a horse and cart milk vendor from Harcourt Street.[5] It was the same house in which the widow Walters had lived with her daughters. Next door on the James Street side lived the Greek Bavas family, who had begun a business making confectionery.

> WE HELPED THEM *wrap their Easter eggs at night and had many enjoyable musical evenings with them. Our friendship lasted for four generations and when my husband was dying in the 1970s, they moved in with us to help take care of him.*[6]

Even though the houses in the street were built almost to the edge of each allotment, close living usually engendered a community spirit. Such were the times that if you were out, your neighbours might not only bring in your washing but fold it and iron it too…

Terrace Street had difficulties with drainage and the ground became swampy with prolonged rain. Some residents tried to remedy it themselves:

> ON THE CORNER *of Terrace and James Streets, there was a bamboo swamp that Dan Murphy and his wife filled in so as to build on it. Mrs Murphy complained that*

if you mowed the lawn while she was cooking, it was her firm belief that the cakes would sink in the middle…

The problems of neglect needed to be corrected by Council measures:

THE VACANT LAND *opposite our home at No. 158 became a dump for car bodies, dead animals and car tyres, etc. Once it caught fire and smouldered for weeks. It was totally toxic. During the 1974 floods, the dump was flooded and children came from miles around to swim in the water. They even had small boats on it. The residents had to pull up the access ramp floorboards during heavy storms, otherwise they would be flooded out by water running off the street.*

In past times people would burn everything in their backyards, so the washing would smell of smoke. Dogs would be running in the streets. You would get to know the dangerous ones and take another route home.

Beattie Dawson was a wonderful worker for the area when she was an alderman on the Council. She had the dump problem attended to quickly. When the new owner decided to build on it, they had to decontaminate the site by removing all of the rubbish and replacing it with clean fill.[7]

If Mr and Mrs Charles and their daughter Florence had socialised in very different circles then the name 'Dulcie Markham' may have rung a bell. As it was, they knew nothing of Surry Hills, once Sydney's toughest suburb where legendary crime queen Kate Leigh battled her arch enemy Tilly Devine, and where 'glamour girls' paraded among the sly grog establishments of Devonshire Street, including Dulcie Markham — "blonde and gorgeous, whose gallery of male protectors all came to sudden and violent ends."[8]

Dulcie also made her name in Melbourne. Residents of St. Kilda's Fawkner Street knew that their avenue had no chance of gaining respectability because its most famous resident was 'Pretty Dulcie' Markham who married Leonard 'Redda' Lewis in her Fawkner Street house."[9] It was a bedside ceremony because Dulcie was recovering from a bullet wound inflicted during the fatal shooting of the former boxer in the same house. She was photographed with her new husband, while the multi-tiered wedding cake balanced precariously on the bed beside her.

Dulcie went under many aliases as she graduated to the notoriety of being a Kings Cross underworld figure. Her most famous soubriquet was 'Angel of Death' since at least eight male associates died from gun or knife wounds.

A 1954 newspaper article[10] reported that police records in NSW, Victoria, Western Australia and Queensland showed that she had convictions dating back to 1931. The charges included consorting, vagrancy, soliciting, using indecent language, stealing, assaulting the police and destroying a cell bucket.

* * *

WHAT A SHOCK the Charles' family received when they learned that the 'Angel of Death' had not only come to live in Terrace Street, but that she was none other than the pretty blonde, with the hard face and heavy escorts, who had moved in next door!

Following the bombing of Pearl Harbour, the build-up of military forces in Brisbane to meet the invasion threat from Japan was a magnet for criminals wanting to cash in on the gold mine of providing sly grog and other unlawful services.

> MY MOTHER WAS petrified… It took a long time for them to leave our street. People would come from miles around to view the house. Because I also had long blonde hair, sometimes I was mistaken for her![11]

Before the war Dulcie had already appeared in the *Queensland Police Gazette*, in trouble for impersonating the Under-Secretary of Justice. In April 1936 at the Brisbane GPO, she attempted to send a telegram issuing an official permit to a confederate in Kingaroy, but the telegram clerk became suspicious. She ended up being arrested by well-known detective Bill Cronau and hence became one of the more famous entries in the newspaper series, "The Cronau Casebook".[12] On that occasion, she was fined £10 and soon left Queensland.

By 1943 'Dulcie Bowen' was back and thereafter received several mentions in police records — from unlawful possession of a ration coupon to stealing and consorting with known criminals. These people included a known 'hotel-breaker' (stealing bulk liquor so as to bottle it for sale) who drove a 1939 Chevrolet sedan; a multi-aliased character described as a 'pickpocket, urger, cheat and bludger'; another character on record as 'a false pretender, basher and thief'; along with a woman considered a thief and prostitute.

Dulcie had apparently been raised in a highly respectable family but had run away as a 15 year old. By 1957 crime was no longer paying for her. Aged just 42, with her beauty fading, she found herself penniless, living on handouts and facing charges of vagrancy. She died in 1976.

No wonder some parents in the 1940s instructed their children to avoid Terrace Street when walking to and from the State School. It was a thoroughfare that had always had its fair share of boisterous activity. Others might say that it simply had a rich 'village atmosphere' of the type described by a Browne Street resident:

> GEORGE DOWN THE road would come home drunk again and his missus was waiting. We'd wait and if he was galloping the horse and dray, then you knew he was full — and speeding! We'd race out into the backyard, down to the back fence and listen to the language, the fighting and crockery breaking. This was part of the village atmosphere we had. We knew everyone.[13]

Strangely enough the most outstanding crime during George Kopelke's 15 years on the beat from the local New Farm station during the 40s and 50s happened on the other side of Brunswick Street:

> A RETURNED SERVICE man had come home to find that his wife had been having an affair with a taxi driver. Unfortunately, the affair did not end on his return. When he found the taxi parked outside his Moray Street residence, he grabbed a bayonet that he had brought back from the Middle East and used it to threaten the cabbie. A scuffle developed when the cabbie tried to get hold of the bayonet, and the cabbie

Florence O'Brien (nee Charles) in the backyard at Terrace Street, which was complete with a papaw tree along with a ladder to reach the fruit. Florence was sometimes mistaken for "Pretty Dulcie" Markham, the Charles' family's next-door neighbour in those days. — *Photo: Lorraine Tomlinson.*

was fatally wounded. In court the soldier was found not guilty of the charges against him, including wilful murder.[14]

No doubt thoroughfares such as Terrace and Browne Streets were what inspired one commentator in 1924 to offer the following lament:

THE VERY GREAT contrast between the two parts of New Farm, the too-closely settled, drab, uninteresting section on the one side of Brunswick Street, and the modern residential section, one continuous vista of beautiful homes on the other side, makes one regret that there should be but one name for the whole suburb.[15]

The writer went on to propose that either 'Kinellan' or 'Merthyr' would have been a much more fitting name than New Farm for the smarter side of Brunswick Street. How much more vociferous would the opinion have been, had it been known that a few decades later, the 'Angel of Death' would reside in Terrace Street, New Farm…

Notes

1. John Schiavo, "Land use," *op. cit,* p. 22.
2. The bakery was later sold to Furnos Bakery and then purchased by Queensland Caterers, who owned it for several years, before a fire burnt most of the bakery and house. The ovens were in an historic property in the rear of the yard. A brick storm water drain nearby dates from an early period. Fred Matthews (1974) remembered that the quality of Thomas McMahon's bread had earned silver cups and that replicas of these were attached to the back of McMahon's delivery carts.
3. Among Ernest Charles' ancestors were a well-known London doctor, Old Bailey Judge Sir Ernest Bruce Charles (1871-1950) and an Archdeacon of Westminster Abbey. One of Ernest's living relatives is Bishop Adrian Charles of the Anglican Church in Queensland.
4. Oral History: Florence O'Brien, 2008.
5. Harry and Elsie Broadrick were milk vendors of Harcourt Street. In 2008, Elsie aged 96 recorded her reminiscences in *69 Years in Harcourt Street.*
6. O'Brien, *op. cit.*
7. *ibid.*
8. Frank Crook, "Crime Czars Haunt the Hills", *Daily Telegraph*, Sydney, 11 April 2008.
9. Brian Matthews, "On Writing", *Manning Clark House Newsletter.* No 27: September 2006. Online at <http://www.manningclark.org.au/newsletter/nl27_Matthews.html>.
10. *Sunday Telegraph*, 7 February 1954.
11. O'Brien, *op. cit.*
12. Pat Lloyd, "They called her the Angel of Death", *Telegraph*, 24 Mar 1964; QSA: Cronau, AF7470.
13. Oral History: Dorothy Messinbird, 1992.
14. Oral History: George Kopelke, 1992-1994.
15. *The A. and B. Journal of Queensland*, 7 February 1924, p. 19.

Dulcie was blonde and pretty, but bad luck dogged her boy friends..

They called her the Angel of Death

This was "Pretty Dulcie" the morning she appeared in Brisbane Police Court after her arrest by Cronau. The court proceedings were stormy.

Pat Lloyd, "They called her the Angel of Death", *The Telegraph*, 24 March 1964. — *Reproduced with kind permission.*

MR. W. CRONAU

By polic repo PA LL

DEATH reached out only once for ace Queensland detective Bill Cronau during his adventurous 38 years of law enforcement. That was when a well known criminal tried to cleave him with a razor-sharp tomahawk.

He missed, however, and was pinioned quickly by Cronau and his workmate, Detective Austin Kunst, now a sub-inspector at Cairns.

Much to Cronau's disgust, his assailant drew only four months' hard labor in Court later. Perhaps if that criminal had been able to read the future, he would have aimed a little better, swung a little harder, on behalf of the underworld.

But he didn't, and a bleak future thus was written for hundreds of criminals, for at that time, The Cronau Casebook was less than a quarter complete.

Usually it is only a detective's major cases that make news.

Cronau, retired South Coast police chief, once arrested—an ANGEL!

It did not cause much of a stir. The angel's wings then, back in 1936, were only fledgling swansdown.

Cronau's target was a lovely young blonde named Dulcie Bowen, a bride of only two months, 20 years old.

Dulcie, in a later stormy life, was to be-

been endorsed, and handed it back.

Dulcie boldly signed "Mrs. D. Bowen" on the back.

Already Dulcie had been in trouble with the police of two States, had accumulated some aliases, had been convicted for consorting with criminals, offensive behavior, and beating a watchhouse bucket out of shape.

She had not given a second thought to faking the Under-Secretary's signature to a telegram.

But trouble was brewing for her. The telegram clerk became suspicious and told his superior, who promptly called police.

The case was given to Plainclothes Constable Cronau.

Cronau took one look at the "Mrs. D. Bowen" signature, and went hunting.

He knew Dulcie, knew she had married a young showman named Frank Bowen two months before

He suspected Bowen was working the show circuit at Kingaroy, had been refused a permit, and that Dulcie had found a way to get him one.

Picking up someone he knew was mere routine for Cronau.

Dulcie was sitting perkily in the old George Street CIB by next morning.

She staggered Cronau by frankly admitting she had sent the telegram.

milestone in her life, and one even forgotten by Cronau himself until he opened an early page of his casebook recently.

They never met again. Cronau went from success to success in his police career in Brisbane. Dulcie, too, was rarely out of the headlines, but she was on the other team, and lived in southern States.

Eight of her husbands and boy friends died by gun or knife.

She made her underworld debut at 15 when she ran away from a highly respectable home.

It was not until 1951 that she suffered any personal harm from the underworld.

She was in Melbourne at the murder of a boy friend, Gavin Walsh, and was shot in the thigh.

A month later she was attacked at St. Kilda, and received a black eye, but refused to tell police how.

Next day, she lay on a bed while being married to a man named "Redda" Lewis.

In 1957 the faded beauty finally realised that crime does not pay.

She pleaded guilty in Sydney to a charge of vagrancy.

She had no alternative. She was penniless, living on handouts.

The former underworld queen had pawned the last of her furs and jewels.

She was then 42—and no longer pretty.

A later picture of "Pretty Dulcie," Queen of the Australian underworld. As the years went by, and her men friends died one after another in underworld feuds, her beauty faded, and finally she ended up in court, penniless, on a vagrancy charge.

They Edward Queen entered

From phone watche jeweller came in

The him n ing.

Cron again, trail t Street

The repea two o

Up the t remo them anoth jewel

On then him, into detec time man close

They still gol oth

his Cr fo ar

w n t a c

desperate, and determined."

He was caught in while Cronau

house while his mate kept watch.

Then he emerged more corpulent than when he went in

Out and about when pleasures were simple...

L OOKING AT THE Village Twin Cinema on the corner of Brunswick and Barker Streets today, it is difficult to imagine that this spot was such a hubbub of activity in the days when it was known as the Astor Theatre:

The Village Twin Cinema in 1995. It opened in late 1970 and was a redevelopment of what had once been the Astor Theatre. — *Photo: Betty Smith.*

THE ASTOR WAS a popular place to socialize. We would go on a Thursday (family night) when prices were reduced, or to the Saturday matinee.
It was a 'posh' theatre without any canvas seats. There was a milk bar across the road where you could sit down and enjoy a milkshake or a mixed grill. Across Annie Street, and after the general store which was run by two old ladies, then past the barber shop (good for repairing fishing rods and tennis racquets) was the fish 'n' chip shop.[1]

On Saturday nights, the Liebermans of Merthyr Road regularly went to the Astor:

IT WAS A hub for social activity. Our family booked permanent seats for the Saturday night show, as did other families. There were always friends there and it was a very nice theatre with proper seats. We would have a light tea before the show and then afterwards would go across the road to order fish and chips which were eaten on the walk home. The trams had finished for the night. Mary and Rose were the two daughters who served in the shop.[2]

THE ASTOR THEATRE was a focal point for a large portion of New Farm residents. The Saturday Matinee was mainly for the kids with the regular serials and cowboy movies. If I was lucky and Mum and Dad went to the movies on Friday night, I would be allowed to go with them and then go to the Matinee on Saturday. The theatre was always full at the weekends as it was ideally located to enable everyone in the area to walk to it.[3]

In the same location before World War I, a German band played every Friday night outside R.O. Sands Store in Brunswick Street. On top of that, each August just before the Brisbane Exhibition...

THERE WAS A merry-go-round operated on the corner of Barker and Brunswick Streets, as well as a Blondin Tight-rope Walking Act. Blondin walked along the wire about 20 feet (six metres) above the ground using a balancing pole. In those days, there were no clothes hoists, just clothes lines stretched along the yard and held up with clothes props. After the Blondin performance, the lads would borrow the clothes props for balancing poles and walk along the top of the fences.[4]

* * *

THANKS TO FRED Matthews' detailed reminiscence, New Farm's first picture theatre can be outlined in more detail:

> THE EARL'S COURT, *on the corner of Brunswick and Kent Streets, was the first motion picture show in New Farm and operated only at night. The owners erected a searchlight on top of the building. Its wide beam would sweep around New Farm houses and make it known that a film was to be screened that night.*
>
> *Charles Chaplin, Cowboy William S Hart and Max Senate comedies were popular. The building was later remodelled and renamed the Rivoli Theatre. It became one of Brisbane's leading film theatres, complete with a four piece orchestra and ushers to show you to your seat. Canvas chairs with head bands were first introduced here and for its day, it was a high-class theatre. The only problem was that it was open to the sky and when it rained, everyone sheltered for cover. The Arcadia opened in Moray Street but operated only for a short time.*

The Rivoli was the popular venue for the New Farm State School's annual fancy dress ball. The other keenly anticipated yearly event was the boat trip to Redcliffe on the *SS Koopa*, departing from the Sugar Refinery wharf. Inhaling sea breezes on the

Two views, dating from around 1980, of the Rivoli Theatre (formerly Earls Court Picture Show). The site enjoyed a major redevelopment in 2008. — *Photos: Fred Matthews, NFDHS.*

open deck while crossing the bay, carrying the picnic lunch from Redcliffe Jetty, then having a swim at Suttons Beach was all a world away from suburbia.

* * *

TENNIS WAS SO popular in New Farm that some residents could readily list the dozen or more locations around the suburb where courts were available. Those with room in their yards even set about making their own…

The Merthyr Café on the corner with Hawthorne Street ca. 2000. — *Photo: NFDHS.*

> IN 1938 FATHER *decided to build a tennis court, which I thought was a wonderful idea as I loved tennis but I had no idea of the work involved. I can't remember where the ant bed came from but I certainly remember that it was full of bull ants, almost an inch long (25mm) and they bit like hell.*
>
> *The ant bed came in big clumps and had to be broken up with a rammer which consisted of a block of hardwood with a long brown handle. The breaking up wasn't too bad except for the ants. We'd wear long trousers, tie the bottom of the legs with cord (like the old country bojangs), which was reasonably effective in keeping the ants at bay. We'd distribute the broken up ant bed to various parts by wheelbarrow, level out, then finish off by watering and rolling many times.*
>
> *Erecting the fence was a big job, along with the concreting involved. There was one very strange happening when doing this. Prior to building the court, we never ever saw a willie wagtail but they always arrived when a load of ant bed came on the scene…*[5]

The modern generation could hardly imagine that the Astor Café, and the Merthyr Café on the corner of Merthyr Road and Hawthorne Street, were the only two establishments that served traditional meals to local workers and residents of rooming houses. In the 40s, there were the two hotels, the Brunswick and the Queen's Arms, but no restaurants, coffee shops or bars.[6]

Notes

1. Oral History: Brian Hjelm, 2008.
2. Oral History: Judith Benjamin, 2008.
3. George Cowin, Talk, 1998.
4. The original French-born Blondin (Jean Francois Gravelet, 1824-1897) made his first Australian appearance at Brisbane's Botanical Gardens on 25 July 1874, later followed by the 'Australian Blondin' James Alexander. The performer that Fred Matthews saw was likely to have been one of many imitators.
5. Oral History: Bryan Oxlade, 2008.
6. Hjelm, *op. cit.*

Taking a walk on the historical side...

Tᴴᴇ ʙᴇɢɪɴɴɪɴɢ ᴏꜰ the New Farm and Districts Historical Society goes back to a Saturday morning in February 1994 when 40 residents responded to an invitation by Councillor David Hinchliffe to join him on an historical walk around New Farm. Arch Trail recorded the event:

The Brunswick Hotel dating from 1889 on the Kent Street corner across from the old Rivoli Theatre. — *Photo ca. 1980: Fred Matthews.*

Tʜᴇ ᴍᴇᴇᴛɪɴɢ ᴘʟᴀᴄᴇ was the Holy Spirit School and participants included local MLA member, Peter Beattie and former Alderman for Merthyr, Beattie Dawson.

The walk took in the 1889 Brunswick Building at 710 Brunswick Street (Annie Street corner) followed by the Brunswick Hotel dating from the same year. Next was 'La Scala' on the corner of Brunswick and Harcourt Streets, known locally as 'the chocolate layer cake house.' It is a timber-framed structure of

La Scala on the corner of Brunswick and Harcourt Streets is diagonally across from *Avalon*. It was built for Dr Thomas Henry Reeve Mathewson, who was the son of Jane (Reeve) and Thomas Mathewson (d. 1934), described as the "Grand Old Man of Queensland Photography." — *Photo: G. Benjamin*

three stories that was designed by T.R. Hall and built in 1914-15 for Dr. Thomas Mathewson.

We walked along Harcourt Street and turned into Bowen Terrace to Wilson's Outlook, looking over the quarry, which provided the stone used for the cutting in Ann Street for All Hallows'. This quarrying also made way for wharves on the waterfront.

Further down Bowen Terrace at the corner of Balfour Street, we viewed 'Cairnsville', built by Charles Le Brocq. This house was rented to Albert Victor Drury, a public servant and prominent figure in government circles. The owner told us the home's story and invited us inside. The cast iron lacework on the verandah and porch dating from the 1880s was very Victorian. From there, we walked down Bowen Terrace past Queenslanders, colonial semi mansions and 1920 post-sewerage apartments.

On the corner of Moreton Street and Bowen Terrace, we were invited into a large, substantial residence named 'Winterburn', which was for sale. A New Farm thespian entertained us with recitals from Colonial and Irish folklore.

Further along Moreton Street were four solid blockhouses built in the late 1890s. This was a speculative development catering for the wealthy professionals on the 'right' side of Brunswick Street.

The walk concluded with morning tea at Holy Spirit School where Jan Power, the food critic, journalist and broadcaster addressed us all on the subject of 'Early New Farm Days.'

Councillor David Hinchliffe thanked participants for attending and said that there was much history to delve into, and research to be carried out on New Farm. He intimated that a grant could be available to a Society and invited interested people to form a committee.

The outcome of this walk was the formation of the New Farm & Districts Historical Society Inc. Its inaugural meeting was held on 18 June 1994 at the New Farm Library. Maureen Baillie was elected President and she was assisted by Patricia Whyte, Penny Davies and Bob Ferguson.

Subsequent presidents of the Society have included Maida Lilley, Virginia Balmain, Peter Walpole and Ross Garnett, while vice-presidents John Schiavo and Fraser Petrie performed the duties during one year when there was no president.

* * *

FOURTEEN YEARS LATER, the current President Ross Garnett was able to report at the Society's AGM on 23 August 2008 that membership had increased by 25 percent and that around 40-50 attended the regular monthly meetings.

Visitors are always welcome at the Society's office next to the New Farm Library. The office at the front of the Ron Muir Room is open on Thursdays from 2pm to 4pm. If you have an interest in New Farm's remarkable history, then please consider joining the New Farm & Districts Historical Society. Membership details are available by emailing: newfarmhistory@yahoo.com.

Wilson's Lookout, ca. 1995, as it would have looked to the New Farm walkers in February 1994. There was no Riverwalk and Dockside was only just beginning at Kangaroo Point. — *Photo: Betty Smith.*

An inaugural general meeting
to establish the New Farm &
Districts Historical Society
will be held at:

The New Farm Library
135 Sydney Street
New Farm 4005

18 June 1994 at 2.30 p.m.

All Welcome.

This simple notice, illustrated by photos of Thomas McMahon's bread cart and No. 28 Moreton Street, marked the start of the New Farm & Districts Historical Society in 1994.

Bibliography

Abrahams, Audrey, *Brothers of Bribie Heritage.* Wavell Heights, 1999.

Allen, Jim & Peter Corris (editors), *Journal of John Sweatman*, Uni. of Qld Press, St Lucia, 1977.

Armanno, Venero, *Firehead*, Random House, Milsons Point, NSW, 1999.

Australian Dictionary of Biography, Melbourne University Press. (online). Various entries.

Ball, Peter, "Wynberg", 2005 (a paper)

Barr, Todd & Rodney Sullivan, *Words to Walk By: Exploring Literary Brisbane,* Uni. of Qld Press, St Lucia, 2005.

Bartley, Nehemiah. *Opals and Agates, or Scenes under the Southern Cross & the Magelhans — Being Memories of Fifty Years of Australia and Polynesia.* Gordon & Gotch, Brisbane, 1892.

Bennett, Helen & John Schiavo, *New Farm Timeline*, Brisbane History Group Inc., 1999.

Besley, Jo, "Powerhouse History" paper; source unknown.

Biographical Record of Queensland Women, Webb, Elliot & Co., Brisbane, 1939.

Boland, T.P. , *James Duhig*, Uni. of Qld Press, St Lucia, 1986.

Brandle, Maximilian, editor. *Multicultural Queensland 2001: 100 years, 100 communities, A Century of Contributions.* Brisbane : Multicultural Affairs Qld, Dept of the Premier & Cabinet, 2001 (Essays by Jan Dickinson, Don Dignan & Morris Ochert)

"Brisbane's Suburbs: New Farm" in *The A. and B. Journal of Queensland*, 7 February 1924, pp 17-19.

Broadrick, Elsie, *69 years in Harcourt Street: A Conversation with Elsie Broadrick, aged 96,* rec. by Gerard Benjamin, Newstead, 2008.

Buckridge, Patrick & Belinda McKay (Eds.), *By The Book: A Literary History of Queensland*, Uni. of Qld Press, St Lucia, 2007.

Buckridge, Patrick, "Home of the 'Nice People': Brian Penton's Vision of New Farm in the Late Nineteenth Century." Talk given to NFDHS, 24 May 2008.

Calthorpe, K. D. and K. Capell, *Brisbane On Fire: A History of Firefighting 1860-1925*, Holland Park, Qld, 1997.

Cole, John R. *The Making of Men: A History of Churchie, 1912-1986.* East Brisbane: Boolarong for the Anglican Church Grammar School, 1986.

CSR Limited, *1893-1993 The Spirit of New Farm — Celebrating A Hundred Years at CSR's New Farm Sugar Refinery.* New Farm, CSR Limited, 1993.

Duchesne College 1937-1989. Boolarong Publications, Bowen Hills, 1989.

Evans, Raymond, "On the Utmost Verge: Race and Ethnic Relations at Moreton Bay, 1799-1842", in *Queensland Review*, Vol. 15, No. 1, 2008.

Felipe, Ricardo (ed.), *Avalon: Art and Life of an Apartment Building.* Museum of Brisbane, Fortitude Valley, Qld. Vanity Publishing, 2005.

"Fifty Years in Queensland: Living Pioneer Colonists." Supplement to *The Queenslander* Jubilee Issue, 7 August 1909.

Fisher, Rod & Barry Shaw (editors), *Brisbane — The Ethnic Presence since the 1850s*, Brisbane History Group, 1993.

France, Christine, "Mary Miriam Dods, in *Dictionary of Australian Artists Online* <http://www.daao.org.au/main/read/2255>"

Garnett Family, *A History of The Garnett Family Grocery Store 1887-1972*, New Farm, 1999.

Hanlon, Percy. *Oh-ver: A History of the Brisbane Cross River Ferries.* Brisbane, 2000.

Hallam, Fr Tony, "George Charles Willcocks", 1999 (a paper)

Hayes, Kevin, "135 James Street", A talk given to NFDHS, July 2005.

"History to 2006", New Farm Neighbourhood Centre, 2006.

Jack, Stephen Wellstood, *S.W. Jack's Cutting Books (various)*

Johnston, W. Ross, *Brisbane: The First Thirty Years*, Boolarong, Bowen Hills, 1988.

Jones, David & Peter Nunan, *U.S. Subs Down Under: Brisbane, 1942-1945.* Annapolis, Md. Naval Institute Press, 2004.

Journey of Faith: Merthyr Uniting Church (based on *An Historical Review of the Merthyr Parish Mission*, compiled by Paul H. Bennett. 1983)

Joyce, Roger B., *Samuel Walker Griffith*, University of Qld Press, St Lucia, 1984.

Kissick, D. L., *All Saints' Church, Brisbane 1862-1937*. All Saints' Parish, Brisbane, 1937.

Kopelke, Michael, *75 Years of Memories: Church of the Holy Spirit*. New Farm Parish, 2005.

Lord, Florence E., Regular series on Brisbane's Historic Homes in *The Queenslander*, 1930-1933.

Lowis, Kate, "135 James Street" ('Old Farm' column), *New Farm Newspaper*, June 1993

McCann, John, *How It Happened*. A personal memoir, 1993.

McKellar, A.R. *McKellar's Official Map of Brisbane & Suburbs*, 1895 and 1917.

Mackenzie-Smith, John, *Caring For Young Women in War and Peace: A History of GFS House, New Farm 1942-76*, Brisbane, 2008.

Mackenzie-Smith, John, "GFS House, New Farm 1829-1942". Paper given to NFDHS, 2008.

Metcalf, Bill, "Dr Thomas Pennington Lucas: Queensland Scientist, Author, Doctor, Dreamer and Inventor", in *Journal of the Royal Historical Society of Queensland*, Vol. 19(5), pp. 788-804, Royal Historical Society of Queensland, 2006.

McPherson, Jim, "Mine Watching Along The Brisbane River – Forgotten Women Volunteers of WWII" in *Australasian Coin & Banknote Magazine*, April 2008.

Marks, Roger, *Brisbane—WW2 v Now: No. 12: Nudgee Junior and Stuartholme*, RR & AJ Marks, Brisbane, 2006.

Martin, D. W., *Cyclists, Doctors and Others: The Introduction of The Motor Car to Queensland*. Church Archivists' Press, Virginia, Qld, 2001.

Martin, D. W., "Wynberg", 1998 (leaflet)

Memories of New Farm State School, 2001.

Milne, Rod, "Brisbane's Newstead Branch" in *Australian Railway History*, Vol. 56, No. 816, October 2005, pp. 403-423.

Nelson, S., 'Mural depicts local children', *Courier Mail*, 1 May 1987.

New Farm News, various issues.

New Farm & Teneriffe Hill Development Control Plan. 1995. Brisbane City Council, pp. 12-19.

Nunan, Peter, "The Story of the New Farm Wharf WWII Submarine Base." Talk to NFDHS, April 2008.

O'Shea, Patricia. *In A League of Our Own*, The Cerebral Palsy League of Qld, Brisbane, 2001.

Oxlade, Bryan, *Oxlade Brothers Pty. Ltd. 1894-1994: 100 Years of Service*. Bowen Hills, Qld, 1994.

Penton, Brian, *Inheritors*, Angus & Robertson, Sydney, 1936.

Petrie, Constance Campbell, *Tom Petrie's Reminiscences of Early Queensland*, Uni. of Qld Press, 1992.

Qld Heritage Register. Many New Farm sites appear on the register < http://www.epa.qld.gov.au>

Rayner, Sam, *Sid & Gladys Rayner of New Farm, Brisbane & Their Ancestors*, Brisbane, 1992.

Richards, Arthur, "A little school that time forgot", *The Courier Mail*, 27 June 1960, p. 2.

"Riverside Drive was a haven for the rich," *Sunday Sun*, 22 May 1983, page 20.

Roberts, Beryl, "Horse-drawn Buses and Cabs: New Farm". An address to NFDHS, 2002.

Roper, Tom, "The Old Colonialist" from <http://users.bigpond.net.au/skyring-homestead/thomas roper.htm>.

Russell, Henry Stuart, *The Genesis of Queensland*, Turner & Henderson, Sydney, 1888.

Schiavo, John, "New Farm: A Study of Land Use and Settlement To 1999," Brisbane City Council — Local Community History Grants Program.

Schiavo, John, *Information Plaques in New Farm Park*, Brisbane City Council.

Steele, John G., *Brisbane Town in Convict Days 1824-1842*, Uni. of Qld Press, St Lucia, 1975.

Stewart, Jean, *The Life and Times of Dr Brockway and The Brockway Cup*, J and D Stewart, Kenmore, 2007.

Stewart, Jean & David J. Hassall, *The Hassall Family History*, The Hassall Family Bicentenary Association Inc., 1998, <http://www.hassall.org/index.html>.

The Colonial Diaries of Frances Sophia Jones and her Daughter Cecilia Mary Jones, Qld Women's Historical Association, Miegunyah, 35 Jordan Terrace, Bowen Hills, Qld, 2000.

Watson, Donald and Judith McKay, *Queensland Architects of the 19th Century: A Biographical Dictionary*, Qld Museum, Brisbane, 1994.

Weir, Nancy & Tamsin O'Connor, "An Art Deco Marvel", *Village News*, April 2008.

Windsor, Harry, *The Heart of a Surgeon: The Memoirs of Harry Windsor*, Uni. of NSW Press, Sydney, 1987.

75 years: New Farm State School: 1901-1976. 2001, Erinport, Deagon, Qld, 2001.

Acknowledgements

THE COMMITTEE of the New Farm & Districts Historical Society Inc. is gratefully thanked for its faith in entrusting us with this historic project. President Ross Garnett, Vice-President Gordon Neilsen, committee members Bruna Burello-Day, Lois Kennedy, Susan White and Beryl Wogan have been constant with their ongoing assistance and encouragement.

BEATTIE DAWSON'S prodigious memory has been an invaluable resource. Born in 1916, she has lived in New Farm most of her life and represented Merthyr Ward as Alderman during 1973-1976. She was instrumental in the establishment of the New Farm Library which opened in October 1975. She was also involved in local flood mitigation work. Her efforts on behalf of those needing low cost housing received recognition by the naming of 92-94 Welsby Street as Beattie Dawson Place, and Dawson Lane off Gibbon Street has been named in her honour. Beattie has been unstinting in her community work and for this she will always be remembered by New Farm residents.

JOHN SCHIAVO'S upbringing in Moray Street clearly inspired a strong desire to investigate the earliest days of New Farm. The time and energy he has invested in researching the peninsula's past and his generosity in communicating his finds have provided an essential foundation for this book. Also underpinning it is the work of **JENNIFER BARRKMAN** who

conducted detailed interviews with long-time residents in 2007 which were incorporated into her article "Memories of New Farm: The Interwar Years." Thanks also to **JUDY BELL**, a local resident of 35 years who very kindly made available her unpublished work "New Farm: The Suburb and Its History." Much appreciated was the effort of **SUSAN WHITE** who admirably assisted with many contacts and interviews, six of which are featured herein.

ARTWORK SHOWING the CSR Refinery by **SHIRLEY MILLER,** adapted for the Front Cover, is very much appreciated. Thanks also to **PHILIPPA WEBB** <philippadon@optusnet.com.au> for her contribution to the Back Cover. Her depiction of New Farm Park in 2000 now has historic value, showing the previous childrens' playground and city sky line, as well as jacaranda trees, many of which have been cut down. Thanks to **GLADYS BLUNDELL** for her artistic contributions on the Back Cover as well as within the book.

DAVID HINCHLIFFE is sincerely thanked for generously contributing such a comprehensive Foreword along with his artwork and ongoing support for this project.

ASSISTANCE FROM researchers, curators and librarians has been particularly useful. They include: Rev. Olaf Anderson, Rector of St Michael and All Angels' Anglican Church; writer Dr

Venero Armanno for local background to his novel *Firehead;* Lisa Jones, Curator of the Queensland Police Museum, and Duncan Leask, Museum Assistant; Nanette Kay, Principal of Duchesne College; Father Denis Martin and Carolyn Nolan of the Catholic Archdiocesan Archives; Kaye Nardella, Curator of the Museum of Lands, Mapping and Surveying, for going the extra mile on many an occasion; Peter Nunan, researcher at the Queensland Maritime Museum along with David Jones, his co-author of *US Subs Down Under, 1942-1945;* Rebekah Pick of the New Farm Neighbourhood Centre; Mrs Jean Stewart, President of the Royal Historical Society of Queensland; Lena Volkova, President of the Oral History Association of Australia, Qld Branch; Librarians at The State Library of Queensland, John Oxley Library and the Mitchell Library; The Curator of the Brisbane City Council Archives; the Courier Mail; as well as proof-reading by Judy Bell, Bruna Burello-Day, Deirdre Fox, Desley Garnett, Lois Kennedy, Gordon Neilsen, John Schiavo and Beryl Wogan.

GRATEFUL THANKS for information or photos connected to past New Farm residents are due to Evelyn Bancroft, Jen Barrkman, Jim Bavas, Robert Blaikie, Patrick Buckridge, Anne & Richard Clarke, George Cowin, Isabelle Davis, Jan Doherty, Deirdre Fox, Sandy Dunstan, Ross Garnett, Paul Lewis, Thomas Clyde Love, Angela McLean, Annie Midgley, Stephen Midgley, Paul Moody, Betty O'Connor, Bryan Oxlade, Fay Rayner, Sam Rayner, Don Sargeant, Robert Riddel, John Schiavo, Betty Smith, Pat Smith, Evie Stanley, Rosemary Stirling, Lorraine Tomlinson and June Tregear.

View from Kingsholme ca 1889, looking towards Merthyr Road and the river beyond. The house on the right hand side may mark the intersection of Annie and Kingsholme Streets. To the right of the row of six dwellings in the centre of the picture, are homes on the upper side of Lechmere Street, including *Briar House*, built by Andrea Stombuco in 1888. — *Photo: John Oxley Library 100020.*

Oral History Contributors
(including year of interview and interviewer)

ARDEN, JOY *nee Le Brocq* (1917-2002)
• 1997, Paul Rollo

BARKER, HARRY • 1992, Deirdre Fox

BAVAS, JIM • 2008, Susan White

BENJAMIN, JACK & JUDITH *nee Lieberman*
• 2008, Susan White

BISHOP, BRIAN & CATHERINE *nee Carey*
• 2007, Jen Barrkman

BLAIKIE, ROBERT • 2008, Susan White

BOYD, ELAINE • "What New Farm Means
to Me"; letter dated March 1992

BROADRICK, ELSIE
• 2008, Gerard Benjamin

BROWN, LEONARD • 1993, Paul Rollo

COWIN, GEORGE • 1998

CRAWFORD, MAIDA
• 1994, Rachel Kennedy

DAWSON, BEATTIE • 1993, Bob Ferguson;
2006, Snippets; 2007, Jen Barrkman

DAVIS, ISABELLE • 2008, Gerard Benjamin

DUNSTAN, SANDY • 2008, Susan White

FLEMING, DULCIE *nee Twible* (b. 1914)
• 2007, Jen Barrkman

GILMOUR, MARGARET
• 2007, Jen Barrkman

GRACE, GRACE • 2008

GRANT, RON • 2002, Deirdre Fox

HAMER, ALISON
• 1992-94, Robert Ferguson

HENDERSON, IVY • 1992, Alex Prior

HJELM, BRIAN • 2008, Susan White

HUGHES, LEW • 1997, Paul Rollo

JOHNSON, ALAN (along with John Cuk &
Norm Waye) • 1992, Alex Prior

KOPELKE, GEORGE
• 1992, Robert Ferguson

KOPELKE, JOAN
• 2008, Gerard Benjamin

MATTHEWS, FRED T. (b. 1904) "New
Farm, The Way It Was: 1904-1924"
• 1974, Barbara Dawson

MESSINBIRD, DOROTHY (1933-2004)
• 1992, Alex Prior

MILLER, GRAHAME
• 1994, Rosanne Dedman

NORMAN, BLANCHE (1915-2001) and her
sister MARJORIE PITT
• 1992, Alex Prior

O'BRIEN, FLORENCE *nee Charles*
• 2008, Susan White

OXLADE, BRYAN • 2007, Jen Barrkman
• 2008, Gerard Benjamin

POWER, JOSEPHINE *nee Wilkinson*
(1908-2004) • 1994, Rosanne Dedman

RAVALESE, SIGNORA • 1992, Alex Prior

RINAUDO, GIUSEPPE • 1992, Alex Prior

ROSENSKJAR, FATHER JOHN
• 2008, Gerard Benjamin

STEVENS, RUSSELL
• 1992-94, Robert Ferguson

"TAIPAN" • 1992, Alex Prior

TRAIL, ARCH (1917-2005)
• 2002, Margaret Ross and Deirdre Fox

MANY OF these contributions have
featured in earlier compilations of New
Farm Oral Histories including *Living
in New Farm, an Oral History Project*
arranged by Alex Prior in 1992, Brisbane
City Council Community Arts Unit,
New Farm Neighbourhood Centre and
the Brisbane City Council's New Farm
Library, as well as in the columns of *New
Farm News*.

THE WORK of Alex Prior, Robert D.
Ferguson, Penny Davies, Paul Rollo,
Margaret Ross and Deirdre Fox is
gratefully acknowledged.

The Compilers

GLORIA GRANT (nee Nonmus) was brought into the world by Doctor Edward Row of Windsor in 1929 at Nurse Austin's Maternity Hospital on the corner of Upper Bowen Terrace and Barker Street, New Farm.

A Buderim upbringing, high school at Nambour, teacher training at Kelvin Grove, eight teaching posts around Queensland , marriage and raising a family were a prelude to family printing works first at Ross Street, then Stratton Street, Newstead.

Gloria is the author of *Divining Wisdom* (2002) and just when she thought that she had chosen teaching and publishing all by herself, her family history research showed otherwise. Her forebear Hannah Nonmus had her story published in London in 1798, and Hannah's descendant (Gloria's great-grandfather) was a Sunday School superintendent on the Victorian goldfields in the 1860s and later conducted his own school in Ararat. It seems that writing and teaching were in her genes all along…

GERARD BENJAMIN attended St. Joseph's College, Gregory Terrace and completed degrees at the Universities of Queensland and Lancaster (UK). After teaching at Ipswich, Carlisle (UK) and McAulay College of Teacher Education, 25 years ago he switched to typesetting, editing and publishing. Staying up-to-date has meant maintaining dexterity with programs such as InDesign, Photoshop and Illustrator.

In common with Sir Samuel Griffith, Gerard's Benjamin forebears came from Merthyr Tydfil in Wales. He has recently transcribed an unpublished 1865 manuscript of his great-great-grandfather J.C. Wood from Shropshire. It may be just the second novel written in the newly-separated state of Queensland.

Gerard finds that family and local history provide an ideal springboard for the larger study of history. This is especially relevant considering that the Federal Government is due to make the study of history compulsory from prep to Year 10 across the country.

Redevelopment in New Farm has not always meant the demolition of a grand house. Some were removed to other locations. The Cowin family's Villiers Street home was refurbished, extended and built-in underneath and currently resides at Mactier Street, Fig Tree Pocket.
— *Photo: George Cowin IV*

Index

A typical New Farm worker's cottage dating from the 1860s. The high-pitched gable roof, the low setting, brick side walls and the small scale of the building, demonstrate early housing design in Brisbane. The front verandah has been built in. Workers' cottages of this kind would have once filled the valley between James and Brunswick Streets. — *Photo and text: John Schiavo 1998.*

Your History for Future Generations